THE
PSYCHEDELIC
EXPLORER'S
GUIDE

"James Fadiman, one of the foremost pioneers of scientific research of the potential of psychedelic substances for therapy, self-discovery, spiritual quests, and creative problem-solving, has written an invaluable guide for safe and productive sessions. Based on more than forty years of the author's experience in the field and presented in a clear, easily understandable style, this book is a breath of fresh air, dispelling the mis-information that has been disseminated over many decades by sensation-hunting journalists and fear-based antidrug propaganda. The publication of *The Psychedelic Explorer's Guide* could not be more timely; it coincides with a major renaissance of interest in psychedelic research worldwide. The information that it provides will thus be useful not only for the hundreds of thousands of people involved in self-experimentation but also for the new generation of psychedelic researchers."

STANISLOV GROF, M.D., AUTHOR OF
LSD: DOORWAY TO THE NUMINOUS

"James Fadiman was the Forrest Gump of the psychedelic sixties. He witnessed the first flowerings of that amazing era of mind-expansion, then kept popping up for cameo appearances whenever the action got particularly interesting and enlightening. Now, riding a new wave of scientific research into the beneficial use of these misunderstood substances, Fadiman is back with a practical and at the same time inspiring guidebook for the next generation of entheogenic explorers."

DON LATTIN, AUTHOR OF THE BESTSELLING
THE HARVARD PSYCHEDELIC CLUB

"This is some of the most thoughtful, wise, heartfelt, and essential instruction for the use of sacred medicine."

JACK KORNFIELD, AUTHOR OF
A PATH WITH HEART

"Fadiman knows what he is talking about. This is the book we have needed."

HUSTON SMITH, AUTHOR OF THE WORLD'S RELIGION AND
CLEANING THE DOORS OF PERCEPTION

"Approaching his subject from intimately historical, psychological-cultural, and accessibly authoritative perspectives, Fadiman's psychedelic magnum opus establishes the benchmark reference for anyone interested in understanding, experiencing, or supervising the effects of this unique family of psychoactive substances."

RICK STRASSMAN, M.D., CLINICAL ASSOCIATE PROFESSOR OF
PSYCHIATRY AT THE UNIVERSITY OF NEW MEXICO SCHOOL OF
MEDICINE AND AUTHOR OF DMT: THE SPIRIT MOLECULE

"James Fadiman's manual offers helpful and well-informed guidance for those who seek 'the divine within' through sacred plants and psychedelic substances."

DANIEL PINCHBECK, AUTHOR OF 2012: THE RETURN OF
QUETZALCOATL AND BREAKING OPEN THE HEAD

"At last, there's a practical, commonsense manual for mindful therapeutic sessions using psychedelics, one that's informed by the latest science and unfettered by arcane platitudes. It will be a boon to personal transformation and a road map for avoiding trouble along the way for all who use it. Bon voyage!"

CHARLES HAYES, AUTHOR OF *TRIPPING: AN ANTHOLOGY OF TRUE-LIFE PSYCHEDELIC ADVENTURES*

"Finally! A comprehensive guide not only to psychedelic use in a therapeutic setting but also, even more bravely, to psychospiritual exploration and cognitive enhancement. We are fortunate to reap the benefits of Professor Fadiman's years of cumulative knowledge and experience as well as to hear from a cadre of 'who's who' in the psychedelic cognoscenti."

JULIE HOLLAND, M.D., EDITOR OF *THE POT BOOK* AND *ECSTASY: THE COMPLETE GUIDE*

"Psychedelics have been part of native cultures for centuries and remain so in many areas of the world. Properly used, they offer a one-step guide to enlightenment and connection with intuition as well as the soul and the Divine. Dr. Fadiman's book offers the best information and guidance available today. Everyone interested in exploring the world of inner consciousness will find this work indispensable."

NORM SHEALY, M.D., PH.D., FOUNDER OF THE AMERICAN HOLISTIC HEALTH ASSOCIATION AND COAUTHOR OF *SOUL MEDICINE* AND *LIFE BEYOND 100*

"The prohibition of psychedelic drugs in the twentieth century unfortunately restricted a most promising and profound inquiry into the religious mysteries of consciousness. This brave and encouraging book goes a long way toward restoring our constitutional right to explore these mysteries. By encouraging individual responsibility and intelligence in this era of purported health care reform, James

Fadiman takes a bold and refreshing step toward reclaiming our freedom of religion, which is the very essence of democracy and the American dream."

ROBERT FORTE, EDITOR OF *ENTHEOGENS AND THE FUTURE OF RELIGION* AND *TIMOTHY LEARY: OUTSIDE LOOKING IN*

"*The Psychedelic Explorer's Guide* is a brave and uniquely valuable book. Written by one of the most highly respected and innovative researchers from the 1960s, this extraordinary book covers topics not found in any other book on the subject. Fadiman offers us a beautifully written, insightful summation of important early research on creativity, problem solving, and psychospiritual development, tragically cut off by government edict, as well as new research on the use of sub-threshold doses of LSD to enhance normal functioning, in the process creating a road map for the future of psychedelic research. *The Psychedelic Explorer's Guide* wisely focuses not on pathology but on human potential for health and, as such, shows us how these transformative substances can improve the future of psychology—and the future of society. Throughout this radical yet evidence-based volume, Fadiman uses a combination of the research and his own broad personal experiences working with Leary, Alpert (Ram Dass), Kesey, and other seminal figures in psychedelic research and practice to make the convincing case that psychedelics offer the power to transform society and reintegrate unitary spirituality into Western civilization. *The Psychedelic Explorer's Guide* is written with a wry humor that brings Fadiman's sincere, soulful intentionality immediately to the reader, integrating and transforming from the moment one opens this important, mature, and absolutely essential book. If you are interested in the safe, effective, and transformative use of psychedelics to improve our lives and our society, you will devour this book. Fadiman's *The Psychedelic Explorer's Guide* is the finest book ever written on the topic—a must read.

NEAL GOLDSMITH, PH.D.,
AUTHOR OF *PSYCHEDELIC HEALING*

THE
PSYCHEDELIC
EXPLORER'S
GUIDE

Safe, Therapeutic,
and Sacred Journeys

JAMES FADIMAN, Ph.D.

Park Street Press
Rochester, Vermont • Toronto, Canada

Park Street Press
One Park Street
Rochester, Vermont 05767
www.ParkStPress.com

Text stock is SFI certified

Park Street Press is a division of Inner Traditions International

Note to the Reader: The information provided in this book is for educational, historical, and cultural interest only and should not be construed as advocacy for the use or ingestion of LSD or other psychedelics. Neither the author nor the publisher assumes any responsibility for physical, psychological, or social consequences resulting from the ingestion of these substances or their derivatives.

Library of Congress Cataloging-in-Publication Data

Fadiman, James, 1939–
  The psychedelic explorer's guide : safe, therapeutic, and sacred journeys / James Fadiman.
    p. cm.
  Includes bibliographical references and index.
  Summary: "Psychedelics for spiritual, therapeutic, and problem-solving use"—Provided by publisher.
  ISBN 978-1-59477-402-7
  1. Hallucinogenic drugs and religious experience. 2. Hallucinogenic drugs. I. Title.
  BL65.D7F33 2011
  200.1'9—dc22

                                                                    2011000549

Printed and bound in the United States by Lake Book Manufacturing
The text stock is SFI certified. The Sustainable Forestry Initiative® program promotes sustainable forest management.

10 9 8 7 6 5 4 3 2 1

Text design and layout by Priscilla Baker
This book was typeset in Garamond Premier Pro with Agenda used as a display typeface

To send correspondence to the author of this book, mail a first-class letter to the author c/o Inner Traditions • Bear & Company, One Park Street, Rochester, VT 05767, and we will forward the communication, or contact the author directly at **www.psychedelicexplorersguide.com** or **Jfadiman@gmail.com**.

For Dorothy, my partner in all ways.

୭

Thank you to those, among others, who helped me along this path:

Albert Hofmann, who in 1943 acted on his intuition to look again at the twenty-fifth derivative of lysergic acid, which he had put aside five years earlier as being of "no special interest."

Richard Alpert (Ram Dass), who first opened my eyes to the wonders of the ten thousand worlds.

Willis Harman, who led me past those worlds to the interconnectedness of all things.

Ken Kesey, Tim Leary, and Al Hubbard—destroyers of structures and complacency, who made it all both possible and impossible.

> *For it appears to me that among the many exceptional and divine things your Athens has produced and contributed to human life, nothing is better than those [Eleusinian] mysteries. For by means of them we have transformed from a rough and savage way of life to the state of humanity, and have been civilized. Just as they are called initiations, so in actual fact we have learned from them the fundamentals of life, and have grasped the basis not only for living with joy but also for dying with a better hope.*
>
> MARCUS TULLIUS CICERO
> *DE LEGIBUS* 2.14.36

CONTENTS

ACKNOWLEDGMENTS

So many people have helped that this is, at best, a partial list.

My writing teachers and friends:

Shelly Lowenkauf   Leonard Tierney

Members of the psychedelic world:

Sasha Shulgin   Aldous Huxley
Peter Webster   Alan Watts
Robert Forte   Robert Jesse
Huston Smith   Alicia Danforth

*Those who taught me at the International Foundation
for Advanced Study:*

Myron Stolaroff   Norman Sherwood
Don Allen   Charles Savage
Bob Lehigh   James Watt
Mary Allen   Robert Mogar

*Those professors committed to real academic freedom and who supported
my then very unpopular research:*

Nevitt Sanford   Jack Hilgard

Those who helped get this manuscript completed:

Tony Levelle—my wise in-house editor

Anthony Austin—gifted novelist himself who was determined to be sure that in spite of all my education, every line of this book would be written in English. My gratitude is enormous.

Sophia Korb—who made clouds of information into useful data

Mike and Mary of the Windmill Café Grill—who created a perfect place for me to edit and refuel

Special thanks to the team at Inner Traditions. Each of you made this book better.

Jon Graham—who believed in it enough to acquire it

John Hays—who helped re-title it and showed me the wisdom behind this decision

Peri Swan—who created a beautiful, honest cover

Erica Robinson—who made the jacket copy sing

Jeffery Lindholm—who firmly corrected almost all of my errors

Jeanie Levitan—who made everything fit

And a bouquet of thanks to Anne Dillon—amazing, wise, word-loving, writer-soothing editor

OVERVIEW—WHY THIS BOOK?
And Frequently Asked Questions

I gather from Don Juan's teachings that psychotropics are used to stop the flow of ordinary interpretations and to shatter certainty.

CARLOS CASTANEDA, *VOICES AND VISIONS*

Why This Book?

Each of us must decide for ourselves whether to put into our bodies what affects our minds, be it micrograms of a chemical, milligrams of a mushroom, ounces of an alcoholic beverage, or smoke from burning tobacco. This book explores the beneficial uses of psychedelics, LSD in particular. It does not advocate illegal activities of any kind.

To become more aware is your birthright. Denying anyone access to any facet of reality in the name of religion, science, medicine, or law serves neither the individual nor society. Whenever opportunities for self-realization are suppressed or are in danger of being lost, there is a moral imperative to protect and restore them. This book has been written so that certain knowledge, experiences, and techniques for increased awareness would not vanish.

The Psychedelic Explorer's Guide describes well-researched uses of psychedelics to advance a spiritual quest, for healing, for personal exploration and psychotherapy, and for facilitating scientific exploration and invention. It

1

includes a first report on an emerging use: enhancing overall functioning.

The book contains guidelines for spiritual and scientific sessions so that those who choose to take or offer a psychedelic may do so with greater confidence and safety. These guidelines may also be helpful to those who have previously taken psychedelics for pleasure, insight, or wisdom as well as to those who have never taken them.

> *What we ordinarily call "reality" is merely that slice of total fact which our biological equipment, our linguistic heritage and our social conventions of thought and feeling make it possible for us to apprehend. . . . LSD permit[s] us to cut another kind of slice.*
>
> ALDOUS HUXLEY, *MOKSHA*

LSD and many psychedelic plants and chemicals are currently illegal in the United States and many other countries. However, by 2006, according to the U.S. government's own figures, at least twenty-three million people had tried LSD in the United States alone. This number has been increasing by about four to six hundred thousand people every year.[1] Neither criminal penalties nor blatant misinformation over the past forty years appears to have curbed personal experimentation. Factual information that could reduce misuse and enhance known benefits can't help but be useful.

In the future, there should be research and training centers for psychedelic experience that are safe and secure, with both secular and sacred settings to ensure adequate training for wise and compassionate use.[2] Such institutions would restore the care and respect that psychedelics have been accorded in almost every other culture over thousands of years. Until the remaining barriers to accurate information and training for the use of these substances are finally removed, resources like *The Psychedelic Explorer's Guide* can be helpful.

How and if ever you use a psychedelic is your own decision. If this book helps you make a more informed decision, it will have more than served its purpose. If it prevents you from doing something foolish, it will have been invaluable.

What This Book Contains

If shamanistic reports—similar over continents, cultures, and eons—are to be seriously considered, it appears that certain plants have the capacity to induce specific states of awareness in humans to transmit information deemed necessary to retain and restore the natural harmony of the biological kingdoms. The ethnobotanist and entheogenic researcher Terence McKenna[3] and others speculate that to some degree civilization evolved or was developed by those who ingested these substances.

Today, the harmony that once existed is in tatters. The disruption between our species and the rest of nature has never been wider, its effects never more pronounced. "By having disconnected ourselves emotionally from the Earth and plants we have lost our understanding of those links and mutual relationships," writes Stephen Harold Buhner.[4]

Part 1, "Transcendent Experience," is one attempt among many to buttress the forces of restoration. The first two chapters are guidelines for how to conduct or be guided in sacred sessions. In chapter 3, Alan Watts describes what characterizes an entheogenic (from Greek, literally "becoming divine within") experience. Chapter 4 concludes part 1, with major figures in the science of consciousness recalling and evaluating their early psychedelic sessions.

Part 2, "Personal Growth and Self-Exploration in Psychedelic Sessions," is based on well-documented data, research, and experience. The current research renaissance has focused on patients with extremely serious physical and mental conditions rather than those with the broader range of psychotherapeutic concerns. From ibogaine (a plant from West Africa) helping people overcome cocaine and heroin addiction, to MDMA (ecstasy, ADAM, X, and many other names) alleviating the torments and healing the wounds of posttraumatic stress (along with supportive therapy), to psilocybin reducing the anxiety of patients with advanced-stage cancer, there is ample evidence that, wisely administered, these substances lessen the suffering caused by addiction, disease, and mental anguish.[5]

Part 2 includes information about the earlier, more established use of psychedelics with adult outpatients and with healthy, well-functioning individuals interested in personal exploration. It also includes a chapter by David Presti and Jerome Beck covering the myths surrounding LSD. Chapter 6, written by the psychotherapist Neal Goldsmith, is a resource guide of what to do if things go wrong—and they do.

Part 3, "Enhanced Problem Solving in Focused Sessions," covers psychedelic sessions to facilitate problem solving for scientific and technical problems. Before 1966, when the U.S. government terminated almost all research, a few groups had learned how to use these substances to aid creativity, although that research has since been neglected.[6] Part 3 contains a description of running such sessions that are quite different from the recommendations for therapy or for spiritual experience and includes a chapter by Willis Harman and myself about that breakthrough research.

Chapters 10 through 13, including chapter 12 by Willis Harman and chapter 13 by George Leonard, illustrate the diversity of individual and group results achieved in sessions.

Specialized use of psychedelics has already changed our culture. Two Nobel Prize winners attributed their breakthroughs to their use of LSD. Near his death, Francis Crick let it be known that his inner vision of the double helix of DNA was LSD enhanced. The chemist Kary Mullis reported that LSD helped him develop the polymerase chain reaction to amplify specific DNA sequences, for which he received the prize. The last chapter in part 3 is my personal account that begins the day the government discontinued LSD research.

Part 4, "New Horizons," covers some emerging directions of psychedelic use. Users of sub-perceptual doses (10 micrograms or less) reveal surprising results that are discussed in chapter 15. Astonishingly, beyond the data described in chapter 16, there have been no other surveys of current psychedelic users' drug histories. Those surveys asked:

- What have you taken? (Many different substances are available.)
- Why (e.g., social, spiritual, fun, being with friends, etc.)?
- What effects did it have?

- What good or harm has it done you?
- What are your future intentions (to take or not take again)?

Part 4 also includes how psychedelics affected my career, personality, and worldview (chapter 17) and a chapter about current trends and positive possibilities for psychedelics (chapter 18). The second wave of psychedelic exploration has begun.

Part 5, "The Necessary, the Extraordinary, and Some Hard-Core Data," presents areas of more specialized interest. The checklist in chapter 19 (which boils down chapters 1 and 2) is for someone seriously intending to be a guide or have a guided experience to be able to quickly and easily be sure that all bases are covered. Chapter 20 contains three personal reports, by Michael Wiese, "Anatole," and Lindsey Vona. The first two reports are ayahausca sessions. The third is a profound mystical sojourn experienced during fourteen days in total darkness.

The final two chapters of part 5 are for data lovers who, not satisfied with individual examples, ask for and expect to be given group data. Chapter 21 lists specific behavior changes after a single-dose therapeutic session, as described in chapter 5. Chapter 22, written by Willis Harman and myself, tallies the results of a questionnaire study about guided psychedelic experiences. The responses offer ample evidence of the value people place on well-guided journeys.

As you can see, a number of chapters have been contributed by other, fellow researchers, though unless otherwise noted, the chapters in this book were written by me. If something is missing that you want told, taught, or corrected, then, as the contemporary Zen sage Scoop Nisker said, "If you don't like the news, then go out and make some of your own." Add it to the website at www.entheoguide.net and/or contact me at www.psychedelicexplorersguide.com and accept my thanks.

Frequently Asked Questions

After 1966, why didn't medical and scientific psychedelic research continue while the government was trying to limit its misuse in the general population, as has been the case for many other drugs?

Initially, researchers were puzzled why research wasn't allowed to continue. Restricting the use of an apparently successful intervention, be it a psychotherapy, a teaching, a training, a procedure, or a pharmaceutical, contradicted common sense.

A partial answer is that radical revisions in human thought do not come easily, especially to any institution whose own structure or status might be endangered. For example, when hypnosis was first used to mitigate pain during an operation, it was seen as a curiosity or a sham. To overcome the resistance in the medical community, an operation was performed before a large number of members of the British College of Physicians and Surgeons. A man's leg was amputated while he was under hypnosis. The patient remained conscious and did not cry out during the entire procedure.

When the attending physicians were leaving, one was heard to say to another, "What did you think?"

"I think the patient was faking," the other replied.

His companion agreed.

Soon after, ether was discovered and was quickly accepted as an effective anesthetic, probably because its action was entirely physiological and, therefore, did not demand a revision of any previously held belief. Hypnosis is still not part of the core medical curriculum, even in psychiatry.

Early, positive results using psychedelics were received, as those for hypnosis had been, with disbelief. The U.S. government never supported research into therapeutic uses of psychedelics, even though it underwrote generous funding of the Central Intelligence Agency's secret research into LSD's possible uses as a weapon.

Today, a new generation of scientists is exploring these materials, and a new, more open-minded generation of regulators has allowed them to complete a few small but telling studies. The trend seems to be to allow more research to continue.

You're writing about mystical adventures, scientific breakthroughs, therapy, and personal growth, but you haven't said a thing about using psychedelics for just plain fun.

The Psychedelic Explorer's Guide does not discuss using psychedelics for recreation or entertainment precisely because there is so much information out there, from knowledgeable to opinionated, that I had nothing to add to that area of use.

This book describes some ways to use psychedelics. You have been fine-tuned over millions of years to desire to be in harmony with the natural world, to be curious about your own mind, and to recognize the essential unity of which you are a part. Whether or not you ever choose to use psychedelic experiences as part of your self-discovery, your decision should be an informed one.

A Vision of a Whole Earth

Stewart Brand

When I'm asked "Can you give me your best example of the magic that LSD can impart?" I share this experience of Stewart Brand's. One session, one person, 100 mcg. From his session a vision arose, one that forever changed the way we look at the earth. The following excerpt, "Why Haven't We Seen a Photo of the Whole Earth Yet?" is from the book The Sixties: The Decade Remembered Now by the People Who Lived It Then, *edited by Lynda Obst and published in 1977 by Random House and Rolling Stone Press, which can also be found at www.smithsonianconference.org/expert/exhibit-hall/spi. In it, Stewart Brand, founder, editor, and publisher of* The Whole Earth Catalog, *recounts his activism on behalf of the planet, and how it influenced the creation of the time-honored image of the earth from space.*

It was February 1966, one month after the Trips Festival at Longshoreman's Hall, when the "whole Earth" in *The Whole Earth Catalog* came to me with the help of one hundred micrograms of lysergic acid diethylamide. I was sitting on a gravelly roof in San Francisco's North Beach. I was twenty-eight.

In those days, the standard response to boredom and uncertainty was LSD followed by grandiose scheming. So there I sat, wrapped in a blanket in the chill afternoon sun, trembling with cold and inchoate emotion, gazing at the San Francisco skyline, waiting for my vision.

The buildings were not parallel—because the earth curved under them, and me, and all of us. . . . Buckminster Fuller had been harping on about this—that people perceived the earth as flat and infinite, and how that was the root of all their misbehavior. Now from my altitude of three stories and one hundred mikes, I could see that it was curved, think it, and finally feel it.

It had to be broadcast, this fundamental point of leverage on the world's ills. I herded my trembling thoughts together as the winds blew and time passed. A photograph would do it—a color photograph of the earth from space. There it would be, for all to see, the earth complete, tiny, adrift—and no one would ever perceive things quite the same way again.

How could I induce NASA or the Russians to finally turn the cameras backward? We could make a button! A button with the demand "Take a photograph of the entire Earth." No, we had to use the great American resource of paranoia and make it into a question: "Why haven't they made a photograph of the entire Earth?"

But there was something wrong with "entire," and something wrong with "they."

"Why haven't we seen a photograph of the whole Earth yet?" Ah. That was it!

The next day I ordered the printing of several hundred buttons and posters. While they were being made I spent a couple hours in the San Francisco library looking up the names and addresses of all the relevant NASA officials, the members of Congress *and* their secretaries, Soviet scientists and diplomats, UN officials, Marshall McLuhan, and Buckminster Fuller.

When the buttons were ready I sent them off. Then I prepared a Day-Glo sandwich board with a little sales shelf on the front, decked myself out in a white jumpsuit, boots and a costume top hat complete with a crystal heart and flower, and went to make my debut at the Sather Gate of the University of California in Berkeley, selling my buttons for twenty-five cents apiece.

It went perfectly. The dean's office threw me off the campus, the *San Francisco Chronicle* reported it, and I had my broadcast.

I kept returning. Then I branched out to Stanford, and then to Columbia, Harvard, and MIT. "Who the hell's that?" asked an MIT dean, watching hordes of his students buying my buttons.

"That's my brother," said my brother Pete, an MIT instructor.

It is no accident of history that the first Earth Day, in April 1970, came so soon after color photographs of the whole Earth from space were made by astronauts on the Apollo 8 mission to the moon in December 1968. Those riveting Earth photos reframed everything.

For the first time humanity saw itself from outside. The visible

features from space were living blue ocean, living green-brown continents, dazzling polar ice and a busy atmosphere, all set like a delicate
jewel in vast immensities of hard-vacuum space. Humanity's habitat
looked tiny, fragile and rare. Suddenly humans had a planet to tend
to. The photograph of the whole Earth from space helped to generate a lot of behavior—the ecology movement, the sense of global
politics, the rise of the global economy, and so on. I think all of those
phenomena were, in some sense, given permission to occur by the
photograph of the earth from space.

This photo of Earth was taken by Apollo 8 *crew member Bill Anders on
December 24, 1968. The image is provided courtesy of NASA.*

▼

TRANSCENDENT EXPERIENCE

Entheogenic Sessions

Introduction to Part One

There is a door within the self. When this door is opened, a unity is revealed that encompasses all beings and transcends all boundaries. Mystics in every religious system in every culture and in every age have reported this to be the highest truth. Those who have had such an experience agree that the state is elusive and usually recalled only in fragments. However, those who have achieved even a moment of this visionary understanding consider it of incalculable value.

Cultures have developed dozens of ways to apprehend this unitive state. Paths include physical austerities, cycles of prayer, meditation, devotions, breathing rituals, and physical postures. A significant number have used plants in combination with other practices. For some, the use of a psychedelic makes the experience suspect. But there are those of us who believe that however one ascends the mountain, the view from the summit is the same. What one gains from that vista and from the climb will depend, as it always has, on how one incorporates such moments into one's life.

> *This is how a human being can change:*
> *there's a worm addicted to eating*
> *grape leaves.*
> *Suddenly. He wakes up,*
> *call it grace, whatever, something*
> *wakes him, and he's no longer*
> *a worm.*

He's the entire vineyard,
and the orchard too, the fruit, the trunks,
a growing wisdom and joy
that doesn't need
to devour.

RUMI, "THE WORM'S WAKING"
(TRANSLATION BY COLEMAN BARKS)

1

MEETING THE DIVINE WITHIN
Part One: Guidelines for Voyagers and Guides

THE GUILD OF GUIDES*

There is an almost sensual longing for communion with others who have a larger vision. The immense fulfillment of the friendships between those engaged in furthering the evolution of consciousness has a quality almost impossible to describe.

PIERRE TEILHARD DE CHARDIN

Why This Material Was Created

In a study of nearly one hundred people who took a psychedelic and were guided as outlined in this chapter, 78 percent reported, "It was the greatest experience of my life.[1]" This response was true even for those people who had taken a psychedelic many times before. This chapter describes

---

*The guild is an informal, largely invisible fellowship, international in scope. Its members include practitioners from major religions as well as the arts, health sciences, and mental health professions. The term *guild* refers to the practice of training by which a guide accepts apprentices. Only when a person's level of work is close to that of his or her mentor is he or she encouraged to work independently. The guild does not maintain a public web presence under this name.

how to benefit from having an experienced guide having sufficient psychedelic material, and being in a supportive setting.

Many people who hope to have a spiritual or an entheogenic experience using a psychedelic don't know how to reach and stay open to those levels of consciousness. And few people who wish to help others on that voyage have had the benefit of being taught how to serve as effective guides. This chapter has been written to offer useful tested suggestions to guides and voyagers. The guidelines are intended to promote spiritual, rather than recreational, use.

This chapter brings together the insights of a number of psychedelic guides who have been working discreetly over the past forty years to facilitate maximally safe and sacred entheogenic experiences. This compilation is being made available to support increased spiritual understanding and to minimize negative experiences.

Many of those who have never had a guided session appreciate how psychedelic experiences have impacted and improved their lives. However, the presence of a knowledgeable guide greatly facilitates the probability of reaching expanded levels of consciousness and recalling and integrating the experiences.

The fact that a guide makes a significant difference in the quality of the experience underscores the difference between psychedelics and almost all other medications. That difference is not only that the plant or "drug" opens one to a wider range of experiences, but also that the direction, content, and overall quality of the experiences can be focused and enhanced with guidance.*

To establish the best possible environment for spiritual psychedelic sessions, it is critical to keep in mind six primary factors that most affect the nature and value of these experiences:

- Set
- Setting

---

*Set and setting have long been ignored in medical research, but the growing literature on placebo effects, for example, is forcing some long overdue attention to the obvious fact that much about our reactions to any stimulus depends on the actual context and the way we perceive it.

- Substance and quantity (dose)
- Sitter and guide
- Session
- Situation

Glossary

Entheogen: Any psychedelic used specifically to enhance the probability of spiritual experience.

Etymology: Derived from a Greek term meaning "that which causes God to be known or experienced within an individual."

Guide: Someone with considerable personal experience and knowledge of altered states of consciousness, with and without the use of psychedelics. A guide helps others experience the full range of entheogenic states and provides support when experiences are challenging. It is assumed that a guide does not take a psychedelic during the session, or any other drugs or alcohol—before or during the session.

Psychedelic: The general term for the spectrum of natural and synthesized conscious-altering substances. These include LSD-25, mescaline (and the peyote cactus that contains mescaline), and psilocybin (and the mushrooms that contain psilocybin) as well as other plants and substances. We will focus primarily on LSD-25 (simply called LSD here), generally regarded as the most potent psychedelic and the one that facilitates access to the broadest range of experiences. (See "Dose" in the guidelines for information on related psychedelics.)

Session: The time for a voyage (six to twelve hours).

Set: The preparation and expectations of the voyager and the guide.

Setting: The surroundings, primarily physical, but also the atmosphere of the space for the session itself.

Sitter: The terms *sitter* and *guide* are sometimes used interchangeably. Here, the sitter is the person, often but not necessarily a close friend, who cares for the voyager after a session as well as during the initial reentry period.

Situation: Post-experience integration. The relationships and support available, especially after a session (e.g., home, work, friends, environment).

Substance: The particular psychedelic used to facilitate the journey.
Voyager: The person taking a psychedelic.

Preparation for a Guided Session

Once a decision is made to work together, even if the guide is familiar with how to manage a session, it will be useful for the voyager and the guide both to review the suggestions in chapters 1 and 2. By reviewing the sections each deems important, together they can better align their intentions and increase their rapport.

Why a Guide?

For most people, the predominant feeling during a session is not of discovering something new, alien, or foreign, but of recalling and reuniting with an unassailable clarity that had been latent in one's own mind. Despite the intensely personal nature of the experience, the importance of a guide cannot be overstated. During the experience of awakening to oneself, it is invaluable to be with someone who supports you. Your guide knows the terrain, can sense where you are, and will be able to advise or caution you as appropriate.

It cannot be emphasized enough that we are not talking about "a drug experience," but about how best to become open to your own inner worlds and make use of a vast range of experiences after taking these substances. In the words of one guide discussing the role of psychedelics in relation to other practices, "It enhances mind states also accessible from intense practice and focused attention discoverable through yoga, meditation, fasting and other disciplines." Seemingly universal, this opening is often experienced as reuniting one's self with an eternal flow of energies and understandings.

Aldous Huxley, the author and philosopher, writing about his first psychedelic experiences, talked about "the heightened significance of things." Objects he had seen countless times but rarely noticed fascinated him as if for the first time. The psychedelic gave his mind freer play to see myriad connections, linking formerly mundane items to an ocean of ideas, memories, feelings, and attitudes. Huxley also described vibrant visions and ancient archetypal constellations that he felt had been present but unnoticed in his mind.

After reviewing many different spiritual breakthroughs, William James, the first important American psychologist, came to the following conclusion, which is especially true of the entheogenic experience:

> One conclusion was forced upon my mind at that time, and my impression of its truth has ever since remained unshaken. It is that our normal waking consciousness, rational consciousness as we call it, is but one special type of consciousness. Whilst all about it, parted from it by the filmiest of screens, there lie potential forms of consciousness entirely different. We may go through life without suspecting their existence; but apply the requisite stimulus, and at a touch they are there in all their completeness, definite types of mentality which probably somewhere have their field of application and adaptation. No account of the universe in its totality can be final which leaves those other forms of consciousness quite disregarded.[2]

Albert Hofmann, the chemist who created LSD and discovered its entheogenic potential, echoed James's statement. He wrote, "The first planned LSD experiment was therefore so deeply moving and alarming, because everyday reality and the ego experiencing it, which I had until then considered to be the only reality, dissolved, and an unfamiliar ego experienced another unfamiliar reality."[3]

Initial Experiences

It is natural to hope that one's first full sexual experience will be loving and pleasurable. However, for many people that initiation can be awkward and uncomfortable—even traumatic. Unfortunately, self-administered psychedelics also can have severely disturbing, long-lasting effects. A well-structured session makes it far more likely that early psychedelic experience will be meaningful, healthy, and life enhancing.

What You Need to Know to Guide a Journey

Set: Preparation for the Session

Suggestions for the Voyager

If possible, approach a voyage as a three-day process.[4] Ideally, on the first day, stay quiet and unhurried. Reserve time for self-reflection, spending a portion of the preparation day in nature. Set aside the second day, all day, for the session. Try to take as much as possible of the day after the session to begin to integrate the experience and to record your discoveries and insights.

Prior to the session, it's wise to clarify your personal preconceptions about psychedelic experiences, sacred plants, and entheogens in general. In addition, consider and reflect on your understanding of mystical experience, cosmic consciousness, or whatever else you may have heard described that might arise. Share your expectations, concerns, and hopes with your guide or guides. This will help you stay attuned with one another during the session.

Discussing the range of possible experiences in advance enables the session itself to go more smoothly. Whether you are a novice or an experienced voyager, internal experiences that may be entirely novel for you may occur. These might include:

- Cascading geometric forms and colors (usually early in the session)
- Alteration of felt time (expansion and/or contraction of "clock time")
- Finding yourself in a different reality, as if you had lived or are living in another time or place
- Being in a different body of either sex
- Becoming an animal, plant, or microorganism
- Experiencing your own birth

As a session progresses, it is not uncommon to find yourself encountering entities that some refer to as "the presence of spirits." In most cases, these meetings are positive. However, if you become upset or frightened, let your guide know.

To maximize the usefulness of realizations that may occur during your psychedelic voyage, it is invaluable to write out beforehand what you hope to learn, experience, understand, or resolve. Whatever you've written should be available to you and your guide during and after the session. Some experienced guides have observed that a voyager can, in fact, direct his or her own journey by choosing a small number of questions beforehand in order to organize the direction of the session. One can use this opportunity for a focused inquiry into very specific psychological, spiritual, or social concerns. At the same time, one can be open to engaging with whatever arises from a new encounter.

In addition to clarifying questions, for some people, it is helpful to identify your goals. Your goals may be spiritual: to have direct experience with aspects of your tradition or another tradition, to transcend prior beliefs, even to transcend belief itself. You may hope to have what is called a "unity experience," in which there is no separation between your identity and all else.

Your goals may be social: to improve relationships with your spouse, children, siblings, parents, colleagues, friends, and spiritual and secular institutions.

Your goals may be psychological: to find insight into neurotic patterns, phobias, or unresolved anger or grief. If you know you want to work in these areas, these guidelines may be insufficient. For these goals, additional preparation is recommended, and it would be best to work with a guide who has psychological training.

Because in many cases a single individual is guiding a session, this material was written as if there is only one guide. Ideally, if possible, there should be two guides, a man and a woman. At times and unpredictably, a voyager may prefer the support of one gender or the other. Having two guides makes the task of guiding easier for the guides and allows them to take short breaks during the session. The presence of both male and female energies is the optimal situation.

Suggestions for the Guide

Guiding someone on a psychedelic journey is sacred work. You are there to ensure that the session is maximally safe and beneficial, to increase the probability of the voyager entering into transpersonal or transcendent states, to minimize difficulties, and to honor the trust placed in you. It is not necessary to have a great deal of specialized information to be a superb guide. The essential prerequisites are compassion, intuition, and loving-kindness.

However, in addition to those qualities, it is valuable to have basic knowledge in certain areas: the range of possible effects, the basic principles of various spiritual traditions, and a sense of how and when to share useful ideas and concepts with the voyager. Your suggestions at the right moments may help the voyager make a pivotal discovery or retain an important insight.

Range of effects: Any psychedelic experience might include a wide range of responses, reactions, visions, and internal dramas, from ecstatic to terrifying. At times, you may need to reassure the voyager that a certain experience, even if troubling, is normal and that it will pass. In other cases, you may need to help an individual cope with a physical symptom. Rarely, it might be necessary to get outside help. A significant body of disinformation about psychedelics has been circulated. Therefore, as part of the preparation for any journey, it is essential to dispel untrue ideas about the effects of psychedelics. A well-kept-up site that discusses misinformation about LSD and other mind-expanding substances is found by going to http://en.wikipedia.org and searching on "urban legends about illegal drugs." See also www.snopes.com.

Remaining centered: The more centered you are as a guide, the more effective you will be. The more you know about yourself and whomever you are guiding, the more likely you are to be able to stay centered and tranquil throughout the session. When you yourself are more comfortable, it will be easier for the voyager to transition from one state of awareness to another. After reviewing hundreds of sessions in different settings, Timothy Leary and Richard Alpert (Ram Dass), while still teaching at Harvard, concluded that in most situations a voyager became distressed when the guide had become unsettled, uncertain, or upset.

Sacred traditions: Voyagers may or may not begin with their own religious orientation. In addition, it is not unusual for a voyager to encounter beings or experience states of consciousness described in traditions other than his or her own. You can reduce any anxiety about such encounters should they occur by preparing to be supportive and respectful of any tradition that emerges. Because every tradition has its own symbols and descriptions of higher states, it is unlikely that you can know about them all. The highest levels of all traditions may be essentially the same, but each individual's capacity to fathom and integrate altered states will be unique.

For example, each of these approaches toward being closer to God arises from a different tradition: wanting to be aware of God and still remain separate; yearning to love and interact with God, yet not lose one's personal identity; or dissolving and merging with God. Your support of the voyager's initial intention about spiritual or religious experience is the best possible way to begin. However, be willing to realign your support with the voyager's shifting experiences as well. In other words, remain open and present to whatever occurs.

A useful response to any experience that stretches a voyager's sense of reality during the session is to gently invite that person to go deeper by saying, "Yes! That's good. Would you like to know more?" When a voyager feels secure, the capacity to reach greater heights, and also to remember and integrate the experience, is most likely.

Working with fear: If a voyager has limited experience with altered states, he or she may be frightened as familiar dimensions of identity begin to dissolve. A guide can alleviate this fear, by discussing this possibility as part of the preparation.

When a voyager looks directly at a complex tangle of memories, desires, insecurities, and other unresolved inner threads, a natural reaction can be to become frightened. Be reassuring; clarify that the feeling of fear is normal and will pass. Your reassurances will make it possible for the individual to process the fear more easily.

During fearful moments, you can use a gentle touch and suggest deep breathing. Notice any shift in the depth or pattern of breathing.

Shallow breathing or panting suggests resistance, while deep, slower breathing usually occurs when a barrier is being dissolved.

> *If you are in an ethnocentric stage of development and you have a unity-state experience of being one with everything, you might interpret that as an experience of oneness with Jesus and conclude that nobody can be saved unless they accept Jesus as their personal savior. If you are at an egocentric stage and have the same experience, you might believe that you yourself are Jesus. If you are at an . . . integral stage . . . you are likely to conclude that you and all sentient beings without exception are one in the spirit.*
>
> KEN WILBER, *THE TRANSLUCENT REVOLUTION*

Common Issues for Guides

Intentions: Review your own hopes and fears for the voyager and for yourself before the session begins. Be careful not to intend or hope for a specific outcome. Your assignment is to hold the space for your voyager's journey, not to set the goals.

Point of view: You may hope the person you're guiding will agree with you about certain issues, especially spiritual ones. It is natural to want this (you are human, after all), but it is distracting to express those opinions during the session. Discuss this beforehand if you feel your own point of view might be an issue that could interfere with your objectivity.

Relationship to voyager: If you are the voyager's lover or spouse, think carefully before being that person's guide. If the relationship is an issue for either of you, allow someone else to be the guide. If sexual feelings arise in you or in the voyager (and they often do), allow the feelings to exist as you would any other part of the experience. However, don't be sexual even if asked. In an entheogenic setting, any acting out will narrow the voyager's experience and can be confusing.*

---

*A guide recalled a session in which a woman in her late forties, over the course of a day, had more than fifty separate orgasms. She would not discuss her experience with her guide, but when evaluated psychologically six months later, she was rated as much improved.

Social boundaries: Be wary of your own judgments about the voyager's personal relationships. It's important not to suggest an assessment of any particular relationship during the session unless this intention has been agreed on beforehand. Your approval or disapproval of any relationship can easily disrupt the voyager's own process of discovery.

Transpersonal expression: During entheogenic sessions, voyagers will usually experience realms beyond their personal egos. As a result, they may undergo transformational transitions. Keep in mind that there are an infinite number of ways to find God as well as innumerable ways to describe that discovery. Let the voyager stay with his own realizations. As a general practice, encourage the voyager to collect experiences, save discussion about them for later review and reflection, and not even try to figure them out as they occur.

When to cancel or postpone: For whatever reason, if you have an intuition that the timing is wrong, that the person is not well prepared or hasn't done what you feel has been the necessary preparation, or that you're not the right guide, don't hesitate to delay or cancel the session. Specifically, in preparing for a session, if someone expresses that his or her intention is to delve deeply into suffering, darkness, or the nature of evil, be cautious. Unless you have psychotherapeutic training related to altered states, you should seriously consider not guiding that person. People who begin with these intentions often become stuck in hellish parts of their own psyches and can damage themselves. If you're not sure that you can deal with problems that may arise, you are right and should not guide such a session. Suggest that this individual work in a nonpsychedelic therapeutic context instead. This is not to deny the value and utility of extremely negative experiences, but entering that realm as a primary focus for a psychedelic experience with an inexperienced guide may be treacherous.*

---

*A guide named B.R. stated, "Yet, there are powerfully positive sessions that entail the courageous movement in and through personal suffering towards transcendence. It is of critical importance that the voyager accepts whatever presents itself in his/her field of consciousness as a potential gift, even if it initially appears dark or threatening."

Setting

The following factors are important in the determination of setting.

Immediate environment: All that is necessary for a safe journey with infinite possibilities is an uncluttered, comfortable room with a couch or bed on which the voyager can rest, a comfortable chair for the guide, and easy access to a bathroom. Having a variety of soft pillows and blankets on hand is usually a good idea. The room should also have some kind of a music system. It is better if the room can be insulated from outside sights and sounds, including people's voices, pets, and phones. Your goal is to create and maintain a simple environment that supports inner quiet. When in doubt, make the space even simpler. Most experienced guides prefer to begin the session indoors with music so that the voyager's mind is the primary source for what unfolds.

That being said, an outdoor setting has its advantages. Wind, stirring leaves, birds, streams, rivers, ocean waves—the connectedness of nature can become an essential part of the session. When questioned about taking a psychedelic, Albert Hofmann had only one recommendation: "Always take it in nature." If you do decide on an outdoor setting, the experience may be extroverted. However, even outside, music is helpful.

With a sufficient entheogenic dose, indoors or out, the voyager tends to want to spend much of the time, day or night, lying down. An ideal balance might be to allow the more intense segments to take place indoors, then to go outside later in the session. What is critical is maintaining physical, personal, and psychological safety and support.

Incense: For centuries, incense has been a part of many entheogenic rituals, and it can serve as another way to orient and accompany the voyager.[5]

Music: Most cultures that use plants for healing, divination, or spiritual revivification use music to facilitate the transition from one level of awareness to another and to enhance the feeling of safety by providing nonverbal support. With or without the ingestion of psychedelics, drumming, chanting, dancing, and singing are used worldwide to guide changes in consciousness. Music proves to be invaluable in helping people travel beyond their usual thought patterns. Music supports and suggests, so choose wisely.

During a session, music becomes a richly layered tapestry of sound and often evokes strong emotions. For most people, the music seems to come from inside one's own body and is not just felt as sound, but also may be perceived as color, shape, texture, odor, or taste.

Headphones or ear buds are fine. Stereo speakers near a person's head are good and allow freer movement. Discuss beforehand what music may be played. Music selections may be suggested by guides and by the voyager.

If any selection does not feel right during the session, the voyager should be able to signal or say, "Please change the music." Stay with whatever is playing for a few more minutes to be sure that the request is appropriate and not just a way for the voyager to voice a reaction or simply try to stay in control. Explain in the preparation session how you will be handling the music. In deeper states of consciousness, the voyager may not even hear the music. However, even then, music serves a protective purpose, like the net of a trapeze artist. Have at least eight hours of music on hand to be able to choose or change selections as needed.

Musical recommendations: When the psychedelic first begins to take effect, put on the person's choice of starting music. Many guides have their own collection of music from prior sessions that can be used from that point on. In any case, use music on which you and the voyager have agreed or make sure that the voyager trusts your choices.

Classical music tends to feel appropriate to most people, even if they have not chosen it. Hovhaness's *Mysterious Mountain,* Fauré's *Requiem,* Gregorian chants, solo piano, piano with one or two other instruments, unaccompanied flute, ragas, and indigenous drum recordings can all be used effectively. Anything with words the voyager can understand may be distracting and should not be played after the first hour. Music that could be considered emotionally leading or manipulative is potentially problematic.[6] By mid-afternoon (after about six hours), almost any musical choice will be enjoyed, but during the most intense early hours, the selection of music is important. Near the end of the session, if requested, play any music the voyager wishes, including pieces with words.

Listening to music with closed eyes increases its value and its potential impact. An eyeshade, an eye pillow, or a folded washcloth or scarf makes it easier for the music to be experienced internally. (There are valuable facets of consciousness to enter with the eyes open or closed, but many guides recommend that a voyager spend most of the time, especially during the period of intensely heightened awareness, with closed eyes. As one guide said, "It's amazing how much one can 'see' with eyes closed.")

Substance

LSD itself is almost completely metabolized well before its peak effects are felt.[7] It seems to act as a catalyst, creating an environment in which other reactions can then occur. LSD serves as a lubricant, allowing certain capacities to interact with one another more easily, thus enabling latent brain functions fuller expression. The resulting experiences range from a subtle shift in perception to breathtaking plunges into other realities. Other psychedelic substances are metabolized at different rates; however, each substance allows consciousness to expand beyond its customary limits.

Dose: Obviously, using any plant or plant extract precludes exact measurement. However, there are some parameters. From 150 to 400 micrograms of LSD is a normal range. While this book focuses on LSD, a full range of similar experiences can occur with mescaline or psilocybin. If the voyager is taking mescaline, 1 microgram of LSD is equal to 1 or 2 milligrams of mescaline. If psilocybin is used, 30 milligrams has been called "a safe high-dose."[8] Body weight and metabolism do not appear to be, in and of themselves, deciding variables in selecting the right dose for an individual. A reliable resource of information about doses for a range of psychedelics can be found at www.erowid.org/psychoactives/dose/dose.shtml.

THE ENTHEOGENIC VOYAGE

Part Two: Guidelines for Voyagers and Guides

THE GUILD OF GUIDES

In LSD inebriation, the accustomed worldview undergoes a deep-seated transformation and its integration. Connected with this is a loosening or even suspension of the I–you barrier.

ALBERT HOFMANN, *LSD: MY PROBLEM CHILD*

The Psychedelic Session

LSD and other entheogens have the capacity to open an infinite number of doors. The following descriptions represent stages that have been reported for many different voyages; however, a spectrum of variations can and do occur. The approximate amount of time given for each stage is typical for LSD, mescaline, or peyote. These times are usually shorter, though in the same sequence, for psilocybin and mushrooms.

Stage One: Ingesting the Psychedelic
Considerations for the Voyager

After you have ingested the psychedelic and while you are waiting to begin your voyage, feel free to talk with the guide about any residual anxiety or considerations you may have. When you feel that the actual experience is beginning, you will probably want to lie down. If you feel comfortable doing so, put on an eyeshade or eye pillow. Once settled, allow yourself to:

- Relax
- Listen to music
- Observe your breathing and pay attention to any sensations you have in your body
- Notice how the music is affecting you

You may now begin to move in and out of an awareness of being in the room. That "in-and-out" feeling is natural; it is a sign that your journey has begun. Again, if you become concerned with anything you are experiencing, share this with your guide. If it feels right to you, you might simply put your hand out, asking for it to be held. Observe what is going on inside your mind and body, but do not try to control the flow of images and sensations. Allow your mind to take its natural course; relax and observe as your thoughts unfold without any effort. Affirm that all experiences are welcome.

It is not uncommon, for example, to feel as though your thoughts are coming more swiftly than you can process them. This rush of images and impressions can be disconcerting, but if simply observed, it can be experienced as pleasurable—with wonder or even amazement. This sensation of heightened intensity frequently comes when you are about to change levels, preparing to shift into a higher gear. Allow it to happen. As you let go, the discomfort will pass.

Remain in a prone position, with eyes closed, using the eyeshade and focusing on your breath. If you feel extremely uneasy, sit up and tell the guide what you are experiencing. You may even wish to stand up, notice how you feel, and look at your guide before lying back down and relaxing. Your body will naturally prefer and find a restful position as your mind's capacity expands.

Considerations for the Guide

Know that you and the voyager are about to create a sacred space together. Early on the day of the session, a light, easily digestible breakfast of fruit or toast, if desired, is fine. If the voyager wishes to say a prayer, express gratitude, or invoke any spiritual tradition, you might set up an altar or just sit in silence together. (See suggestions for rituals at the end of this chapter.)

Some guides offer the psychedelic in a formal way, serving the tablets, capsules, or plant materials in a small, attractive dish or bowl, and offering water in a crystal wineglass or even a metal goblet.

Stage Two: Initial Onset (twenty to fifty minutes)

After ingesting the psychedelic, some voyagers may want to move around the room and converse normally. If possible, it is better for the person to be quiet and reflective. However, you need to be responsive and allow the voyager to do whatever comes naturally, especially if there is some anxiety. As the substance takes effect, the voyager should be invited to lie down, and begin to listen to his or her own music or the guide's choice of music. If, after the initial onset, a person continues to sit up and talk or move around, he or she may need a booster dose. This can be given an hour or more into the session without any problems. A second dose should be about one half of the initial dose. Before giving the booster, check in and find out what the person is experiencing. If a deep spiritual journey is going to unfold, it will almost always begin before the second hour is over.

If after two hours, with or without the extra dose, the voyager is still up and interacting, do not give another dose. Needing to continue to move around or relate to someone else is usually a sign of resistance to going inward and should be respected. Suggest walking outdoors, listening to music sitting up. Do not continue to press for an entheogenic session.

Dosage: A dose that is too low may diminish the intensity or depth of the experience; too large a dose can prevent what happens from being recalled or even understood. If in doubt, begin with a lower dose with the possibility of a booster.

Stage Three: Opening and Letting Go (three to four hours)
Considerations for the Voyager

About halfway through the session, you will be able, if you are willing, to let go of whatever thoughts, feelings, and concerns you don't need for this journey. Your guide will play music for you, unless you ask for silence. At this point, you will be able to:

- Let go of expectations about the session
- Let go of personal concerns
- Let go of concerns about personal issues such as problems in your relationships and habit patterns
- Let go of each experience, feeling, or visual event as it occurs
- Let go of your concerns about your personal identity
- Experience and deepen your awareness of other dimensions of reality

For some people, this is an effortless, ecstatic period; for others it can be disorienting. At some moments, you may be frightened or confused by the content or intensity of your visions. You may experience unusual feelings associated with letting go. These might be physical ("My arm is melting") or emotional ("Am I going crazy?"). You may feel unsafe, not trusting yourself, the situation, or even your guide. Some people feel as if they are dying. Your guide may remind you that this is an inner experience of your mind and that your body is fine and that your guide or guides are there to help you ride it through, not to stop it.

Therefore, if something concerns you, ask for help. Remember, your guide is there to support and re-center you. (The sensation of dying, for example, may be your personality's initial reaction to the recognition that "you" are greater than your personal identity.)

This dissolving of boundaries happens at the stage when you may feel as though you are in the presence of spirits. These experiences are usually positive. However, if they disturb you, be sure to tell your guide.

Considerations for the Guide

Listen, watch, and be sensitive to the voyager's shifting mental states. During this period, you do little more than monitor the music and remain close by, being supportive. If you need to calm the voyager's anxieties, a reminder that he or she chose to have this experience can be helpful.

It is during this stage that the voyager is most likely to be in touch with the underlying unity of all existence. Some people will describe this as "seeing God," others "joining with God," while for still others it becomes an experience of "being God." Sometimes this state includes the realization that not only you but also everyone else is God. Whatever form it takes, your primary responsibility is to support the person having the realization.

Especially at this point, it is not uncommon for guides to experience what is known as a contact high. Without taking any substances, a guide may recall vivid memories or have sensations of being tuned back in to expanded states of consciousness. Hearing certain music and/or being with someone undergoing experiences and exhibiting behaviors you may have done in the past can ignite sensations that echo or re-create your own past voyages. These states are natural, usually enjoyable, and do not need to interfere with your role as the guide.

Throughout the day, if you need to go to the toilet, go. If a guide waits too long, the voyager may pick up his or her discomfort and become confused. Even if you are the only guide, be sure to go when you need to and tell the voyager that you are leaving for a few minutes. When you return from the bathroom, if it seems necessary, mention that you have only been gone a few minutes. In those few minutes, a great deal of inner time may have transpired for the voyager.

Stage Four: Plateau (one to two hours)

Following the period of entheogenic recognition, music is optional. The guide may gradually lower the volume until it is off or alternate periods of silence or music as requested.

Considerations for the Voyager

Feel free to sit up, check in with the guide, or continue to listen to the music. You may focus on the music or the images you see internally. You can let go and enjoy the interplay and variety of what has been called the "ten thousand worlds" of shifting realities. You may need to ask for assurance that what you recall and have experienced is valid. Generally, a guide can explain to you that what you have seen on your journey is real, in that it is real to you, while at the same time unique to you. Others who take a psychedelic will have had their own, and perhaps similar, experiences—unique according to their interests, capacities, and frame of mind.

Considerations for the Guide

The voyager may report that he or she has had or is still having a vast expansion of identity, of being part of the creation of the universe or the formation of the stars. The voyager may report having experienced a recapitulation of personal creation, going from sperm and egg on through birth. Others will have entered what seemed to be evolution itself or what appeared to be past lives. Wherever the voyager reports having been or being, your role is to listen, be supportive, and clarify only if asked to.

Keep conversation at a minimum. If the voyager is confused or upset, offer reassurance. Place your hand gently on his or her arm and say something like, "You can let it go; you're doing well." That comforting touch is often all that is needed. Experienced guides learn to intuit when it is appropriate to say something. Usually, it is more than enough just to be with the voyager. If the voyager needs to use the toilet, you may need to help the voyager stand up and walk to the bathroom because his or her external visual world may be in flux.

Stage Five: The Gentle Glide (next three hours or until the guide and the voyager agree it is time to move on)

Simple finger food (e.g., fresh or dried fruits, nuts, crackers, juice) should be offered. Water should be available all day. The voyager may or may not choose to eat something. (If an apple is included, you might hear a comment about Adam and Eve.) The guide should eat if hungry.

Considerations for the Voyager

After the peak of your experience, as you are reentering your world, is often an excellent time to do personal work. You will be aware of your usual identity, but not be as attached to your usual habits, templates, or distortions. If you wish—and your guide agrees—this is also a good time to go outside. If there is no outdoor setting that is safe and inviting, you may enjoy observing a flower or plant in the room or even looking through large-format photography books about nature.

Considerations for the Guide

If you've been asked to help create a bridge between the mystical experiences earlier in the day and the voyager's personal self, excellent tools to make this connection include a flower, a mirror, and family photographs.

The preferred flower is a rosebud, ideally one that is just beginning to open. Encourage the voyager to look into it as long as that feels appealing. This may be as long as half an hour. If the voyager merely glances at it, smells it, and hands it back, offer a second opportunity and suggest a deeper look. However, if there is no interest, be ready to move on.

Another way to deepen the connections made during the session is to invite the voyager to gaze into a full-size handheld mirror. The voyager may see his or her own face aging or becoming younger, and may also see people of different sexes, ages, and races from different historical periods. If this occurs, encourage the voyager to continue looking into the mirror. If the voyager becomes concerned or fearful, suggest that he or she focus on the eyes in the mirror. Eyes usually remain constant through the changes and are reassuring. Even if you have had a similar experience on a journey of your own, don't offer an interpretation of what is being seen.

If the voyager wishes to do more personal work, offer photos of people and places that have been brought to the session. The voyager may stare into a single picture for as long as an hour. After either commenting or sitting in silence, the voyager may put that photo down and ask for another one. Do not intrude with your ideas or opinions, especially if you know the individuals in the photos.

A person asking for his or her glasses back is an indication of the return to more familiar perceptual limits. The person is still only lightly identified with his or her personality but has reidentified with their body. If a voyager arrived with a cold, an allergy, or pain of some kind, these symptoms often disappear during the session and may come back about this time.

Complete or partial cures of physical conditions may happen. For example, Dr. Andrew Weil, the most widely known advocate of complementary medicine, who had suffered from a severe and lifelong cat allergy, had that allergy disappear during an LSD session and it never reappeared.

If the voyager brought music to the session, this is an excellent time to listen to that. This is also a good time to review goals or questions written before the session. Read one item at a time aloud. As with the photographs, discuss or interpret as little as possible. Don't suggest an answer or even a direction unless asked. Some people will want to discuss their insights and realizations; others will not.

Stage Six: The End of the Formal Session

The guided portion of the day of the session should come to an end six to eight hours after taking a shorter-acting substance such as psilocybin or eight to ten hours after taking a longer-acting substance such as LSD or mescaline.

Considerations for the Voyager

You may dip in and out of the experience for the rest of the evening. Don't feel any obligation to be sociable. You may feel extremely loving toward your spouse or children or others close to you but not especially demonstrative. If you wish to call people, limit those calls to people who know what you've been doing and, ideally, who have experience with psychedelics. Don't worry if some parts of your session are difficult to recall. The major events will stay with you, both consciously and unconsciously.

You will probably want to spend time starting to integrate what you've experienced. You may still see the world as flowing or sparkling. Enjoy these visual gifts from your own mind. Eat lightly, and be sure you drink enough liquids to replenish yourself. It's wise to avoid caffeinated beverages because they can interfere with your ability to fall asleep.

Considerations for the Sitter

As stated earlier, the sitter is a friend or relative, ideally someone who has had experience with psychedelics, who minds the voyager when the session is over. He or she should arrive to take the voyager from the session room to the voyager's home, if possible, or to the sitter's. During the voyager's evening of reentry, the sitter should be nonjudgmental, gentle, open to listening, and comfortable with silence. Long periods of silence indicate that the voyager is still moving in and out of the experience and may be having significant insights. The sitter should take notes if asked to.

It is a good idea to offer a light meal of simple foods. If the voyager takes medications regularly, remind him or her to take them. After a session, a person may go in and out of sleep for most of the night. If a person would like to go to sleep but cannot relax enough to do that, warm milk, chamomile tea, or just a single glass of wine may help. Most people prefer not to take anything, allowing the session to end naturally with normal sleep.

Situation: Post-Experience Integration

Considerations for the Voyager

In the first few weeks after your journey, take time to distill out what matters the most to you from your experience. Don't rush. It is likely that you will find your life flows more easily than before. Some people will be curious and open to hearing about your experience; others will be afraid for you, apprehensive that you may be changing your worldview or disturbing theirs. Don't try to convince anyone of anything. Few people will want to hear too many details about your session. As your realizations become integrated into your own life, you will feel less need to describe your journey to others.

You may become more aware than ever before that some people in your life are nourishing and nurturing to you while others are not. Stay with what nourishes you, as you would with food. Stay away, if possible, from anyone who belittles you or tries to diminish your experience.

Do not make major life changes for the first few weeks. Some people, for example, prematurely reevaluate their primary relationships. Give yourself time to integrate your experience first. The exception would be to stop toxic behaviors such as excessive drinking and taking harmful drugs. There is ample evidence that what drives many people to excessive use of alcohol or hard drugs is a vague awareness of their spiritual estrangement and isolation. When people feel reconnected, as they often do after an entheogenic experience, they may stop their excessive drug use or drinking without effort or withdrawal symptoms.

Considerations for the Guide

It's good to meet with the voyager at least once soon after the session to help with the integration process. Beyond that, be available as needed.

Knowing you are there if needed seems to be almost as valuable as your actually doing or saying anything in particular.

Prior to the session, make sure you learned about your voyager's support system: family, friends, people at work, and people at church, mosque, or temple as well as therapists or spiritual teachers. If it is appropriate at any later meetings, suggest that some of these people can be helpful while others might not, at least for a while.

Frequency: How Soon Again? How Often?

As with most other positive experiences, we usually want to do it again. However, psychedelic voyages are not like other most other experiences. If you take them again too soon, you cannot expect that they will have the same effect. The rule of thumb is *the more profound the experience, the longer you should wait before doing it again.* The Guild of Guides suggests a minimum of six months between entheogenic journeys because it takes at least that long for the learning and insights to be absorbed and integrated into your life.

Research conducted at the International Foundation for Advanced Study in Menlo Park, California,* over a six-year period found that it took at least a full year for deep-seated personality changes to stabilize. Many people who had truly profound experiences had no desire for some years, or even ever again, for any subsequent sessions.

Another caveat in response to those questions is that "chasing the high" almost never works. It is like taking a photograph on top of another photograph on the same frame of film—a double exposure. The two images will obscure each other. However, if you advance the film so that an unexposed frame is available, the next captured image will be fresh and can be as meaningful in its own way as the first one was.

If you feel you absolutely *must* take a psychedelic again as soon as possible, it's likely that you need to face some issue that you're avoiding. That feeling is not a command from your highest self to take a psychedelic, no

---

*The International Foundation for Advanced Study is where I worked and studied for seven years, beginning in 1961. Research done there will be referred to throughout the book.

matter how much you want it to be. One option is to arrange a session with a therapist to look at what was uncovered or discovered. Keep in mind that your experience was not simply "drug-induced," but was facilitated by a blend of the substance, the guide, your intention, and other factors unique to your situation at the time. Neglecting any of these variables may lower the value to you of any subsequent session.

Wait at least another month and then see what feels right.

Watering the Celestial Tree

These guidelines are a living entity made up of the collective experience of a number of guides from different cultures. Fuller versions plus a great deal of additional material can be found and added to at www.entheoguides .net, a Wiki site established and maintained by guild members for the general public.

> *The door*
> *between the worlds*
> *is always open.*
>   RUMI

3
QUALITIES OF TRANSCENDENT EXPERIENCE
Four Dominant Characteristics

ALAN WATTS

Alan Watts (1915–1973), a very important early popularizer of Eastern thought, was an Episcopal priest turned philosopher, writer, and speaker.* The author of more than twenty-five books, he also wrote many articles and recorded hundreds of audiotapes, all of which are still broadcast on noncommercial radio. When he and I were on early panels that presented pro and con arguments about psychedelics, he was never angry but only amused at the folly of others. He modeled that good living and good thinking went well together. For a sample of Watts talking about "nothingness," go to www.youtube.com and search on "Alan Watts–On Nothingness."

The following selection by Alan Watts is excerpted from his article titled "Psychedelics and the Religious Experience,"[1] which was in the January 1968 issue of California Law Review. *Almost all the readers of this*

*Please note that the italic text included at the head of many chapters of this book, or contained in the discussion therein, is my (James Fadiman's) commentary on that particular author and his work.

39

book will have had their own psychedelics experiences and may wonder why this particular selection has been included. One answer is that not everyone who has used psychedelics has experienced existence at its core. A second reason is that this selection assumes that readers have not had the experiences he speaks of. Therefore, he needed to be as exact and as lucid as possible in describing states that other writers stumble over, calling then ineffable or noetic or, even worse, "indescribable." What makes this article especially valuable is the manner by which Watts suggests how the world might appear to someone who has felt the revelatory nature of these experiences.

For the purposes of this study, in describing my experiences with psychedelic drugs, I avoid the occasional and incidental bizarre alterations of sense perception that psychedelic chemicals may induce. I am concerned, rather, with the fundamental alterations of the normal, socially induced consciousness of one's own existence and relation to the external world. I am trying to delineate the basic principles of psychedelic awareness, but I must add that I can speak only for myself. The quality of these experiences depends considerably upon one's prior orientation and attitude to life, although the now voluminous descriptive literature of these experiences accords quite remarkably with my own.

Almost invariably, my experiments with psychedelics have had four dominant characteristics. I shall try to explain them—in the expectation that the reader will say, at least of the second and third, "Why, that's obvious! No one needs a drug to see that." Quite so, but every insight has degrees of intensity. There can be obvious-1 and obvious-2, and the latter comes on with shattering clarity, manifesting its implications in every sphere and dimension of our existence.

The first characteristic is a slowing down of time, a concentration in the present. One's normally compulsive concern for the future decreases, and one becomes aware of the enormous importance and interest of what is happening at the moment. Other people, going about their business on the streets, seem to be slightly crazy, failing to realize that the whole point of life is to be fully aware of it as it happens. One therefore relaxes, almost luxuriously, into studying the colors in a glass of water or listening to the now highly articulate vibration of every note played on an oboe or sung by a voice.

From the pragmatic standpoint of our culture, such an attitude is very bad for business. It might lead to improvidence, lack of foresight, diminished sales of insurance policies, and abandoned savings accounts. Yet this is just the corrective that our culture needs. No one is more fatuously impractical than the "successful" executive who spends his whole life absorbed in frantic paperwork with the objective of retiring in comfort at sixty-five, when it will all be too late. Only those who have cultivated the art of living completely in the present have any use for making plans for the future, for when the plans mature they will be able to enjoy the results.

I have never yet heard a preacher urging his congregation to practice that section of the Sermon on the Mount which begins, "Be not anxious for the morrow. . . ." The truth is that people who live for the future are, as we say of the insane, "not quite all there" and also not quite here: by overeagerness they are perpetually missing the point. Foresight is bought at the price of anxiety, and when overused it destroys all its own advantages.

The second characteristic I will call "awareness of polarity." This is the vivid realization that states, things, and events that we ordinarily call opposite are interdependent, like back and front or the poles of a magnet. By polar awareness one sees that things which are explicitly different are implicitly one: self and other, subject and object, left and right, and male and female, and then, a little more surprisingly, solid and space, figure and background, pulse and interval, saints and sinners, police and criminals, and in-groups and out-groups. Each is definable only in terms of the other, and they go together transactionally, like buying and selling, for there is no sale without a purchase and no purchase without a sale. As this awareness becomes increasingly intense, you feel that you yourself are polarized with the external universe in such a way that you imply each other. Your push is its pull and its push is your pull, as when you move the steering wheel of a car. Are you pushing it or pulling it?

At first, this is a very odd sensation, not unlike hearing your own voice played back to you on an electronic system immediately after you have spoken. You become confused and wait for it to go on! Similarly, you feel that you are something being done by the universe, yet that the universe is equally something being done by you, which is true, at least in the neurological sense that the peculiar structure of our brains translates the sun into light and air vibrations into sound. Our normal sensation of relationship to the outside world is that sometimes I push it and sometimes it pushes me. But if the two are actually one, where does action begin and responsibility rest? If the universe is doing me, how can I be sure that, two seconds hence, I will still remember the English language? If I am doing it, how can I be sure that, two seconds hence, my brain will know how to turn the sun into light?

From such unfamiliar sensations as these, the psychedelic experience can generate confusion, paranoia, and terror, even though the individual is feeling his relationship to the world exactly as it would be described by a biologist, ecologist, or physicist, for he is feeling himself as the unified field of organism and environment.

The third characteristic, arising from the second, is an awareness of relativity. I see that I am a link in an infinite hierarchy of processes and beings, ranging from molecules through bacteria and insects to human beings and, maybe, to angels and gods—a hierarchy in which every level is in effect the same situation. For example, the poor man worries about money while the rich man worries about his health: the worry is the same, but the difference is in its substance or dimension. I realize that fruit flies must think of themselves as people because, like us they find themselves in the middle of their own world—with immeasurably greater things above and smaller things below. To us, they all look alike and seem to have no personality—as do the Chinese when we have not lived among them. Yet fruit flies must see just as many subtle distinctions among themselves as we do among ourselves.

From this, it is but a short step to the realization that all forms of life and being are simply variations on a single theme: we are all in fact one being doing the same thing in as many different ways as possible. As the French proverb goes, *Plus ça change, plus c'est la même chose* (the more it varies, the more it stays the same). I see, further, that feeling threatened by the inevitability of death is really the same experience as feeling alive and that all beings are feeling this everywhere; they are all just as much

"I" as I am. Yet the "I" feeling, to be felt at all, must always be a sensation relative to the "other"—to something beyond its control and experience. To be at all, it must begin and end. But the intellectual jump that mystical and psychedelic experiences make here is in enabling you to see that all these myriad I-centers are yourself—not, indeed, your personal and superficially conscious ego, but what Hindus call the *paramatman,* the Self of all selves.[2]

As the retina enables us to see countless pulses of energy as a single light, so the mystical experience shows us innumerable individuals as a single Self.

The fourth characteristic is awareness of eternal energy, often in the form of intense white light, which seems to be both the current in your nerves and that mysterious *e* which equals *mc*[2]. This may sound like megalomania or delusion of grandeur—but one sees quite clearly that all existence is a single energy and that this energy is one's own being. Of course, there is death as well as life because energy is a pulsation, and just as waves must have both crests and troughs, the experience of existing must go on and off. Basically, therefore, there is simply nothing to worry about because you yourself are the eternal energy of the universe playing hide-and-seek (off and on) with itself. At root, you are the Godhead, for God is all that there is. Quoting Isaiah just a little out of context: "I am the Lord, and there is none else. I form the light and create the darkness: I make peace, and create evil. I, the Lord, do all these things."[3]

This is the sense of the fundamental tenet of Hinduism, *Tat tram asi* ("That art thou"),[4] with "that" being the subtle Being of which this whole universe is composed.

A classical case of this experience, from the West, is recounted by Alfred Lord Tennyson in *A Memoir by His Son.*

A kind of waking trance I have frequently had, quite up from boyhood, when I have been all alone. This has generally come upon me thro' repeating my own name two or three times to myself silently, till all at once, as it were out of the intensity of the consciousness of individuality, the individuality itself seemed to dissolve and fade away into boundless being, and this not a confused state, but the clearest of the clearest, the surest of the surest, the weirdest of the weirdest, utterly beyond words, where death was an almost laughable impossibility, the loss of personality (if so it were) seeming no extinction but the only true life.

4
EXPERIENCES OF PSYCHEDELIC PIONEERS
In Their Own Words

How did the pioneers of psychedelics assimilate their early experiences? What is common to almost all of their reports included here is that their experiences shifted their respective life directions, for most of them with a single exposure. In the lull between the prior research period and this current one, a generation has lost sight of the reason these substances had such an impact on individuals. These experiences radically reformulated the worldview of whoever was undergoing the journey, which led in turn to major changes in that person's career, relationships, and interactions with the larger culture. Because many of the people in this chapter recorded their observations about their experiences, links to videos and other Web sources have been given when available.

There have been three waves of psychedelic experiences in the West. When Albert Hofmann first tested LSD on himself, no one had any idea of its remarkable properties. The first round of guesses, that it caused a model and containable psychotic episode, turned out to be wrong.

The initial experiences of the first wave of pioneers—Albert Hofmann, Aldous Huxley, and Stanislav Grof—were totally unexpected. With all that we now know about set and setting, we can see that Hofmann and Grof took LSD in far from ideal situations, yet both had, all in all, a positive experience that changed their lives. By the time

Huxley tried LSD, he had already taken mescaline several times at home with a good guide.

The exemplars of the second wave—Alexander Shulgin, Timothy Leary, Ram Dass, Ralph Metzner, and Huston Smith—had all been promised something special and profound, but unknown.

The third wave is illustrated here by reports from Rabbi Zalman Schachter-Shalomi, Charles Tart, Frances Vaughan, Bill Wilson, and Peter Coyote. These people approached their own sessions as explorers, but as explorers who were entering terrain that they knew others had visited before them.

In writing this book, I know that a large number of people worldwide have had some level of experience with one or more psychedelics in a wide variety of settings. The larger culture is aware of their existence. However, the larger culture has also lost some of the understanding about the depth and levels of experience presented here. The experiences of these individuals are as relevant today as they were when they initially occurred.

The First Wave
ALBERT HOFMANN, ALDOUS HUXLEY, AND STANISLAV GROF

The first wave began with the creation of the semisynthetic compound LSD, derived from lysergic acid, a naturally occurring compound. Hofmann, Huxley, and Grof strongly or directly influenced the major figures of the second and third waves of pioneers who followed them.

Albert Hofmann

Albert Hofmann, Ph.D. (1906–2008), was a Swiss biochemist known best for being the first person to synthesize, ingest, and experience the effects of LSD. In 1938, he was employed by the Sandoz Pharmaceutical Company in Basel, Switzerland, and worked with lysergic acid in the hopes of developing a stimulant for blood circulation. Because LSD-25 had no effect in animals, it was put aside, but in 1943, he decided to reexamine it (as described below). He later synthesized psilocybin and authored more than one hundred scientific articles and a number of books, including LSD: My Problem Child.

He regretted that LSD became popular and that medical research was banned for so long. He told me that his advice to the thousands who had asked him how to use LSD was simple and direct: "Always use it in nature." While he did not attribute his living fully till he was 102 to the use of these substances, they were central to his life and worldview. To view a video of Hofmann, at 101 years of age, reflecting on his initial experiences, please go to www.youtube.com and search on "Albert Hofmann" and read the interview by "elmercuriodeinternet." The following material is from an interview with Hofmann in High Times *magazine and from his book* LSD: My Problem Child.[1]

This substance, lysergic acid diethylamide, which I first synthesized in 1938, was given to the pharmacological-medical department at Sandoz laboratories for testing. The animals that were used for the test had no special reaction with this compound, and further research was stopped with this substance.

Five years later, in 1943, I decided to prepare a new batch of the lysergic acid diethylamide. . . . From the very beginning, I thought this substance was something special. It was just a feeling I had. . . . Then, at the end of the synthesis, when I was crystallizing the LSD, I suddenly went into a very strange, dreamlike state. Everything changed, everything had another meaning, unexpectedly. I went home and lay down and closed my eyes and had some very, very stimulated fantasies. I would just think something, and that was what I saw. It was wonderful.

But I didn't know why I was having this strange experience. . . . Three days later I . . . I thought that maybe in some strange way I'd gotten some of this lysergic acid diethylamide in my body, and I decided to experiment on myself with it. I started by taking the equivalent of only one-quarter of a milligram, 250 micrograms.

Within half an hour, I began to experience similar symptoms to those I'd had three days earlier. But quite quickly they became very strong, very intense, and I became anxious, so I asked my laboratory assistant to accompany me home.

As it was wartime and I had no car, we went home by bicycle, and the bicycle ride was strange. My condition began to assume threatening forms. Everything in my field of vision wavered and distorted as if in a curved mirror. I also had the sensation of being unable to move from the spot. I had the feeling that time was standing still. It was a very strange feeling, one I'd never had before. There was a change in the experience of life, of time. But it was the most frustrating thing. I was already deep in the LSD trance, in LSD inebriation, and one of its characteristics, just on this bicycle trip, was of not coming from any place or going anyplace. There was absolutely no feeling of time.

At home I asked my assistant to call for a doctor. . . .

I was in a very odd state of consciousness. The outer world had changed. The room seemed to be full of life in the light, and colors were more intense. But I also had the feeling that I was changed, that my ego had changed. And then it became such a strange experience that I was afraid that I had gone insane. And sometime during that experience, at the climax, I had the feeling I was out of my body.

I had the feeling I was going to die. I had no sensations in my body and thought I'd already left it, was already out of my body, which was something I couldn't explain to the doctor. I couldn't really speak rationally to explain that I had made an experiment, either. So he sat with me through that very difficult experience—horribly difficult—and after about four or five hours, the feeling began to change. I felt that I was coming from this very strange other world back to our normal world. And I had the feeling, when I came back from this strange world, that our normal world, which ordinarily we don't think is wonderful, was a wonderful world. I saw it in a new light. It was a rebirth.

But this happy feeling was only at the end of the experience. And when I came back I closed my eyes and had beautiful, colored visions. There was a transformation of every sound into an optical figure. Each noise produced a corresponding colored figure, which was very enjoyable.

Finally I went to sleep, and in the morning I was completely fresh. A sensation of well-being and renewed life flowed through me. Breakfast tasted delicious and gave me extraordinary pleasure. When I later walked in the garden, in which the sun shone now after a spring rain, everything glistened and sparkled in a fresh light.

Aldous Huxley

Aldous Huxley (1894–1963) was an English writer who spent the later part of his life in Los Angeles, from 1937 until his death in 1963. His best-known novels include Brave New World *and* Island, *but he also produced a wide-ranging output of novels, essays, short stories, poetry, travel writing, and film scripts. Almost legally blind since he was a teenager, Huxley was especially delighted with the visual intensity of his psychedelic experiences. When his library of four thousand books and almost all of his unfinished manuscripts were destroyed in a fire late in his life, I heard him say only, "It seems strange to be starting over."*

Huxley's best-known book about psychedelics, The Doors of Perception, *is a detailed description and discussion of his initial experiences with mescaline. He knew nothing about LSD until shortly before his first experience with it. In these selections from his letters (from the book* Moksha: Aldous Huxley's Classic Writings on Psychedelics and the Visionary Experience[2]*), he reveals his own experiences, not incident by incident, but how the revelations about the nature of being had made a deep impression on his understanding of culture, of humanity, and of the cosmos.*

Go to www.youtube.com and search on "Huxley's LSD Death Trip" for a short video about his asking for and receiving LSD to help him at the time of his death.

23 December 1955

My Dear Humphry [Humphry Osmond, who had given Huxley mescaline],

The psychological effects, in my case, were identical with those of mescaline, and I had the same kind of experience as I had on the previous occasion—transfiguration of the external world, and the understanding, through a realization involving the whole man, that Love is the One, and that this is why Atman is identical with Brahman, and why, in spite of everything, the universe is all right. . . . We played the Bach B-minor suite and the *"Musical Offering,"* and the experience was overpowering. Bach was a revelation. The tempo of the pieces did not change; nevertheless they went on for centuries, and they were a manifestation, in the plane of art, of perpetual creation, a demonstration of the necessity of death and the self-evidence of immortality, an expression of the essential all-rightness of the universe—for the music was far beyond tragedy, but included death and suffering with everything else in the divine impartiality which is the One, which is Love, which is Being or Istigkeit . . . let me advise you, if ever you use mescaline or LSD in therapy, to try the effect of the B-minor suite. More than anything, I believe, it will serve to lead the patient's mind (wordlessly, without any suggestion or covert bullying by doctor or parson) to the central, primordial Fact, the understanding of which is perfect health during the time of the experience, and the memory of the understanding of which may serve as an antidote to mental sickness in the future.

Affectionately,

Aldous

19 July 1956

Dear Victoria [Victoria Ocampo, editor of the distinguished literary review *Sur*],

. . . How strange that we should all carry about with us this enormous universe of vision and that which lies beyond vision, and yet be mainly unconscious of the fact! How can we learn to pass at will from one world of consciousness to the others? Mescaline and lysergic acid will open the door; but one doesn't like to depend exclusively on these chemicals, even though they seem to be more or less completely harmless. I have taken mescaline about six times now and have been taken beyond the realm of vision to the realm of what the mystics call "obscure knowledge"—insight into the nature of things accompanied by the realization that, in spite of pain and tragedy, the universe is all right, in other words that God is Love. The words are embarrassingly silly and, on the level of average consciousness, untrue. But when we are on the higher level, they are seen to stand for the primordial Fact, of which the consciousness is now a part. . . .

Ever yours affectionately,

Aldous

20 November 1956

Dearest Ellen [Ellen Huxley],

Thank you for your fascinating account of the mescaline experience.
. . . Did you get what I have got so strongly on the recent occasions
when I have taken the stuff—an overpowering sense of gratitude, a desire
to give thanks to the Order of Things for the privilege of this particular
experience, and also for the privilege—for that one feels it to be, in spite
of everything—of living in a human body on this particular planet? And
then there is the intense feeling of compassion for those who, for whatever reason, make it impossible for themselves to get anywhere near the
reality revealed by the drug—the reality which is always there for those
who are in the right state of mind to perceive it. . . . Some of the compassion and some of the gratitude remain, even after the experience is over.
One can never be quite the same again. . . .

Your affectionate, Aldous

11 February 1962

Dear Tim [Timothy Leary],

I forgot, in my last letter, to answer your question about Tantra. . . . [He
gives Leary a list of books and suggestions on what to read in them.]
The therapy is not merely for the abnormal, it is above all a therapy for
the much graver sickness of insensitiveness and ignorance which we call
"normality" or "mental health." LSD and the mushrooms should be
used, it seems to me, in context of this basic Tantric idea of the yoga of
total awareness, leading to enlightenment within the world of everyday
experience—which of course becomes the world of miracle and beauty
and divine mystery when experience is what it always ought to be.

Yours, Aldous

Stanislav Grof

*Stanislav Grof, M.D., born in 1931, is a psychiatrist with more than fifty
years of experience researching the healing and transformative potential
of non-ordinary states of consciousness. He is a founder of Transpersonal
Psychology and the International Transpersonal Association, a professor of
psychology at the California Institute of Integral Studies and the Pacifica*

Graduate Institute in the United States, and the author of many books, includ-ing Beyond the Brain, LSD Psychotherapy, Psychology of the Future, The Cosmic Game, When the Impossible Happens, *and* The Ultimate Journey.

You can see Grof discussing his initial LSD experience by going to www .youtube.com and searching on "Stan Grof about His LSD Experience." The following excerpt is from an interview that Grof did for Yoga Journal.[3]

I couldn't believe how much I learned about my psyche in those few hours. I experienced a fantastic display of colorful visions, some abstract and geometrical, others figurative and filled with symbolic import. The sheer intensity of the array of emotions I felt simply amazed me. I was hit by a radiance that seemed comparable to the epicenter of a nuclear explosion or perhaps the light of supernatural brilliance said in oriental scriptures to appear to us at the moment of death.

This thunderbolt catapulted me out of my body. First, I lost my aware-ness of my immediate surroundings, then the psychiatric clinic, then Prague [Czechoslovakia], and finally the planet. At an inconceivable speed, my consciousness expanded to cosmic dimensions. I experienced the big bang, passed through black holes and white holes in the universe, identified with exploding supernovas, and witnessed many other strange phenomena that seemed to be pulsars, quasars, and other cosmic events.

I was able to see the irony and paradox of the situation. The divine manifested itself and took me over in a modern scientific laboratory in the middle of a scientific experiment conducted in a Communist country with a substance produced in the test tube of a twentieth-century chemist.

The Second Wave
ALEXANDER SHULGIN, TIMOTHY LEARY, RICHARD ALPERT (RAM DASS), RALPH METZNER, AND HUSTON SMITH

Alexander Shulgin

Alexander "Sasha" Shulgin, Ph.D., who was born in 1925, is a pharma-cologist and chemist best known as a drug developer. Shulgin discovered, synthesized, and bioassayed (specifically, he tried out on himself) over

230 psychoactive compounds. In 1991 and 1997, he and his wife, Ann, authored the books PiHKAL: A Chemical Love Story *and* TiHKAL: The Continuation, *collections of personal stories and descriptions of how to make, and the effects of, many of these compounds. He is interested in creating what he calls "tools," but leaves it to others to study their effects. To ever so many of us, he has been an easygoing, endlessly supportive, unassuming friend. To see a video in which Shulgin explains what he does and why he does it, go to www.youtube.com and search for "Alexander Shulgin: Why I Discover Psychedelic Substances."*

The following excerpt is from the biographical section of PiHKAL: A Chemical Love Story.[4]

I had read all the recent literature about it, but it was not until April of 1960 that a psychologist friend of mine, and a friend of his . . . provided me with the opportunity to be "babysat" on an experience with 400 milligrams of mescaline sulfate. It was a day that will remain blazingly vivid in my memory, and one which unquestionably confirmed the entire direction of my life.

The details of that day were hopelessly complex and will remain buried in my notes, but the distillation, the essence of the experience, was this: I saw the world that presented itself in several guises. It had a marvel of color that was, for me, without precedent, for I have never particularly noticed the world of color. The rainbow had always provided me with all the hues I could respond to. Here, suddenly, I had hundreds of nuances of color which were new to me, and which I have never, even today, forgotten.

The world was all so marvelous in its detail. I could see the intimate structure of a bee putting something into a sac on its hind leg to take to its hive, yet I was completely at peace with the bee's closeness to my face.

The world was a wonder of interpretive insight. I saw people as caricatures which revealed both their pains and their hopes, and they seemed not to mind my seeing them this way. More than anything else, the world amazed me, in that I saw it as I had when I was a child. I had forgotten the beauty and magic in the knowingness of it. I was in familiar territory of space wherein I had once roamed as an immortal explorer, and I was recalling everything in it that had been authentically known to me then and which I have abandoned, then forgotten, with my coming of age. Like the touchstone that recalls a dream to a sudden presence, this experience reaffirmed a miracle of excitement that I had known in my childhood but had been pressured to forget.

The most compelling insight of the day was that this awesome recall had been brought about by a fraction of a gram of a white solid, but in no way whatsoever could it be argued that these memories had been contained within the white solid. Everything I had recognized was from the depths of my memory and my psyche.

I understood that our entire universe is contained in the mind and the spirit. We may choose not to find access to it, we may even deny its existence, but indeed it is inside us, and there are chemicals that can catalyze its availability. It is now a matter of history that I decided to devote whatever energies and skills I might possess to unraveling the nature of these tools for self-exposure. . . .

I had found my learning path.

Timothy Leary

Timothy Leary, Ph.D. (1920–1996), taught psychology at the University of California, Berkeley, and Harvard University (which fired him in 1963) and was a hugely controversial figure during the 1960s and 1970s because he supported the widespread use of psychedelics for self-discovery. Described as "the most dangerous man in America" by President Richard Nixon, he spent almost eight years in prison and exile, more for his beliefs than for any crime. Author William Burroughs referred to Leary as "a true visionary of the potential of the human mind and spirit." Poet Allen Ginsberg proclaimed him "a hero of American consciousness." Novelist Tom Robbins said that Leary is "the Galileo of our age." Leary wrote 27 books and monographs and 250 articles and gave more than 100 published interviews. Everyone who spent time with Leary—friend or enemy—agreed that he was friendly, funny, smart as all get out, and overwhelmingly charming. He is given far too much credit for causing the cessation of psychedelic research and not enough credit for his insistence on the centrality of a safe set and setting in using any of these materials.

Leary's autobiography, Flashbacks, *and a collection of writings about him,* Timothy Leary: Outside Looking In, *edited by Robert Forte, are the best books to read in order to begin to understand him. Tim's first experience was with mushrooms, soon followed by psilocybin and then LSD. Five hours after eating the mushrooms, Leary said it was all changed. The revelation had come. It was the classic vision, the full-blown conversion experience.*

In his book *High Priest*, Leary wrote, "We [Leary and Alpert] had moved beyond the game of psychology, the game of trying to help people, and beyond the game of conventional love relationships. We were quietly and serenely aware of too much. . . . I've never recovered from that shattering ontological confrontation. I've never been able to take myself, my mind, and the social world around me seriously.

"From the date of this session it was inevitable that we would leave Harvard, that we would leave American society . . . tenderly, gently disregarding the parochial social inanities."[5]

In the book *Birth of a Psychedelic Culture*, Ram Dass said, "When Tim first took LSD he didn't speak for weeks. I went around saying, '. . . we've lost Timothy, we've lost Timothy.' I was warning everybody not to take the drug as Tim wasn't talking. . . ."

Leary said his first LSD experience was "the most shattering experience of his life."[6]

Ram Dass (then Richard Alpert)

Richard Alpert, Ph.D., who was born in 1931 and is better known as Ram Dass, is a contemporary spiritual teacher and the author of a number of books, including The Only Dance There Is, Be Here Now, *and* The Psychedelic Experience *(with Leary and Metzner). After serving as a visiting professor at the University of California, Berkeley, he accepted a position at Harvard University, where he worked with the Social Relations Department, the Psychology Department, the Graduate School of Education, and the Health Service, where he was a therapist. He was also awarded research contracts with Yale and Stanford until, along with Leary, he was fired in 1963. Ram Dass is also known for his relationship with his guru,*

Neem Karoli Baba, and for helping found two charitable groups, the Seva Foundation and the Hanuman Foundation.

When asked if he could sum up his life's message, Ram Dass replied, "I help people as a way to work on myself, and I work on myself to help people." He was my mentor at Harvard before he had any involvement with psychedelics, and later (as described in chapter 17), he gave me my first psychedelic experience. He changed the direction of my life. This book is, in some ways, a partial thank-you to him. If you go to www.youtube.com and search on "Richard Alpert—The LSD Crisis," you will see a very young Richard Alpert discussing his early psychedelic insights. He has been an important worldwide spiritual teacher for many years. The following excerpt is from his chapter in the book Higher Wisdom.[7]

My introduction to psychedelics was via Tim Leary. . . . I was very eager. . . . In March of 1961, we took some psilocybin pills at his big fancy house in Newton. Tim and I took the psilocybin pills together with Allen Ginsberg, who was there too.

I left Tim and Allen in the kitchen and went into the living room where it was dark. Eventually, I noticed that there was someone in the corner of the room, and tried to see who it was. And I realized that it was me! Me, in my various roles—pilot, academic—all my roles were out there somewhere. I was living those roles, so it was quite difficult to see them "over there." I thought, "This drug is going to make me not know who I am. If those are my roles over there, what's going to be left?" then I thought, "Well, at least I have my body." That was my first mistake, because I looked down at the couch and I saw the full couch with no body there! That scared me. Being a philosophical materialist at the time, I really considered my body to be solid. With a sort of Jewish humor, I wondered, "but who is minding the store?"

I ended up going inward to a place in myself where I had never been before. It was a feeling/tone that conveyed the message of being "home." It was a safe home, an ecstatic home. . . .

Eventually I came out of that experience, and realized that we'd had a snowstorm. Tim's house was on a hill, and I rolled down the snowy hill, ecstatic. . . . Tim's house was only about three blocks from my parents' house, where I grew up. So I walked to their house in the snow. When

I came to their walk and saw that it was not shoveled, well, I felt that as the young buck in the family, I should shovel the walk for my dear old parents. So I shoveled the walk.

Unfortunately, it was about four in the morning. My father and mother appeared at their window with a look on their faces that said: "what's wrong with you, you damn little fool?"

Now, ever since I was a baby, I always looked to my parents' attitudes to determine my behavior. Later in life, I looked to their surrogates for this: professors and heads of departments. But in my inner self, in this "home" inside, it felt very good to shovel their walk. And so I danced a jig down below, and I waved, and I shoveled snow. That was the first time I had ever bucked authority. That was the key "aha" during that psilocybin trip.

Very shortly after this, Aldous Huxley gave us a copy of the *The Tibetan Book of the Dead*. Here was a book designed to be read to dying monks, so for me to identify with it so strongly was a shocker.

The Tibetan Book of the Dead gave me a feeling that eastern psychology described the internal workings of this feeling of "home" that I had experienced. I became fascinated by what "the moment" included. It was like multilayered baklava. Like planes upon planes, and some of them were nuts, and some of them were honey. For example, there was an ecstatic state, where colors and music became so incredibly vivid that it seemed as though Mozart must have had access to, and listened in on, these realms. And I liked it very much.

Ralph Metzner

Ralph Metzner, Ph.D., born in 1936, is a psychologist, writer, and researcher who participated in psychedelic research at Harvard University in the early 1960s with Leary and Alpert. Metzner is a psychotherapist and professor emeritus of psychology at the California Institute for Integral Studies in San Francisco, where he had also been the academic dean and academic vice president. He and I have been friends since we were research assistants for Richard Alpert (before psychedelics), and we have remained close ever since. In spite of almost all of my own work being with laboratory-produced psychedelics, Ralph is one of the people who has put me back in touch with the older, nature-based traditions.

To see a video of Metzner giving a presentation at the World Psychedelic Forum in Basel, Switzerland, in 2008, go to www.YouTube and search for "Metzner" and "World Psychedelic Forum." The following excerpt is from the book that he coauthored with Leary, Outside Looking In.[8] *Although a graduate student at the time of this experience, Metzner soon became an equal partner with Leary and Alpert after they left Harvard. He is now a co-founder and the president of the Green Earth Foundation, a nonprofit educational organization devoted to healing and harmonizing the relationship between humans and the earth.*

I lay down on the floor and stretched out, feeling very relaxed and yet very alert . . . all of a sudden I found myself in completely new and magical worlds . . . when I closed my eyes, fantastically beautiful and intricate geometric depth patterns were interweaving behind my eyelids, watching, colliding, streaming by at great speed . . . my skin was embracing me, enwrapping me, in a kind of alternatively wet and dry, hot and cool almost unendurably pleasurable embrace. . . .

. . . at a certain point I noticed that the intensity of the experiences began to diminish, like a slow gliding down. The body felt very warm and relaxed. I understood how my normal perception of the world was constricted and limited by many prohibitions I had somehow accepted. . . .

This was perhaps the most significant revelation of this experience: that I was basically in charge of what I could perceive and think about, but I was not bound by external forces but rather made choices that determine the extent and quality of my awareness.

Huston Smith

Huston Smith, Ph.D., was born in Suzhou, China, in 1919 and spent his first seventeen years there with his parents, who were Methodist missionaries, and his siblings. He taught at the University of Denver from 1944 to 1947 and Washington State University in St. Louis from 1948 to 1958 before becoming the chair of the Philosophy Department at the Massachusetts Institute of Technology, from 1959 to 1973. While there, he took psychedelics and worked with Leary and Alpert. He moved to Syracuse, New York, and worked at Syracuse University until his retirement in 1983.

During his career, Smith not only studied but also practiced Vedanta Hinduism, Zen Buddhism, and Sufism without losing his Christian roots. One of my great joys is to approach Huston and to see him seemingly fill with light before he hugs hello.

Huston is best known for his book World Religions, *which is a textbook for colleges around the country and remains the most widely read book of its kind. He is less well known for his role in trying (unsuccessfully) to shape the early work in psychedelics done at Harvard. By going to www.youtube.com and searching on "Huston Smith on 'How to Study a Religion,'" you will learn how to learn about a religion: by full immersion. Many full-length videos of Huston teaching about the world's major spiritual traditions are also available. The following excerpt, about his first psychedelic experience, is from his book* Cleaning the Doors of Perception.[9]

New Year's Day, 1961. Kendra and I reached the home of Dr. Timothy Leary in Newton, Massachusetts, about 12:30 p.m. Present in addition to Leary were Dr. George Alexander and Frank Barron.

After coffee and pleasantries, Tim sprinkled some capsules of mescaline [probably psilocybin] onto the coffee table and invited us to be his guest. One, he said, was a mild dose, two an average dose, and three a large dose. I took one; after about half an hour, when nothing seemed to be happening, I too took a second capsule.

After what I estimate to have been about an hour, I noticed mounting tension in my body that turned into tremors in my legs. I went into the large living room and lay down on its couch.

It would be impossible for me to fix the time when I passed into the visionary state, for the transition was imperceptible. From here on time becomes irrelevant. . . . The world into which I was ushered was strange, weird, uncanny, significant, and terrifying beyond belief. Two things struck me especially. First, the mescaline acted as a psychological prism. It was as if the layers of the mind, most of whose contents our conscious mind screens out to smelt the remainder down into a single band we can cope with, were now revealed in their completeness—spread out as if by spectroscope into about five distinguishable layers. And the odd thing was that I could to some degree be aware of them all simultaneously, and could move back and forth among them at will, shifting my attention to now this one, now another one. Thus, I could hear distinctly the quiet conversation of Tim and Dr. Alexander in the adjoining study, and follow their discussion and even participate in it imaginatively.

But this leads to the second marked feature. Though the five bands of consciousness—I say five roughly; they were not sharply divided and I made no attempt to count them—were all real, they were not of equal importance. I was experiencing the metaphysical theory known as emanationism, in which, beginning with the clear, unbroken Light of the Void, that light then fractures into multiple forms and declines in intensity as it devolves through descending levels of reality. My friends in the study were present in one band of this spectrum, but it was far more restricted than higher bands that were in view. Bergson's notion of the brain as a reducing valve struck me as accurate.

Along with *"psychological prism,"* another phrase occurred to me: *empirical metaphysics.* Plotinus's emanation theory, and its more detailed Vedantic counterpart, had hitherto been only conceptual theories for me. Now I was seeing them, with their descending bands spread out before me. I found myself amused, thinking how duped historians of philosophy had been in crediting the originators of such worldviews with being speculative geniuses. Had they had experiences such as this, they need have been no more than hack reporters. But beyond accounting for the origin of these philosophies, my experience supported their truth. As in Plato's myth of the cave, what I was now seeing struck me with the force of the sun, in comparison with which everyday experience reveals only flickering shadows in a dim cavern.

It should not be assumed from what I have written that the experience was pleasurable. The accurate words are *significance* and *terror.* . . . The experience was momentous because it showed me range upon range of reality that previously I had only believed existed and tried without much success to imagine. Whence, then, the terror? In part, from my sense of the utter freedom of the psyche and its dominion over the body. I was aware of my body, laid out on the couch as if on an undertaker's slab, cool and slightly moist. But I also had the sense that it would reactivate only if my spirit chose to reenter it. Should it so choose? There seemed to be no clear reason for it to do so. . . .

Later, after the peak had passed and I had walked a few steps, I said to Tim, "I hope you know what you're playing around with here. I realize I'm still under the influence and that things probably look different from your side, but it looks to me like you're taking an awful chance in these experiments. . . . I feel like I'm in an operating room, having barely squeaked through an ordeal in which for two hours my life hung in the balance."

I have said nothing about the visual. Where it was important, it was abstract. Lights such as never were on land or sea. And space—not three or four dimensions but more like twelve.

The Third Wave
RABBI ZALMAN SCHACHTER-SHALOMI, CHARLES TART, FRANCES VAUGHAN, BILL WILSON, AND PETER COYOTE

Rabbi Zalman Schachter-Shalomi

Rabbi Zalman Schachter-Shalomi, Ph.D., was born in 1924 in Zhovkra (then Poland). He is one of the founders of the Jewish Renewal Movement. Raised in Vienna, he was interned in detention camps under the Vichy French and fled to the United States in 1941. He became an Orthodox rabbi in 1947 and subsequently earned a doctorate from Hebrew Union College. He was initially sent out to speak on college campuses by the Lubavitcher Rebbe, but was expelled from Chabad for praising the sacramental value of LSD.

Schachter-Shalomi eventually left the Lubavitch movement altogether and founded his own organization, known as B'nai Or, meaning "Children of Light." For many years, he helped many rabbis and others better understand the intersection between their faith and psychedelic experiences. A joyful and exuberant man, I recall his conducting a wedding ceremony that went on for hours and hours. At some point, he interrupted the service and told those attending, "Yes it is a long service, but, believe me, they stay married!"

Schachter-Shalomi has held teaching positions at Naropa Institute and Temple University. The following excerpt is from his chapter "Transcending Religious Boundaries," in the book Higher Wisdom: Eminent Elders

Explore the Continuing Impact of Psychedelics, *edited by Roger Walsh and Charley Grob.*[10]

It was a very wonderful journey. I subsequently had some other trips where there were descents into hell, but that first one was just wonderful.

The wonderful thing about psychedelics was the "mind move" that occurred—the recognition of the fluidity of consciousness. My reality maps were no longer absolute. With psychedelics, I could see how all cosmologies are heuristic and it depends on what you want to do. I could get into various viewpoints; if I wanted to see the universe from a Christian perspective, I got it. That was a very important discovery for me.

Another thing I learned was how important it is to do one's contemplative homework afterward. Leary said to me that time, "Imagine how potent this is and what it might do for people. And imagine how, if this is misused, it's not so good." Ram Dass would say in those years, something along the lines of: "For grass you should have the equivalent of a driver's license. And for LSD you should have the equivalent of a pilot's license." He emphasized the preparation and the responsibilities that go with it.

So the experience only opens you up to greater vision. When you have the vision, you have a burden to carry that vision out. In other words, it makes demands on you. But you can also ignore the demands, shut the doors again, and then the places that have become transparent become opaque. It's beneficial to have someone with you who will help you harvest the experience.

After a while the experiences were less momentous, and there seemed to be a need to wait between sessions. In those years I felt that it was important to have a psychedelic experience at least twice a year, once before Yom Kippur and once before Passover, to revisit that place and check out what was happening there.

Charles Tart

Charles Tart, Ph.D., born in 1937, is a professor at the Institute for Transpersonal Psychology and an emeritus professor of psychology at the University of California, Davis. He is among the foremost scientists in the areas of altered states of consciousness and paranormal phenomena, and he has been involved with research and theory in the fields of hypnosis, psychology, transpersonal psychology, parapsychology, consciousness, and mindfulness since 1963.

Tart has authored over a dozen books, two of which, Altered States of Consciousness *(1969) and* Transpersonal Psychologies *(1975), became widely used textbooks; he has had more than 250 articles published in professional journals and books, including lead articles in* Science *and* Nature. *Tart's insistence that real science also includes everything that one finds interesting has often helped me understand my own assumptions and bias. This excerpt is from his chapter titled "Initial Integrations of Some Psychedelic Understandings into Every Day Life" in the book* Psychedelic Reflections, *edited by Lester Grinspoon and James B. Bakalar.*[11]

While finishing my psychology degree at the University of North Carolina, . . . I volunteered to try some mescaline. . . . It was arranged that we would try the experimentation on a Saturday morning in a friend's office at the laboratory. . . .

A few minutes later the most extraordinary event happened. Quite suddenly the room, a dingy office in an old college building, resembled a cathedral of enormous size and beauty. The colors of the furnishings were incredibly beautiful, full of deep texture and hues I had never seen before. Small objects around the office were magnificent works of art. My friends were surrounded by beautiful colored rainbows. Indeed, within a few minutes rainbows were floating through the air everywhere.

The most important thing about that first experience was that for the first time in my life I knew what the word "beauty" meant. True, I had spoken it thousands of times before, had pointed at objects I'd been taught to believe were beautiful and said the word in association with them, and had occasionally had vague, moderately positive feelings in connection with such objects. Now I understand that I had never even begun to penetrate what beauty was all about. While the incredible and intense immediate experience of beauty faded rapidly after the experiment, a door had been opened in my mind and senses that would never close completely.

Frances Vaughn

Frances Vaughan, Ph.D., a psychotherapist and teacher, is the author of the books Shadows of the Sacred, Awakening Intuition, *and* The Inward Arc. *Vaughan is an editor of the* Journal of Transpersonal Psychology *and was one of the founding faculty members at the Institute of Transpersonal Psychology. She has been president of the Association for Transpersonal Psychology and the Association for Humanistic Psychology as well as a trustee of the Fetzer Institute, a foundation whose mission is to foster the awareness of the power of love and forgiveness in the emerging global community. Her psychedelic session, which she reports below, happened at the International Foundation for Advanced Study in Menlo Park, California, where I did all of my training and guiding.*

After careful screening I was given a high dose of LSD combined with mescaline. Then I relaxed and listened to selected music, using earphones and an eyeshade, under the supervision of a well-trained psychiatrist. The experience changed my life.[12]

The perennial philosophy and the esoteric teachings of all time suddenly made sense. I understood why spiritual seekers were instructed to look within, and the unconscious was revealed to be not just a useful concept but an infinite reservoir of creative potential. I felt I had been afforded a glimpse into the nature of reality and the human potential within that reality, together with a direct experience of being myself, free of illusory identification and constrictions of consciousness. My understanding of mystical teaching, Eastern and Western, Hindu, Buddhist, Christian, and Sufi alike, took a quantum leap. I became aware of the transcendental unity at the core of all great religions, and understood for the first time the meaning of ecstatic states.[13]

Bill Wilson

Better known as "Bill W.," the man who founded Alcoholics Anonymous was known to have taken LSD.[14] Less known is who guided his session.

One of his therapeutic journeys led him to Trabuco College in California, and the friendship of the college's founder, Aldous Huxley. The author of Brave New World *and* The Doors of Perception *introduced Wilson to*

LSD in the late 1950s. The drug rocked Wilson's world. He thought of it as something of a miracle substance and continued taking it well into the '60s. As he approached his seventieth birthday, he developed a plan to have LSD distributed at all Alcoholics Anonymous meetings nationwide. The plan was eventually quashed by more rational voices.

To see a straightforward discussion of Alcoholics Anonymous working with other groups, go to www.video.google.com and search for "Bill Wilson" and "singleness of purpose."

Peter Coyote

Peter Coyote is a well-known film actor and is also the valued narrator of several hundred documentaries, including Explorer: Inside LSD *for National Geographic Television in 2009. The following excerpt is part of an essay Coyote wrote for the journal* The Sixties *shortly after Hofmann's death in April 2008 at age 102. Coyote's essay is included here not only because of what he says, but also because he says it so well.*[15]

The first time I took LSD, my roommate volunteered to "mind me." By the time Ravi Shankar's music had transformed me into something as sinuous as smoke, I had gone far beyond what I could recognize as either fear or comfort. Like a wave, I possessed a momentary, individuated expression and yet was simultaneously the sea itself, and understood clearly that I had never, not once, ever been separate from it. When the life force holding my various parts together would finally disintegrate, I understood, without fear, that I would return to what I had always been before I was born.

The next morning, the world appeared fresh and new. Everything made sense, and particularly the art and expression of the counterculture. The psychedelic posters advertising rock shows were visual shorthand for the melding of in-line and out-line precipitated by the LSD. Anyone who had crossed that border recognized those ideograms of inner and outer space—immediately. . . .

I don't mean to suggest that we had all ingested "wisdom" pills and achieved enlightenment, far from it. But the geography of wisdom was now a discernable, available territory. Our feet were firmly pointed toward these shadowy hills and our intentions to explore them fixed.

PART TWO

PERSONAL GROWTH AND SELF-EXPLORATION

in Psychedelic Sessions

The approach to the numinous is the real therapy. And in as much as you attain the numinous experience, you are released from the curse of pathology.

C. G. JUNG, *LETTERS*

Introduction to Part Two

If a process, procedure, or product helps individuals heal themselves and become better partners, lovers, parents, or coworkers, it makes no sense to restrict its availability from those who use it safely and responsibly. Psychedelic therapy has had remarkable effectiveness with a wide range of psychological disorders as well as with more serious conditions including childhood schizophrenia, autism,[1] and chronic alcoholism.[2] Today, psychedelic therapy is available, but only for a small number of patients in a few research settings. In addition, little information or training has been available on how to safely conduct psychedelic psychotherapeutic sessions.

Before all civilian LSD research was stopped in 1966, LSD was the most widely studied psychiatric drug in the world. Although early experimental use pointed to the possibility of it causing a transient psychosis, later research established that such a reaction was typically produced when patients given LSD were not informed about or prepared for the range of likely reactions. As researchers began to learn the importance of the setting, atmosphere, and attitude surrounding the session, they realized that the LSD experience was a valuable psychotherapeutic modality that frequently catalyzed significant episodes of healing and integration.

Psychedelics, when used wisely, can open up consciousness, sometimes spectacularly. When they are misused, such openings can be troubling, frightening, and even sometimes damaging. Real, long-lasting harm can and does occur. The following example of a poorly done and unsupervised series of events was conducted by a physician who, earlier, had been part of legal and better-supervised studies. "My mother was a participant in this study and not only did Dr ——— overdose her on the drugs but refused to offer any real follow-up care. Only to send her more drugs through the mail and try and get her to take them on her own, with no medical supervision! To put someone in that situation and then refuse follow-up care is unconscionable. She had kept a file, which I found recently after she died, and there are many letters from her begging for help as she was having problems maintaining her mind/body connection and was suffering the LSD/flashback experience over and over without the drug. This experience was an absolute nightmare for her as well as her children—she lost everything—her marriage, her children, business, possessions, and peace of mind."[3]

In well-administered psychotherapeutic programs, negative effects have been infrequent.[4] When guides—usually trained mental health professionals—help a patient resolve disturbing psychodynamic material and facilitate new insights, the benefits are sustained over years and decades. For example, an alcoholic who was treated at Spring Grove Mental Hospital in 1966 and whose session was shown in the CBS television documentary *LSD: The Spring Grove Experiment,* was interviewed in 2009 for the in-production film series *The Acid Chronicles.* He reported that not only has he not taken a drink for over forty years, but also, since the therapy, he has had no desire to do so.

Therapy-oriented psychedelic sessions, like every other therapy, are not suitable for every sort of patient. It is as important to screen out unsuitable candidates as it is to establish a safe and supportive environment. However, when a candidate is suitable and well prepared and the situation is right, there is a high rate of success. Recent clinical studies, including a double-blind study that encouraged spiritual experiences, attest to its therapeutic value.[5]

This section does not include guidelines for mental health professionals or others who would act as therapists or guides because each person and group varies in how it chooses to work. This section does include an overview and resources about what to do if things go wrong. It also reviews popular notions of the dangers of unsupervised psychedelic uses. Most of these warnings have been proved to be false or exaggerated. Many of the "harmful consequences" presented as facts in textbooks, at health clinics, and in government publications perpetuate myths long contradicted by accepted research.

Many popular and scientific publications describe changes in beliefs and attitudes induced by psychedelic therapy. What has been missing is an objective examination of what happens in a patient's daily life after the therapy ends. This section concludes with a detailed report of changes in the behaviors and lifestyles of adults given a single dose of LSD or mescaline by trained guides in a safe clinical setting.*

Anthropologists and archaeologists have learned that shamans and other traditional healers have successfully used psychedelic agents for healing for thousands of years. In the West, attitudes about these traditional uses have progressed from rejection and demonization, to doubt and disbelief, to gradual acceptance and legal protection.[6] There is now a growing interest in learning how to tap these agents' potential for healing and spiritual experience.[7]

---

*A much more detailed review of these findings can be found in chapter 21, "Behavioral Changes After Psychedelic Therapy: Lasting Results of High-Dose Single Sessions."

5
THERAPEUTIC USES
OF PSYCHEDELICS
Psychotherapy and Healing

Psychedelic Psychotherapy

Psychedelics enable us to help others and ourselves become more aware. It is wonderful that they exist, and like any other powerful intervention, they work better when used correctly. To push them aside because they can be damaging when used badly is no wiser than to eliminate headache tablets because overdoses are harmful to the liver.

Given the wide range of benefits from proper use, why were these substances ever banned? The most generous explanation I know is that the government was caught between the laws protecting religious experience and the obligation to regulate drug use. Psychedelic experiences were religious, and psychedelics were "drugs." The easiest solution, if the most simplistic, was to pretend that the uses of psychedelics were all medical, then to ban them outright, even though all of the uses that were freaking out the government were nonmedical. But no one has ever accused governments of acting wisely under pressure. Another probable reason for their ban was that the results of psychedelic sessions and statements from users implied that "the belief-and-value system implicit in our 'scientific' culture is not uniquely true and not even optimally wholesome."[1]

Why have psychedelics been so tightly restricted until recently?

Perhaps because they were repeatedly classed with drugs like heroin and cocaine, perhaps because of their easy availability and the relatively few prosecutions, perhaps because, like General Motors or the U.S. Department of Defense, the government did not adjust to new conditions, but maintained the same rules and regulations past their usefulness. In any case, it appears that the cultural wind is starting to blow in the right direction.

The medical profession has no need to be afraid of these substances, the psychological profession has no need to deny the reality of the experiences they uncover, and the regulatory agencies have no need to deny anyone the right to proper treatment, especially for conditions for which psychedelics have proved to be not only helpful but also the treatment of choice.

Any careful review, however, of what is known and what has been published about psychedelics makes it clear that our understanding of their therapeutic use is still a cognitive mess and a philosophical morass. One reason is the abiding confusion between the intentions of the therapists, the actuality of the experiences, and the way the results are measured, described, and reported. Sad but true, researchers tiptoe ever so carefully around federal oversight, deliberately muting the far-reaching implications of their findings. Despite their fine results, they still hedge their accounts, decrying a lack of generalizability and almost always concluding that what is needed is a slightly larger, slightly broader, and usually more expensive study.

Their goal is to move therapeutic psychedelic use beyond research into basic medical and psychological practice. However, while this sensible forward movement continues, people around the planet who are already taking psychedelics have more immediate needs. Both concerns need to be addressed.

What I find personally difficult is how often current researchers, most of whom are personal friends, dismiss all prior research, even when their own work replicates it. They state, almost as gospel, that all early research was inadequate, inferior, used too small a sample, lacked control groups, and so on. My guess is that they do this so they will not be considered wild-eyed, drug-toting, drug-using revolutionaries intent on overturning conventional psychiatry's current assumptions. Since my own research no longer depends on grants or government permission, I can speak to concerns they do well to avoid.

Reading the theoreticians on the subject of psychedelics—those familiar with their use as well as those who are not—I am reminded of the early Western writings on acupuncture by researchers with little or no experience with it attempting to argue for or against its efficacy. That it had been used successfully for a myriad of conditions by millions of people over several thousand years was not considered relevant. Psychedelics have suffered somewhat the same fate. While we have clear evidence, for example, that peyote has been used for seven thousand years, this fact is not part of the medical literature.[2] One reason may be that there is a rarely challenged bias against any data collected in eras before our own, data labeled "pre-scientific," as if observation, experimentation, replication, and conclusions were Renaissance innovations.

There are at least two medical categories where psychedelics may help: mental illness and physical disorders. Of course, such a distinction is nonsense in the real world, but in the world of medical, psychiatric, and psychological research, that distinction is maintained. The reality of the unified field of mind-body-spirit at the core of shamanistic and other traditions has barely scratched the surface of Western thought and is far from being an accepted operating principle in Western science.

Thus, it is not surprising that until research was terminated by government fiat in the late 1960s, psychedelic research that was labeled "therapeutic" dealt mostly with how psychedelic experience accelerated, improved, or bypassed conventional psychotherapy, as if the benefits accrued were of the same order as those of psychotherapy. Quotes from patients commonly described how months or years of conventional therapy had been compressed into a single high-dose day or a series of lower-dose sessions. Evaluations of the psychotherapeutic benefits rarely recognized them to be secondary effects of transcendent experience. Explanations stressed that psychedelics lowered patients' defenses so that a skilled therapist could help them uncover valuable personal material. This uncovering could lead to insights and eventually to a decrease in symptoms. Here, for example, is a clinician's evaluation: "Mescaline and

LSD [are] essentially anxiety-producing drugs which, because of their magnification of the patient's symptomatology and the accompanying increase in anxiety and fear of loss of ego integration, may lead to the release of repressed material."[3]

The results reported seem little different from what would be obtained more slowly with normal methods. Stated within an implicit pathology model of therapy, the benefits were seen as less illness, almost never as more health.

The reasons for the moderate level of effectiveness described in these reports lie in the choice of setting and dose and in the therapist's orientation: if the set or expectations were that the experience would be like conventional therapy but more intense, if the setting was the same office or laboratory where conventional therapy took place, if the therapist believed deeply in the efficacy of his or her interventions, or if the dose was in the low to medium range, a patient's experiences would conform to those limits. Experiences outside this theoretical construction would not appear in the published discussion or would be explained in such a way as to fold them back into the therapist's prior expectations.[4] I recall, for example, a therapist reporting a patient's self-described encounter with Divinity as regressive behavior relating back to mistreatment by his father.

With low enough doses, a forced set, and no way for patients to go inside themselves for long periods, the reported results make sense. However, the results were different when the therapist acted as a guide— and then only if necessary—and when the dose of the psychedelic was sufficient and both therapist and patient presumed that the patient was possessed of everything required for self-understanding and self-healing.

This is not the place to argue for one kind of therapy over another. Too much of the psychedelic therapy literature reads like the Middle Eastern story of the blind men, each allowed to touch part of an elephant, an animal that none of them knew existed. Each man concluded that *his* part of the elephant—the tail, a tusk, a leg—was the whole animal. Up until now, the scientific literature has provided little guidance on how to conduct effective sessions.[5] However, a 2009 survey of people using different psychedelics found that almost 70 percent of users listed self-healing among the reasons for use.[6]

If you wish to give psychedelics therapeutically, I recommend the model and methods described in chapters 1 and 2 and summarized as a checklist in chapter 19. Approach the session with respect. Be prepared for the possibility of a spiritual or transcendent experience. In the afternoon, offer, but don't push for, therapeutic opportunities. Chapters 1 and 2 describe how to use a mirror, photographs, and flowers (a rosebud is best; see the excerpt below). If you can be loving, supportive, and non-interfering—if you can just "be"—you can probably help someone you care for. (Visit www.entheoguides.net for additional, updated information.)

The excerpt below is from a therapy session at the International Foundation for Advanced Study in Menlo Park, California. W.S., an engineer, had been concerned about a lack of connecting in relationships and a need to try to control all parts of his life. He'd had several hours of insightful transcendent experience before being asked to look at the rose.

3:00 p.m.: "Why don't you look into the rose?" M. asked. "It has something to tell you."

"What could it tell me?" I thought. "After all of these tremendous insights and experiences, are we now playing games with rosebuds?" I stared at the rose. "It's pretty." I laughed again. It seemed so trite and insignificant to say it was pretty. I want to go on to other things, but M. kept suggesting I look at the rosebud. "Okay, I thought, if it's that important, I'll look at it." Suddenly the rosebud started to get larger and larger and soon blossomed into a full size rose. The beauty was exquisite. As I kept looking at it, I suddenly said, "I see me!" I was quite shocked at this unexpected comment. I didn't understand what I'd said at the time but afterward the significance came to me that I was really "at one" with the rose, with nature. We are both part of a much larger being or force or power, just like two leaves are part of a tree. Soon the center of the rose changed into a bucket of red-hot glowing coals—the power that I had inside me—controlled power. As I continued looking at the rose, I was completely awed by the effect that it was having on me. The intensity was so overpowering that all I could do was to sit and cry and cry and cry. I kept thinking how wonderful it all was, just wonderful. What was wonderful? It didn't matter. It was all wonderful and that's all that mattered to me at the time.[7]

Chapter 6 discusses conditions that can become worse if a person takes a psychedelic without support or guidance. While some successful work has been done with chronic alcoholics, schizophrenics,[8] and autistic children, those sessions took place in controlled settings and by staff trained to anticipate special difficulties. Don't take on what you don't feel qualified to deal with.

The increased awareness offered by psychedelics comes in different forms. In higher doses taken in safe and sacred settings, they facilitate recognition of one's intimate relationship with all living things. In moderate doses, they facilitate awareness of the intricate psychodynamic structures of one's individual consciousness. In low doses, they facilitate awareness of solutions to technical and artistic problems.

If you intend to guide a session or intend to be guided, at least frame it as self-discovery, not as therapy. Avoid a sense of the "therapeutic" as much as possible. Just as the body is acutely attuned to self-healing, there is ample evidence that the mind is equally adept. A safe, supportive psychedelic session can encompass free and full exploration of whatever arises. A person returning from a transcendent experience and observing his or her personality may break out laughing at the absurd lengths he or she has gone to deny, suppress, or distort his or her healthy core. In sessions focused on personality exploration, it is especially useful to help the voyagers record their most pertinent realizations about themselves.

The Training of Psychedelic Therapists

While the training of psychedelic therapists is seen as necessary in the medical and psychological literature, there have been few opportunities to provide it. For now, the criteria developed in Czechoslovakia in the 1950s remain a good model. For medical professionals, the training included five personal sessions with an accredited practitioner and thirty patient sessions under the same sort of supervision. Such training should give a therapist an understanding of clients' experiences as well as expertise in working with them.

When psychedelic licensing becomes available, there will be endless debates over what kind of training will be required. The training model given above will undoubtedly be central to whatever else is deemed necessary. A number of therapists with considerable experience with different psychedelics have been providing this kind of training. However, one size does not fit all. One of the finest guides in the United States prefers psilocybin to LSD for clinical work. He says he sees the same range of experiences and doesn't have to overcome the client's preconceptions about LSD. Another internationally respected therapist does holotropic breathwork the day before the session to learn more about the client and to resolve some issues before the actual psychedelic session.

A short list of websites and books about psychedelic psychotherapy[9] is included at the end of this chapter. If you're a professional mental health worker, you can learn when your prior training can be helpful and when it would be more useful to set it aside and just be a good listener, compassionate observer, and caring supporter. There are listings of resources for easing people down from bad trips brought on by taking too much of something, being with the wrong people, being in the wrong setting, or all of the above. It is good to know how to reorient someone lost in inner space. A bad experience, even one that has been chaotic and terrifying, can be rechanneled and become beneficial, or at least not harmful. If you move in a recreational-drug crowd, it's good to know how to administer psycho-emotional first aid.

This discussion has been about psychedelics as adjuncts to psychotherapy and about their reintroduction as legitimate healing tools. With all the plausible theories about altered states now available,[10] the fears that gripped the psychiatric profession in the 1960s when psychedelics were first introduced are unlikely to resurface. Many people in the mental health professions have had some psychedelic experience and certainly will have smoked enough marijuana to know that the official scare literature is laughably inaccurate. "This is your brain on drugs" is as hokey today as the movie *Reefer Madness* was in its time. Groups like the Multidisciplinary Association for Psychedelic Studies (MAPS) (www .maps.org) and the Heffter Research Institute (www.heffter.org) continue to support psychedelic research projects and have as their institutional goals the reintroduction of psychedelics into medical and psychiatric practice. Their work is generally well accepted, and news of each study is reported widely and almost always favorably. The population at large seems more open than the politicians to relaxing the restrictions about therapeutic use.

At the same time, there is a need to consider other therapeutic effects that do not have as much theoretical support, especially since some current research projects don't fit psychotherapeutic, biomedical, or pharmaceutical models.

Extended Healing

During some psychedelic sessions, a physical or psychophysical symptom or symptoms have been ameliorated or even cured. Such swift and lasting healings are often mentioned in shamanistic reports from different cultures. Yet those reports have not resulted in this evidence being accepted by conventional medicine. That psychedelic use has alleviated or even eliminated cluster headaches cannot be shoehorned into any psychodynamic theory.[11] That micrograms of a substance, fully metabolized and excreted within several hours,[12] can prevent a recurrence of a physiological syndrome over a period of months or years falls outside of conventional medical thinking. The low success rates that conventional therapy and conventional medications have had with post-traumatic stress disorder (PTSD) make that condition a good candidate for exploratory psychedelic intervention.[13] Many cases of PTSD, especially those spawned by the Iraq War, were brought on because soldiers were driven to behave against their deepest moral convictions while living in constant fear of the people they were supposed to be helping.[14] Offering these veterans a therapy that works at the same level as their wounding seems realistic and has proved to be valuable.[15]

Patients with advanced cancer have been helped with psychedelic therapy.[16] Current permissible research has proved successful in lowering excessive anxiety, perhaps by allowing patients to realize that death is neither as frightening nor as final as they had believed. Their ultimate prognosis remained the same, but their concept of their identity as greater than their body, greater in fact than their life, appears to have enriched their remaining time. Some have outlived their predicted death with an enhanced quality of life; others realize that it is within their own control to put an end to increasing pain and discomfort. These studies may allow the cancer world to look at psychedelics as more than a curiosity.

People with a whole gamut of other physical conditions might be helped by psychedelic intervention. The therapists I've worked with have noted that, in working with several hundred clients, minor physical symptoms such as aches and pains, colds, arthritis, headaches, and allergies would often disappear for the duration of the session. Equally intriguing was that most people did not seem to need their glasses for the first five or six hours of their session, despite long periods of looking closely into a mirror and at photographs of themselves and people close to them. As stated earlier, in running therapy sessions, we could tell when clients were coming down when they requested or reached for their glasses.

None of this has been investigated systematically. We have not fully used or understood the immediate or long-term effects of psychedelics on physical conditions. One therapist did ask about physical changes and recorded some reports. Dr. Morgens Hertz supervised LSD treatments for some sixty people and found that a high percentage claimed alleviation of organic complaints.[17] A few examples include:

- My long-lasting feeling of paralysis of the left part of my whole body has disappeared . . .
- A worried feeling of involuntary urinating has disappeared since I had the feeling I could influence the urinating
- My stuttering of many years has disappeared[18]
- My tendency to feel giddy every time I stood on my feet has gone
- I no longer feel my pulse hammering unpleasantly all over my body when I lie down

Straddling the mental and physical realms are the results of psychedelic therapy with chronic alcoholics who had failed to benefit from other treatments and who have symptoms of physical degeneration attributed to drinking. The results of early Canadian research were sufficiently impressive to have the Public Health Department of Saskatchewan declare that a single high-dose LSD treatment of alcoholism is to be considered "no longer experimental" and "to be used where indicated."[19] When presented to federal research officials in the United States, these same results were rejected as unbelievable.[20] Hopefully, those days are long past. Today, many people in alcoholism research have taken psychedelics recreationally. They are unlikely to react like frightened kittens to the idea that psychedelics can help these sufferers, who are so desperately in need.

A number of these former alcoholics who have not had any problems with alcohol, often for decades, report that they stopped, not because their will to resist temptation was strengthened (as is sought at Alcoholics Anonymous meetings), but because they were no longer attracted to drinking and had nothing to resist. This internal shift was unexpected, but unexpected results are not unusual in the history of therapeutic agents. After all, who would have thought that marijuana, another substance almost totally banned from research, could alleviate the symptoms of multiple sclerosis and relieve cancer and a host of other conditions and, as well, become the treatment of choice for appetite improvement during chemotherapy?

Less widely reported is the work done by Gary Fisher, Loretta Bender, and others with regressed and autistic children.[21] In an analysis of the seven studies available, of ninety-one children aged five to fifteen who were given a wide range of doses of LSD in a variety of settings, seventy-five of the children showed either good or excellent improvement.[22] It is a great sorrow that for decades we have been prevented from trying to release such children from the maze of their physical and mental entrapment.[23]

In a class by themselves are the numerous psychic events that occur during psychedelic sessions. What appears to be telepathy is common, and there are numerous incidents that appear to have precognitive or clairvoyant components. The resistance to even acknowledging the possibility of these phenomena is well understood.[24] Therefore, clinical researchers (and I include myself here) tend not to even mention them in their published reports.

In short, there are a number of therapeutic interventions that go well beyond the psychotherapeutic.

We are body-mind-spirit beings; anything that affects one system affects all. Perhaps what has inhibited our culture from researching psychedelics is that it demands a level of training and personal capacity not required in conventional medicine or psychotherapy, as well as a willingness to relinquish well-established beliefs.

I am not discussing shamanistic practices using psychedelics for physical and mental healing or for divination. Fortunately, the anthropological literature now contains numerous examples of shamanistic treatment, training, and effectiveness. One other reason for my not discussing shamanistic practices is that they do not parallel Western procedures. Shamans sometimes take the materials themselves instead of giving them to patients; they work with a wide variety of plants, many psychedelic, many not, and perform specific rituals for each plant and for each condition. The visionary experiences commonly reported appear to differ from those of people using LSD, mescaline, and psilocybin in non-shamanistic settings. (See chapter 20 for a report of and comments on three ayahuasca sessions.)

The other chapters in part 2 describe research done with people who took a high dose of one of several psychedelics in a setting that encouraged transcendent experience. The results are described in ample detail, so there should be no confusion as to what is meant by "positive results." These not-yet-fully-understood substances have put many people in touch with a more inclusive reality and have improved their daily functioning. Their impact on music and the arts is well known, and some of their impact on computer science has been described.[25] Their contribution to therapy and to the practice of healing has only just begun.

Resources for a Fuller Understanding of Psychedelic Psychotherapy

Originally, I intended to write a companion piece on psychotherapeutic use similar to the entheogenic and scientific problem-solving sections. However, extensive and detailed discussions and descriptions on working therapeutically already exist, such as *The Secret Chief Revealed*.[26] In addition, much of the entheogenic sections (chapters 1 and 2) can be adapted for psychotherapeutic work. A good list of resources can be found at http://primal-page.com/psychede.htm. See the following for more information about psychotherapy using LSD and other psychedelics, plus links to other lists:

> In 2010, Johns Hopkins University was recruiting patients for a study titled "Psychopharmacology of Psilocybin in Cancer Patients." For a formal description of the study, go to www.clinicaltrials.gov and search using the study's title.

> For an article titled "Autistic schizophrenic children: An experiment in the use of D-lysergic acid diethylamide (LSD-25)," go to www.neurodiversity.com and search on the article's title.

Books Describing Shamanistic Healings and Practices

Michael Harmer, *The Way of the Shaman*. New York: Harper and Row, 1980.

Jeremy Narby, *The Cosmic Serpent: DNA and the Origins of Knowledge*. New York: Tarcher/Putnam, 1998.

Robert Tindall, *The Jaguar That Roams the Mind: An Amazonian Plant Spirit Odyssey*. Rochester, Vt.: Park Street Press, 2008.

Wade Davis, *One River: Explorations and Discoveries in the Amazon Rain Forest*. New York: Simon and Shuster, 1996.

Don José Campos, *The Shaman and Ayahuasca*, Studio City, Calif.: Divine Arts, 2011.

6
THINGS CAN GO WRONG
What You Need to Know

NEAL GOLDSMITH, Ph.D.

These best practices, written by Neal Goldsmith, are from his book Psychedelic Healing: The Promise of Entheogens for Psychotherapy and Spiritual Development.[1] Psychedelic Healing *is about, among other things, understanding the use of psychedelics as catalysts for psychotherapeutic and spiritual transformation. Goldsmith is a psychologist in private practice in New York.*

If you know what you're doing, if you've been careful in who you are with, if the setting is good, the substance is pure, and the preparation has been taken seriously, there is little chance of anything going wrong.

However, life is way more uncertain than that. Many people reading this book have used psychedelics in less than ideal situations or have helped people who have taken psychedelics in such situations. It is simple common sense to be aware of what to do when a person needs help staying with his experience or, in rare cases, being helped out of it. The more you understand what can go wrong and how it can be managed, the less you will ever need to make use of your knowledge.

Information and Procedures for Psychedelic Emergencies

Education

People who may be involved in responding to a psychedelic emergency should be familiar with the following resources.

Information about Psychedelic Crises

"Working with Difficult Psychedelic Experiences." This twenty-minute educational video produced by MAPS is a practical introduction to the principles of psychedelic therapy. It teaches psychedelic drug users how to minimize psychological risks and explore the therapeutic applications of psychedelics. Narrated by Donna Dryer, M.D., the video demonstrates examples of when and how to help a friend, peer, or loved one make the most out of a difficult experience with psychedelics. www.maps.org/wwpe_vid

"How to Treat Difficult Psychedelic Experiences: A Manual." Written by a psychedelic therapist for the use of lay volunteers helping those undergoing difficult psychedelic psychedelic experiences. www.maps .org/ritesofpassage/anonther.html

"A Model for Working with Psychedelic Crises at Concerts and Events." This MAPS bulletin article is about the group's "Serenity Tent" at the Hookahville music festival, at which MAPS staff worked alongside a medical team to help concertgoers work through difficult experiences. www.maps.org/ritesofpassage/model_working_with_psychedelic_ crises_concerts_events.htm

Information about Psychedelic Psychotherapy

"Guidelines for the Sacramental Use of Empathogenic Substances": www .maps.org/gateway/%5B55%5D181-197.html

"Sitters or Guides": www.csp.org/nicholas/A59.html

"Code of Ethics for Spiritual Guides": www.csp.org/development/code .html

"Ethical Caring in Psychedelic Work": www.maps.org/news-letters/ v07n3/07326tay.html

"Counter-Transference Issues in Psychedelic Psychotherapy": www.maps
.org/news-letters/v10n2/10204fis.html

"Psychedelic Psychotherapy: The Ethics of Medicine for the Soul": www
.maps.org/media/u_penn_3.17.06.pdf

"Psychotherapy and Psychedelic Drugs": www.psychedelic-library.org/
thermenu.htm

General and Background Information about Psychedelics

For the single best introduction to the facts of psychedelics, try: Lester
Grinspoon and James B. Bakalar, *Psychedelic Drugs Reconsidered*
(New York: Basic Books, 1979; New York: The Lindesmith Center,
1997) (www.drugpolicy.org/library/bookstore/pdrad2.cfm)

An extraordinary intellectual achievement in popular scholarly inquiry
may be found in: Andy Letcher, *Shroom: A Cultural History of the
Magic Mushroom* (New York: HarperCollins, 2006.) It is incisive,
skeptical, brilliantly analyzed, and beautifully written by an insider.

A more scholarly, in-depth overview is found in: Jonathan Ott,
*Pharmacotheon: Entheogenic Drugs, Their Plant Sources and
Histories,* foreword by Albert Hofmann (Kennewick, Wash.: Natural
Products Company, 1993) (www.erowid.org/library/review/review_
pharmacotheon1.shtml)

For a fun, informative cultural history of America's drug-induced visionary history (1870s–1966), see: Jay Stevens, *Storming Heaven: LSD
and the American Dream* (New York: Harper and Row, 1988) (www
.stormingheaven.com)

Psychedelic Psychotherapy, New Research, Ancient Practice (PowerPoint
presentation): (www.maps.org/slideshows/neal/Slide1.html)

There's much more on the topic at the MAPS (Multidisciplinary
Association for Psychedelic Studies) website: www.maps.org. MAPS is
the premier organization and website for up-to-date information about
the clinical research and policy issues.

What Can You Do?

Here is an especially helpful excerpt from Erowid (www.erowid.org), the best and largest information resource for all things psychedelic: "Psychedelic Crisis FAQ: Helping Someone Through a Bad Trip, Psychic Crisis, or Spiritual Crisis." (www.erowid.org/psychoactives/faqs/psychedelic_crisis_faq.shtml)

1. If someone seems to be having a hard time, gently ask them if they would like someone to sit with them. If it seems disturbing to them to have someone sitting with them, have someone nearby keep an eye on them unobtrusively.

2. Relate to them in the space they are in. Oftentimes, the thing which isolates people and creates a sense of paranoia or loss is that others are trying hard to ground them because they are "so far out" of normal awareness. Start off instead by trying to just be there for them. Try to see the world through their eyes.

3. What different ways can you change the setting (noise level, temperature, outside vs. inside, etc.)? A party/rave/concert setting can aggravate a person's state of mind. Consider finding the quietest place if it seems like it will help (taking cues from the experiencer), and ask people to not crowd around. Reassure them the situation is under control, noting those who offer help in case help is needed later.

4. How can you minimize risk of emotional or physical harm? Remember, your concern should be for how the person is feeling, not concern for the situation (as in "oh my gawd, we've got to do something").

5. Paranoia: If the person doesn't want anyone near them, hang back or turn so you aren't staring at them, but keep an eye on them as discreetly as possible. Think about what it would feel like to be in a paranoid state, having some stranger (whether you are one or not) following you around and watching you.

6. What objects/activities/distractions might help the person get through a difficult space (toys, animals, music, etc.)?

7. No Pressure: Just be with them. Unless there is risk of bodily injury, just make it clear you are there for them if they need anything.

8. Touch. Touch can be very powerful, but it can also be quite violating. In general, don't touch them unless they say it's okay or they touch you first. If it seems like they might need a hug, ask them. If they are beyond verbal communication, try to be very sensitive to any negative reaction to touch. Try to avoid getting pulled into any sexual contact. Often, holding hands is a very effective and non-threatening way to let someone know you are there if they need you.

9. Intensity can come in cycles or waves. It also can work as a system— a movement through transpersonal spaces—which can have a beginning, a middle, and an end. Don't try to push too hard to move it.

10. Not Forever: If they are connected enough to worry about their sanity, assure them that the state is due to a psychoactive and they will return to their "home" state of mind in time.

11. Normal Drug-Induced: Tell them they are experiencing the acute effects of a psychoactive (if you know what it is, tell them) and inform them that it is normal (although uncommon) to go through spiritual crises and they (like thousands before them) will be fine if they relax and let the substance run its course.

12. Breathing: Breathe with them. If they are connected enough to be present for assistance, get them to join you in deep, long, full breaths. If they're amenable to it, or really far out and freaking, putting a hand on their belly and saying, "breath from down here," "just keep breathing, you've got it," can help.

13. Relaxing: It can be very, very hard to relax in the middle of dying or being pulled apart by demons, but tell them that you are there to make sure nothing happens to their physical body. One of the most important things during really difficult internal processes is to learn to be okay with the fact that they are happening, to "relax" one's attempt to stop the experience and just let it happen.

14. Getting Meditative: Gently suggesting they try to close their eyes and focus inward can sometimes change the course of their experience.

15. Bare Feet on the Ground: One of the most centering and grounding things to do is to take off shoes and socks and place the feet directly

on the hard ground. Be careful of doing this in toe-dangerous set-tings where the ground is abrasive.

16. Eye Contact: If the person is not acting paranoid and fearful of you, make sure to include a lot of eye contact.
17. Everything Is Fine with Me: Make it clear that the whole world may be falling apart for them, but everything is okay with you.
18. Healthy Process: Crises are a normal part of the human psychological process and one way to engage them is as a process of healing, not a "problem" to be fixed.

The most comforting thing that some people reported as having helped them the most during acute experiences is having a blanket wrapped around them. We cannot recommend highly enough having a thick, weighty blanket for emergencies.

Values and Procedures in the Setting

Those creating a psychedelic-friendly event have (some) responsibility to make it safe and to be able to respond to members of the community who need a safe place to chill, including water, a place to recline, and a staff member aware and facilitating the setting. While there is no "treatment" expected or appropriate, it is important for staff to be able to recognize when an attendee needs outside help and when they can safely continue to be accommodated in the event environment.

- Dosing without the recipient knowing about it or giving permission is like rape: it is not a gift, it is not a psychedelic act, and it is never okay. This value must be actively promoted in the culture of the hosting organization.
- The purpose of sitting with an attendee in crisis is not to reduce effects, but to create and maintain a safe place where the individual can play out the process without coming into conflict with themselves or others.
- While sitting, transference (of fear, of not wanting to get involved, of power, of attraction, etc.) is inevitable and should be acknowledged, talked about in advance, and managed.

- No sexual acting out, ever.
- The community member in crisis deserves discretion and confidentiality.
- The community member in crisis shouldn't be left alone.
- Sitters should be ready to face difficult times and stay around.
- Psychedelic-friendly events should have medical staff on call, but if a safe space is created, they will rarely be necessary.

MYTHS AND
MISPERCEPTIONS

DAVID PRESTI, Ph.D., and
JEROME BECK, Ph.D.

Recently, I was commiserating with an anthropologist friend about some misinformation he noted in a current, thoughtful, and well-produced film about mushrooms. We concurred that misinformation, especially as it passes from a scholar with no actual experience to another scholar who also has no experience and so on, gradually becomes accepted and filters into the general community. Once there, it is devilishly difficult to dislodge and replace with the truth. The wonderful thing about this chapter is that it is totally current; all these misperceptions are out there. The terrible thing about this chapter is that it was written ten years ago. I hope it goes out of date soon.

This material was originally published in the book Psychoactive Sacramentals, *for a chapter written by David Presti and Jerome Beck.[1] Presti is a senior lecturer of neurobiology in the Department of Molecular and Cell Biology at the University of California, Berkeley, and his research focus is on the relationship between chemical processes in the brain and behavior. Beck is a coprincipal investigator at the Institute for Scientific Analysis and serves as a public health, policy, and epidemiology research administrator for the Tobacco-Related Diseases Research Program at the University of California.*

LSD (lysergic acid diethylamide), like many hallucinogenic, visionary, or entheogenic chemicals, is classified by the U.S. government as a Schedule 1 controlled substance. Such substances are deemed to have no medical applications and are not legally available for human use in the United States. As such, LSD is available to users only as an illicit "street drug" of unknown purity and potency. Many so-called street drugs have an associated corpus of myth, but nowhere is this more dramatic and fantastic than with LSD. Although unknown prior to its synthesis in 1938 and characterization in 1943 by Albert Hofmann,[2] to many, LSD represents the prototypical hallucinogen. The remarkable folklore associated with LSD is perhaps to be expected, given its highly controversial nature and its powerful and profound effects on consciousness.

A particularly noteworthy aspect of LSD mythology is its existence among both users of the drug and experts in the substance abuse field. Among professionals, some of these myths are pervasive enough to have received mention as "facts" in prominent professional publications. Although the general public and the media may be hoodwinked by misinformation, users of hallucinogens are often well informed about the substances they use. Despite this, however, some myths are still widely believed by users of LSD.

Most of the LSD myths began in the politically charged era of the 1960s and have multiple origins and methods of propagation, among which have been the media, the street-user subculture, and scare tactics by the government and law enforcement. In this chapter, we address the prominent folklore associated with LSD, giving particular attention to the prevalent belief held both by users and by professional experts that strychnine is a common adulterant of LSD. In addition to this prototypical myth, we reflect briefly on several other widely held beliefs.

Strychnine and Other Adulterants

That LSD is frequently adulterated ("cut") with a number of toxic substances is a long-standing belief that has permeated user and professional networks for more than three decades, despite the lack of any supporting evidence. Prominent among the believed additions to LSD are methamphetamine (the popular synthetic street drug known as speed) and strychnine (an alkaloid from the seeds of a tree native to India, *Strychnos nux-vomica,* historically used as a rodent poison and having nervous-system stimulant properties).[3]

Users will sometimes attribute characteristics of an LSD experience as much to these adulterants as to the LSD itself. For example, an LSD experience may be described as "speedy" because of methamphetamine presumed to be present in the sample. LSD thought to be adulterated with strychnine is sometimes claimed to be the basis for an unpleasant experience (bad trip) or as the source of gastrointestinal distress experienced by some users on LSD. Even *High Times* magazine, a standard reference among users, has reported that "common adulterants [to LSD] are strychnine, amphetamines and whatever else was lying around the bathtub."[4] In a survey administered to more than four hundred university undergraduates in a required health class, students who had used LSD commonly believed that strychnine and methamphetamine were frequent adulterants, while those who had not used LSD were largely unaware of this myth.[5]

It is also widely believed among drug-treatment professionals that LSD is frequently adulterated with strychnine. Even the *Diagnostic and Statistical Manual of Mental Disorders* (4th edition) (*DSM-IV*), the standard reference in the United States on the diagnosis of mental disorders (including drug abuse), mentions strychnine as an adulterant to LSD.[6] *Psychiatric Annals,* a professional journal of continuing education for psychiatrists, devoted an issue to hallucinogens in 1994. Among the numerous inaccuracies in this issue of the journal was a reference to strychnine being added to LSD in order "to increase the potency of its hallucinatory experiences."[7] This article continued with a description of the procedure for the treatment of strychnine poisoning, indicating that this is likely to be an emergency medical need for anyone presenting in acute distress after having ingested LSD.

Strychnine contamination of LSD is also mentioned in leading professional books on substance-abuse treatment[8] as well as recent drug-education textbooks.[9-11] Thus, educational texts continue to propagate the strychnine myth, without reference to any documented analyses or cases.

Compilations of drug slang published by the U.S. Department of

Justice[12] and a professional medical journal[13] list terms that describe combinations of LSD and strychnine, such as "backbreaker," "white acid," and "four way." However, there is no evidence whatsoever that this chemical combination ever existed under any name. The extent of this belief among experts is impressive and makes the strychnine myth unique in the corpus of LSD folklore.

The strychnine myth may have been fortified by Albert Hofmann's report of an analysis (conducted in 1970) of a powder sample purported to be LSD that turned out to be nothing but strychnine.[14] However, all other analyses of a large number of street samples of LSD over the years have consistently revealed that products sold on the street as LSD seldom contain adulterants and have never been found to contain strychnine.[15,16]

Thirty years ago, in the few cases where adulteration was detected, the adulterant was either phencyclidine (PCP) or methamphetamine. Of 581 street samples of purported LSD analyzed by J. K. Brown and M. H. Malone, results showed that 491 (84.5 percent) contained LSD alone, 31 (5.3 percent) contained LSD and PCP, 11 (1.9 percent) were PCP alone, and 5 (0.9 percent) contained LSD plus amphetamine or methamphetamine. The authors stated, "We have analyzed several samples thought to contain strychnine on the basis of toxic symptoms, but in each case only LSD was detected. . . . None of the other groups doing street drug analyses has reported strychnine in any LSD-containing sample."[17]

Even if, historically, adulterants were infrequently detected in street samples of LSD, this possibility has been rendered even more unlikely in recent times by the introduction of blotter paper, which has been by far the most common carrier medium for the distribution of LSD for more than twenty years. This medium evolved because the high potency of LSD demands that a reliable method be used to partition small quantities of the chemical into uniform doses. Exposing absorbent paper to solutions of known concentration works quite well for this. However, in order to produce any significant psychoactivity, the five-millimeter-square dosage units of blotter paper cannot contain sufficient amounts of strychnine or other substances claimed to be adulterants. In addition, the very high potency and continued low cost of LSD make it unnecessary to add adulterants to enhance its effects.

In *Licit and Illicit Drugs,* Brecher[18] claims that strychnine may have been added to LSD as a "bulking agent" and possibly to increase the immediacy of psychoactive effects. Another reason offered for the presumed presence of strychnine in LSD is that it is required to facilitate the bonding of LSD to blotter paper. None of this is true. Other stories say that strychnine is a contaminant of the synthesis of LSD, a breakdown product of LSD, or a metabolite produced after ingestion. These are also myths. While both strychnine and LSD are complex carbon-based compounds, their molecular structures are quite different. Strychnine is not a chemical precursor, by-product of synthesis, degradation product, or metabolite of LSD. There simply has been no strychnine found in street samples of LSD or any reason to expect its presence.

The origin of the strychnine-in-LSD myth is obscure. It was already well established by the late 1960s. In *Acid Dreams,* their otherwise excellent historical review of LSD use, Lee and Shlain[19] state, "Much of the LSD turning up on the street [in San Francisco's Haight-Ashbury neighborhood in the late 1960s] was fortified with some sort of additive, usually speed or strychnine, or in some cases insecticide. But where did this contaminated acid come from?" The authors go on to say that this contaminated LSD was manufactured and distributed by organized crime and came to be called "syndicate acid," a name that was at the time synonymous with bad LSD.

The late 1960s were chaotic times in the hippie scene of San Francisco. Alcohol, heroin, and methamphetamine were increasingly used, and this, together with the influx of large numbers of clueless youth, was rapidly contributing to the demise of the formerly idyllic scene. The resultant chaos undoubtedly added a powerful negative component to the set and setting of the LSD experience. However, there is no evidence from that time indicating the actual presence of strychnine in LSD samples. We suspect that the strychnine myth evolved in the late 1960s to help explain negative aspects of the LSD experience related to the degenerating social scene.

There are claims from experienced users that different samples of illicit LSD can produce subtly different effects. Although such differences may be accounted for by variations of mental set and physical setting, there may also be chemical mechanisms at work. Other ergot alkaloids and chemical relatives of LSD present in an incompletely purified preparation could have psychoactive effects.[20] Breakdown products and metabolites of LSD might also contribute to such reported differences.

However, this remains speculation at this point in time. Clinical study of such possibilities has not been conducted and, indeed, would be virtually impossible to conduct at the present time, given the difficulty of doing human research with LSD and related chemicals.

From the perspective of the government, law enforcement, and the substance-abuse-treatment community, the myth of strychnine as an adulterant remains a convenient scare tactic to dissuade users from experimenting with LSD. From the perspective of the user, this myth remains a convenient external explanation for those experiences that are significantly unpleasant (i.e., the bad trips).

Tattoo Acid

Another myth has been passed around so often between the media, law enforcement, and parents' groups that it has been described as "the most insidious urban drug legend."[21] This is the ever-surfacing myth of "tattoo acid." Since blotter-paper LSD is frequently illustrated with cartoon characters or other artistic designs, some folks have found it to resemble transfer tattoos. This has resulted in the periodic appearance in communities throughout the United States of anonymous fliers warning of the threat this brings to children. A bulletin dated March 31, 1987, from the Emeryville Police Department in California stated, "A new danger has entered our community. . . . This is a new way of selling acid by appealing to our young children. A young child could happen upon these and have a fatal 'trip.' It is also learned that little children could be given a free 'tattoo' by older children who want to have some fun or by others cultivating new customers." The bulletin concludes by warning people not to handle these tattoos because "these drugs are known to react very quickly and some are laced with strychnine."

This particular myth is the only one that has been officially discredited by the Drug Enforcement Administration (DEA). In a memorandum issued in 1991, the DEA stated:

Fliers with warnings against a claimed "new form" of LSD have been circulating throughout the United States for more than a decade. Typically, the warnings, which are usually addressed to parents . . . warn of the dangers of LSD-impregnated decals or tattoos decorated with cartoon characters or other pictures designed to appeal to children. . . . It is claimed that, by licking the decals and applying them to the skin, a child could suffer a hallucinogenic high. . . .

The warnings, which have been found on letters, posters, and fliers, have been reproduced countless times by well meaning persons, school systems, private companies, and the press. The warnings can be particularly troublesome and confusing because they do contain some accurate information about LSD, its forms, and effects. . . . The accidental similarity between children's decals and decorated blotter acid was probably the basis for the erroneous presumption made by some well-meaning individuals that there was a particular danger to small children. Although some high school and college-age children may be purchasing blotter acid and getting high on it, no, repeat, no DEA or state or local authorities have ever, to date, reported any instance of children's decals or tattoos with LSD. . . . It is a hoax.[22]

Chromosome Damage and Birth Defects

One of the preeminent myths of the late 1960s, and one that contributed significantly to the fear and condemnation of LSD, was the belief that LSD use produced chromosomal breakage, other genetic damage, and birth defects (teratogenicity). This story began with a short publication in the reputable journal *Science* in 1967 claiming that LSD added to cultured human white blood cells produced chromosomal abnormalities.[23] The primary author of this article published a similar report in the prestigious medical journal *The New England Journal of Medicine* a few months later.[24] The same issue of this latter journal also contained an editorial article highlighting the discovery of birth defects and genetic damage caused by LSD, emphasizing that the effect of LSD on chromosomes was similar to the damage produced by ionizing radiation.[25] These publications were followed by a spate of work by various researchers claiming more of the same. Such findings were given front-page attention by the media and became a prominent aspect of the public perception of LSD.

Later and more careful studies demonstrated that the conclusions drawn from the initial research were ill founded. A comprehensive review of sixty-eight studies and case reports published in the four years following the initial 1967 article appeared as a major article in *Science* in 1971. The review concluded that "pure LSD ingested in moderate doses does not damage chromosomes in vivo, does not cause detectable genetic damage, and is not a teratogen or a carcinogen in man."[26]

Unfortunately, these refutations of earlier claims were ignored by the media and by government purveyors of drug information. As a result, the myth of LSD as a promoter of genetic damage is still very much alive. One of the better contemporary drug-education textbooks opens with the results from a series of true/false questions on drugs. The questions were presented to a drug education class taught by the author of the book at the State University of New York at Stony Brook. One question states that "women who take LSD during pregnancy, even once, have a significantly higher likelihood of bearing children with birth defects than women who do not take LSD." The answer is false. In a class of 223 students given this question in 1991, only 6 percent chose the correct answer,[27] and in a class of 200 students given this question in 1996, only 9 percent answered correctly.[28] The myth lives on.

Going Crazy
ACUTE AND LONG-TERM ADVERSE REACTIONS

LSD, as well as many other psychoactive drugs, can produce a variety of acute (short-term, during the period of intoxication) behavioral effects. These may include anxiety, euphoria, dysphoria, paranoia, hallucinations, other alterations of perception, and so forth. Alterations of perception and consciousness are, not surprisingly, an anticipated part of the experience. In addition, the initial mental set (e.g., mood, expectations) of the user may profoundly influence the nature of the experience. Someone who is depressed or anxious and takes LSD may experience an exacerbation of depression or anxiety. Someone who is in a positive mental space may have an ecstatic experience, although not necessarily so. Any single experience with LSD can include both positive and negative mood states. Even negative mood states can be psychologically beneficial if material that emerges is therapeutically processed or integrated within a spiritual framework. This is one facet of the psychotherapeutic value of LSD and similar substances.[29,30]

Lasting (chronic) negative psychological effects are a different story. LSD and other hallucinogens are frequently discussed as being associated with a significant and unpredictable risk of "going crazy" as well as a haunting fear of "permanent brain damage." Such folklore includes outrageous statements like "use LSD seven times [or five times or ten times or whatever . . .] and you are legally insane," or "I know someone who took LSD and felt like they turned into an orange, and they still feel like they are an orange." Other effects spoken of are the development of chronic anxiety, depression, paranoia, psychosis, or suicidal and violent behavior, to name but a few.

While we are not disputing the possibility that lasting negative effects of LSD use might occur in particular individuals, reviews of the clinical literature suggest that chronic problematic effects, when they do occur, are most often associated with psychological instability that was present prior to LSD use.[31,32] For example, people with borderline personality functioning (in the language of the *DSM-IV*)[33] or latent mental disorders (e.g., having a positive family history for schizophrenia) may experience activation of symptoms from LSD use and chronic problems thereafter. Such individuals would also be at risk from exposure to a variety of other environmental stressors.

A comprehensive review by Dr. Sidney Cohen of the use of LSD in psychotherapeutic environments during the 1950s (including approximately twenty-five thousand administrations, given to five thousand recipients) reported that the incidence of acute and chronic problematic reactions was extremely low when LSD was administered under controlled therapeutic conditions to individuals not having preexisting severe psychopathology.[34] This argues for psychological screening of potential users (it may be safe for most people, but it is not for everyone) as well as careful attention to the set and setting of the drug session.

Human death from toxic pharmacologic effects of LSD has never been documented.[35] The pharmacologic therapeutic index (the ratio of lethal dose to therapeutically effective dose) for LSD is undoubtedly very large. There is an infamous case of some "scientific research," published in *Science*,[36] in which an elephant who received a very large dose of LSD subsequently died. However, in this situation the elephant was also administered other potent substances, including barbiturate and antipsychotic drugs, which likely contributed to its demise.

We have heard claims that LSD sequesters in the brain, spinal cord, and body fat, and can leak out at later times—even years later—to produce adverse effects (such as "flashbacks," which are the re-experiencing of some aspects of the drug-intoxication experience in the absence of the drug). Recently, we heard from a medical student that she learned this "fact" in a class at one of the country's leading medical schools. There is no basis in reality for this because there is absolutely no evidence suggesting that LSD remains in the body for extended periods of time.

The notion of the flashback is probably one of the more muddled concepts in the literature about hallucinogenic drugs. In their excellent discussion of this phenomenon, Harvard Medical School faculty Lester Grinspoon and James B. Bakalar have this to say:

> Studies of flashbacks are hard to evaluate because the term has been used so loosely and variably. On the broadest definition, it means the transitory recurrence of emotions and perceptions originally experienced while under the influence of the drug. It can last seconds or hours; it can mimic any of the myriad aspects of a trip; and it can be blissful, interesting, annoying, or frightening. Most flashbacks are episodes of visual distortion, time distortion, physical symptoms, loss of ego boundaries, or relived intense emotion lasting a few seconds to a few minutes. Ordinarily they are only slightly disturbing, especially since the drug user usually recognizes them for what they are; they may even be regarded lightheartedly as "free trips." Occasionally they last longer, and in a small minority of cases they turn into frightening images or thoughts.[37]

One framework for thinking of flashbacks is as a kind of memory that is robust and easily activated. Another conceptualization of flashbacks is a psychodynamic one that views them as related to a re-emergence of con-flictual material released from the unconscious mind during the time of the drug action and not fully processed at that time. Stanislav Grof, one of the world's most experienced LSD therapists, makes the following state-ment about flashbacks and other adverse reactions in his classic book, *LSD Psychotherapy:* "Sessions in which the drug activates areas of difficult emo-tional material and the individual tries to avoid facing them can lead to pro-longed reactions, unsatisfactory integration, subsequent residual emotional or psychosomatic problems, or a precarious mental balance that becomes the basis for later 'flashbacks.'"[38]

The *DSM-IV* terminology for flashbacks associated with LSD use is "hallucinogen persisting perceptual disorder," abbreviated "HPPD."[39] The *DSM-IV* takes a particularly narrow definition that focuses on persistent visual perceptual phenomena that cause significant distress to the indi-vidual. This condition may be a real but rare occurrence among individu-als who have used LSD.[40] However, the condition has received only very limited study, and its claimed association with LSD use is confounded by polydrug use as well as other variables.[41]

A major factor in determining the intensity—either ecstatic or problematic—of an LSD experience is the quantity of drug ingested. Along these lines, it is important to note that the average dosage con-tained in street samples has declined dramatically since the early 1970s. While dosage units of street LSD in the 1960s were generally upward of 200 micrograms, the reported average dose of street samples in the 1990s has been closer to 60 micrograms.[42,43]

Acute, adverse psychological reactions are certainly the most signifi-cant concerns associated with LSD use. Unfortunately, these dangers are also the ones that are most enhanced by the myths and dire warnings. The LSD experience is shaped not only by the pharmacologic character-istics of the drug itself, but also by the beliefs that accompany the expe-rience. Because of the highly suggestive nature of the LSD experience, belief in the myths can contribute to self-fulfilling prophecy and increase the likelihood of having an adverse reaction. Cohen called this the phe-nomenon of "excessive initial apprehension" and cited it as a significant factor contributing to bad trips.[44] Given this, it is perhaps not surprising that the number of reported bad trips increased markedly during the media blitz of the late 1960s.

After media coverage died down at the close of that decade, so did the number of negative experiences. This occurred despite the fact that the total number of LSD users was still increasing into the early 1970s.[45-48] An increasingly informed user culture and the predictably lower dosages of street LSD have been among the most significant contributors to this decline in negative experiences.

Henderson and Glass, in their book on the history of LSD, summarize the relationship between adverse reactions and mythos in the following way: "In the popular mythology, LSD users are prone to violent outbursts and bizarre behavior. They may jump off buildings believing they can fly, stare at the sun until they go blind, tear their eyes out, or even become homicidal. It is widely believed that an LSD user may at any moment experience a drug flashback during which any of these events may recur. The literature on LSD does document some bizarre episodes. Given the millions of doses of LSD that have been consumed since the 1950s, however, these are rare indeed."[49]

Spiritual Development

A central theme of the book *Psychoactive Sacramentals* is the entheogenic potential of LSD and similar substances. Indigenous cultures around the world and throughout history have used psychoactive plants as sacramentals in religious rituals that have served to facilitate their connection to the transpersonal. This notwithstanding, it is a myth that the use of these substances will automatically lead to a higher degree of spiritual or religious development. Entheogen use does not necessarily make spiritual development any easier. Skillful and respectful use, with careful attention to intention, set, and setting, may help to foster the spiritual path.

Conclusions

There is more to these myths than simply inaccurate information. They have had a major impact on public, scientific, clinical, and governmental perceptions of hallucinogens as well as on user experiences. These myths were a primary factor in the termination of the clinical research forty-five years ago and continue to interfere with the resumption of legitimate investigation of the therapeutic and entheogenic properties of LSD and similar substances.

Searching for the origins of these enduring drug mythologies often proves to be both a fascinating and frustrating experience that only rarely yields complete elucidation. Possessing a life of their own, these hoary myths are hardly static as they journey through space and time. Reflecting the dynamic and adaptive nature of myths, their elements often undergo changes and embellishments over time as a result of faulty memories or the emergent needs of various interest groups.

The Internet has assumed a central role in the diffusion of drug mythology. While the potential exists for the Internet to further propagate these as well as other myths to a wider population, it appears that the opposite may actually be occurring. Electronic mail exchange, newsgroup discussions, and the information-rich World Wide Web have emerged as correctors of myths that have remained largely unchallenged for decades. Websites such as those of Erowid (www.erowid.org), the Multidisciplinary Association for Psychedelic Studies (www.maps.org), the Psychedelic Library (www.psychedelic-library.org), the Lycaeum (www.lycaeum.org), and the Council on Spiritual Practices (www.csp.org) are exemplars of such founts of accumulated knowledge.

More than half a century after its discovery by Albert Hofmann, LSD remains one of the most powerful and profound psychoactive substances known. The folklore surrounding LSD reflects, in part, fears of this power. LSD has the potential to produce extraordinary effects on consciousness, stripping away psychological defenses and bringing users into contact with the gods and the demons of their own psyches. It deserves the utmost respect for the powerful effects it can produce. There is power enough in this truth.

8
THERAPEUTIC
EFFECTIVENESS OF
SINGLE GUIDED SESSIONS

Janet's (not her real name) smile deepened and her Brooklyn accent, softened by years of living in California, became more pronounced. "It's different. Growing up, nature wasn't part of life. Sure, a tree on the street, flowers in a vase, a walk in Central Park, vacations to Jersey, but nothing special. Now I *feel* it. As if nature notices me. When I'm at the ocean or in Memorial Park, I'm not alone."

"Do you spend more time in nature?" I asked, my pen hovering over the item under "Leisure Activities" on page 11 of the form.

"Sure. Don't you?"

After writing down her comments, I asked the next question. We were into the third hour of the interview. I had over three hundred questions to ask and she had something to say about most of them. I'd scheduled the customary four hours, which usually gave me an hour or more to fill in my summary and make some general remarks.

Not today. Some of these interviews had gone even longer. It was fine with me. I loved the stories.

Three rooms away, another interviewer was asking the same questions. Six to nine months earlier, both participants had a single high-dose, psychedelic therapy–oriented session, part of a therapy regime. Now Janet, who had never met me, was telling me intimate details of her life.

It was 1965, and the interview was part of my dissertation research. There had been dozens of studies in the United States and many more around the world on how LSD and other psychedelics affected everything from the crawling of snails and the building of spiderwebs to people with schizophrenia, autism, alcoholism, and neurosis. In the shadows, the CIA had tried to use these substances to confuse and terrify people. Through front organizations, the CIA also sponsored small conferences and publications where therapists and researchers shared their findings. Timothy Leary and Ken Kesey were both big news, and a worldwide wave of unsupervised use was starting to build.

This research was intended to clear up some of the confusion of researchers talking past each other about wildly different versions of results. Unhappily, even though some results were published, the findings were swept away into obscurity by a flood of culture-changing events and media exaggeration. Now that research is again making tiny steps forward, it would appear to be timely to make the findings available to give researchers, therapists, and potential users a baseline of what to expect.

The Therapeutic Protocol

The therapy I was documenting had consisted of three parts: preparation, a guided psychedelic session, and a series of follow-up meetings with the therapist. Added to that was this final follow-up interview to measure behavior changes that persisted.

In the preparatory meetings, pertinent issues and concerns were discussed while establishing trust and psychotherapeutic rapport. The meetings also included brief experiences breathing a mixture of 70 percent oxygen and 30 percent carbon dioxide, a therapy pioneered a decade earlier.[1] As none of the subjects had any prior psychedelic experience and several inhalations put most subjects into a transient altered state, anyone who found even these micro-experiences very disturbing was counseled out of the program.

Today, it is hard to find someone interested in working with psychedelic materials who has not used one or another psychedelic.* Therefore,

---

*Survey results by James Fadiman, Alicia Danforth, and others are discussed at length in chapter 16.

the amount of preparation can be less than it was for these truly naive subjects.

The psychedelic session lasted an entire day. The patients spent the day listening to music or viewing various visual stimuli such as family photographs or a mirror, while a male and a female guide provided support. The subject was seen for a follow-up interview one day later, with additional follow-ups at one, two, eight, and twelve weeks after the session. The final evaluation was conducted as closely as possible to six months later.[2]

The Sample

Sixty-seven people (forty-four men and twenty-three women) were interviewed for the study; their average age was 35.5 years. The sample was not random; it included everyone who had completed the therapy program over a nine-month period still living in California and who was between six and nine months away from the day of his or her psychedelic session. The median educational level was two years or more of collage. The subjects differed widely in religious upbringing and orientation, clinical diagnosis, and cultural background. It is safe to assume that because they had paid the medical costs for the therapy, they all were highly motivated to seek and attain self-knowledge and self-improvement. Severely disturbed persons were not accepted into the study.

Two-thirds of the group had a range of diagnoses similar to those of the patients at an outpatient mental health clinic. One-third had no presenting symptoms; they were "healthy normals" in their work and personal life and were thus more likely to grapple with ultimate questions of love and death as well as other universal concerns during their psychedelic experience. It was observed that the content and tone of their sessions were markedly different from those of the more neurotic participants, who were more likely to use the session for personal and transpersonal exploration.

A Brief History

How I developed the interview and was able to do psychedelic research at all is symptomatic of the uneasy relationships between academic psychology, mind exploration in general, and psychedelics in particular.

In my graduate years at Stanford University in the early '60s, I carefully tailored my outward characteristics to appear to be one more humble though ambitious psychology student. I dressed as squarely as I could, hoping that my frayed-at-the-elbows sport coat and my worn neckties would persuade the professorate (who could toss me out of the university to be drafted and sent to Vietnam) to ignore my off-campus activities. In my classes and seminars, I hid my continual puzzlement at my professors' parochial understanding of the psyche and their limited exposure to its full range.

Granted that my opinions were fueled by arrogance and ignorance, I could not help feeling as though I were listening to very young children expounding their theories of adult sexual behavior: how very unlikely it was that babies could be made by putting your pee-pee stick into her pee-pee hole, that such acts could never be pleasurable, or that was what one's parents did when they were making all those noises in their locked bedroom. I dutifully made notes, read books, wrote papers (often the same paper with a new front page), and blended in as much as possible.

On my own time, I struggled to understand the larger world-mind I had experienced with LSD. Reading widely in anthropology, Tibetan Buddhism, mysticism, altered states, and parapsychology, I had found clues and partial answers.

By the middle of my third year, I wanted to learn what the lasting effects were of taking psychedelics in a safe, supportive setting. To turn such research into a dissertation, I needed three faculty members to serve as a supervisory committee. To my surprise, finding them became a lengthy process, as professor after professor wanted no part in what they considered fringe or downright dangerous science.

The breakthrough came at a meeting with Professor Jack Hilgard, a major figure in the American Psychological Association, author of major textbooks on learning theory, and the founding director of the Stanford Hypnosis Laboratory—and a gentle avuncular man and a skilled listener. As we sat on opposite sides of his large uncluttered desk, both of us in jacket and tie, I laid out the idea for my dissertation.

Professor Hilgard chided me kindly, saying that if I pursued my project, I would have no future in academic psychology.

"Dr. Hilgard," I replied, "when you decided to study hypnosis, it was in dispute, much the same way that psychedelics are now. It was very much not an acceptable area of study. You took that chance with your career. I'm willing to take a chance with mine."

He leaned back for a long, long time, as if caught up in memory. Then, tipping his chair forward, he spread his hands on the desk and looked at me. "I will be on your committee."

His acceptance gave me my third member, and his stature and reputation gave me protection from any disapproval from other faculty.

The committee chairman was Willis Harman, my mentor (and a contributing author to this book), who had guided me through my most life-changing psychedelic experience. The other member was Nevitt Sanford, who had been fired from Berkeley for refusing to sign a loyalty oath during the fear-ridden McCarthy era. Neither Hilgard nor Sanford had the slightest interest in my research with psychedelics, but both had taken strong, unpopular stands in the past and supported genuine academic freedom. To this day I am grateful for their support.

How Can One Measure Psychotherapeutic Utility?

A few years before the start of this research, there had been a small cascade of papers arguing not only for the effectiveness of psychedelic therapy, but also that the material produced by patients during the therapy sessions validated the theoretical orientation of each individual researcher-therapist, all of whom had radically different ideas about the nature of consciousness. The medley included Freudian, Jungian, behaviorist, existential, and eclectic therapists, each in good standing in his theoretical camp.[3]

One reason for their different reports, or so it seemed to me, lay in their inadequate grasp of the effect of their own mental set on their outcomes.

From sitting in on many psychedelic sessions over several years, it was clear to me that the experience was inspiring and positive. In an earlier study, for example, 78 percent of the subjects called the experience "the greatest thing that ever happened to me."[4] As impressive as that seemed, I was aware that such statements would not satisfy a potential critic.

How could one measure the changes suggested by tributes without getting caught up in the patients' desire to ascribe benefit to the therapy (to be explained away as transference or cognitive dissonance, depending on which critic one read) or being caught by the tar baby of one's own theoretical bias?

The way out of the dilemma seemed obvious once I thought of it. I would measure the changes in the daily lives of individuals who had undergone psychedelic therapy. To my surprise, I found that no one evaluating the effectiveness of psychotherapy, including well-funded, years-long, multi-institution studies ever looked at subsequent behavior. I found the accepted argument for ignoring the patient's behavior and opinions stunningly unconvincing. One researcher, describing her contribution to the longest and best-known study, said, "If theory recognizes such constructs as the ego, in which reorganization may come about with or without direct or immediate reflection in verbal report or behavior, dynamic states and ego variables can be assessed only by the instrument through which they are apprehended: clinical judgment."[5] As this seemed to me to be pure hogwash, I realized that not only was I torpedoing my career by studying psychedelics in the first place, but I was even rejecting the "right way" to go about it.

Yet I did not stop going at it my way. At the Palo Alto Veterans Hospital mental ward, where I had worked with individuals and run groups, the ultimate test of therapeutic effectiveness had been whether a veteran left the hospital and reinvigorated himself into civilian life. That made sense to me.

Developing the Behavior Change Interview (BCI)

I began to ferret out moments of daily life that might change after a therapeutic intervention. I asked the therapy staff to note down any behavior changes reported by clients as well as any changes in their own behavior since their own introduction to psychedelics. Eventually I amassed 433 entries that I divided into nineteen categories. The next step was to create questions for each item to which answers could be very simply scored and counted.

I read how Alfred Kinsey conducted his initial research on sexual behavior. He found that people would say "No" when asked if they had done this or that behavior but would admit to it if the question were posed in a different way. He developed a forced format that assumed, in the structure of the question, that the behavior *had* occurred. So it was not "Do you masturbate?" but rather "How often do you masturbate?" It was not "Have you ever had a have a sexual experience with an animal?" It was "At what age did you first have a sexual experience with an animal?" This approach, modified to suit my needs, was the right one for me.

Thus, I would ask if the person were reading, working, going to parties, dreaming, or engaging in some other activity more frequently, less frequently, or as frequently as before the psychedelic experience. After sifting out behaviors that rarely changed or were difficult to score, I was left with 332 items in eighteen categories.

Administering and Scoring the Behavior Change Interview

The form I developed had one category on each page and a list of the items in that category. Each answer could be recorded as more, less, or the same. The interviewers would write down any additional comments. Below are a few of the questions, each from a different category.

- Do you dream more or less frequently?
- Are you eating more or less meat than before?
- Are you watching more or less television?
- (Couples only) When you quarrel, are your quarrels more or less violent than before?
- Do you do more or less gardening than before?
- Do you have intercourse more or less frequently?
- Do you attend a religious service more or less often?

At the top of each page was a space to include a qualitative summation.* Each looked like this example:

Religious activities	improved	same	worse

Qualitative summation is research jargon for doing what cannot be done by statistical analysis—taking into account not the recorded answers but the tone, body language, and whatever else the subject said or did while answering. One might prefer to think of these decisions as "sensible guesses."

The instructions for these interviewer ratings were: "If the change appears to be in the direction of a flexible, self-aware adaptability and away from the extreme of unrealistic rigidity, it is scored as 'improved.' In cases, however, where movement is from some point of flexibility toward irresponsible or purposeless behavior, it is scored as 'worse.' Withdrawal—religious, social, psychological, or political—is not to be scored as 'improved.' Changes that appear to be predominantly in fantasy or attitude are to be scored 'same.' If there was any doubt or if I did not have enough information in any category, I wrote the words 'unable to judge.'" In practice, in almost every case, it was not difficult to score the direction of change.

The results are summarized in the following table. Since reviewing the changed behavior in each category makes for tedious reading, a summary can be found in chapter 21.[6]

TABLE 8.1. BEHAVIOR CHANGE INTERVIEW[7]

Category	75% + improved	60–75% improved	7–15% worse	Male/Female Difference
Dreams	•			
Eating habits and preferences			•	
Reading and listening habits	•			
Personal habits		•		
Material values	•			
Marriage (48 subjects)	•		•	
Emotional responsiveness	•			
Family relations	•			
Work	•			
Introspection	•			
Health		•	•	
Religious activities		•		
Interpersonal contacts	•			
Physical activities				•
Creative activities				•
Sexual pattern		•		•
Fears		•	•	

Description of Categories and Percentage Changed

Over 75 percent of participants were rated as improved in the following categories.

- **Dreams:** Improvements included frequency, recall, use, and enjoyment of dream material.
- **Reading and listening habits:** Included were television, music, theater, and reading habits. Attending to something for its own sake instead of as a distraction was seen as improvement.
- **Material values:** A shift of emphasis from income and benefits to work itself was viewed as improvement, as was less need for status and recognition.
- **Marriage:** Items included satisfaction, communication, shared interests and activities, and quarrels.
- **Emotional responsiveness:** Items dealt with the ability and capacity to tolerate and exhibit both negative and positive feelings. Other items related to self-concept and dependent or independent relationships.
- **Family relations:** These included relations with parents, in-laws, siblings, and children, and sharing time and interests. Items dealing with children included activities like playing with them and reading to them.
- **Work:** Items related to amount of work, ease of work, time spent working, and various relationships at work.
- **Introspection:** Items related to an individual's ability to observe oneself and to modify one's actions based on one's observations.
- **Interpersonal contacts:** Items covered friendship patterns of all sorts.

From 60 to 75 percent of the participants were rated as improved in the following categories.

- **Personal habits:** Items related to personal hygiene, housework, buying habits, and sleeping habits.
- **Health:** Items included exercise, fatigue, insomnia, and medications.

- **Religious activities:** Items included church attendance, prayer, and interest in religious subjects. Increased religious activities were not rated as improvement unless they seemed to be part of a more mature religious framework, whether the person was more devout or not.
- **Sexual pattern:** Items included interest in and pleasure with sexuality, intercourse, and masturbation.
- **Fears:** Items included fears of falling, insects, darkness, isolation, and death.

More than 6 percent of the participants were rated worse in the following categories. (The figure after each category is the percentage of subjects in each category.)

- **Eating habits and preferences** (10 percent): Items included diet, food preparation, and interest in food. Undesirable weight loss or gain was rated as worse.
- **Marriage** (7 percent): The responses covered two difficult marriages and one man who married and divorced in the six months between the psychedelic experience and the interview.
- **Health** (13 percent): All declines in health were minor; fatigue and indigestion were most common. All but one subject were men.
- **Fears** (10 percent): Participants were rated worse if they reported greater awareness of fears. One subject developed a phobia about car accidents that became so severe that he quit his job as a taxi driver. It remains unclear whether this forced career change was beneficial.

Substantial differences were found between men and women in the following categories.

- **Physical activities:** Factors included hiking, sports, and gardening. One-third of the men and two-thirds of the women were rated as improved.

- **Creative activities:** Items covered various kinds of creative expression. Over half the men showed no change, while two-thirds of the women were rated as improved.
- **Sexual pattern:** Almost twice as many men as women (32 percent versus 17 percent) reported no change.

Conclusions

It appears that behavior changes were real, observable, and pervasive and that most changes were improvements that reflected increased self-worth, reduced anxiety, and lessened feelings of inadequacy. In addition, the subjects formed deeper and more meaningful relationships.

A large majority of the participants reported that the therapy had been among the most intense and meaningful experiences of their lives— some said the most difficult as well. The findings described here and in chapter 21 are clear evidence that just as a single calamitous incident can have a lasting, crippling impact, so a single intense, propitious experience can have lasting therapeutic effects.

At the time this research was done, one question that kept being asked was how this therapy's batting average compared with other therapies. The answer given here, as well as in several linked clinical papers,[8] is that it is a Babe Ruth of therapies, especially given its short duration and the depth and extent of the changes. It is encouraging to see that a new wave of researchers is asking better questions, such as, "Does it work for this or that group (e.g., patients with stage IV cancer who have extreme anxiety)?" Another question being asked is, "Does it work for this or that condition (e.g., cluster headaches or post-traumatic stress disorder)?"[9]

Also beginning to be asked is, "What training and experience should anyone sitting with or guiding a psychedelic session have?" This book attempts some answers for nonprofessionals in informal and, for now, not yet legal settings. There are manuals being produced for authorized studies as well. Both kinds of information will reduce harm and foster therapeutic benefit. Both are long overdue.

ENHANCED PROBLEM SOLVING

in Focused Sessions

Introduction to Part Three

Crick told him [Dick Kemp] that some Cambridge academics used LSD in tiny amounts as a thinking tool to liberate them from preconceptions and let their genius wander freely to new ideas. Crick told him he had perceived the double-helix shape while on LSD.*

The use of psychedelics by scientists and other professionals for enhanced problem solving is a realm where little is known and less has been published. In fact, it has often been argued that psychedelics taken for these purposes cannot possibly produce good results since, for the most part, their major effects bypass or suppress analytic and rational areas of the mind. Even those readers with considerable experience with psychedelics may be skeptical of the evidence in this section that refutes these suppositions. However, the set, setting, dose, expectation, and facilitation can redirect what is assumed to be the natural thrust of these substances. When participants can be induced to become absorbed in their intellectual concerns, they do not get not caught up in self-exploration or self-transcendence. When our research group began to explore this area, we did not know if this was true. Therefore, we were elated by the initial results when participants not only improved their scores on well-

---

*A. Rees, "Noble Prize genius Crick was high on LSD when he discovered the secret of life." *Associated Newspapers, LTD Mail* (Sunday August 8, 2004): Section FB, 44–45.

regarded creativity tests, but also, more important, made significant breakthroughs on professional problems.

A promising line of research abruptly vanished from public view on October 6, 1966, when the U.S. Food and Drug Administration shut down the research before we published our results. (Chapter 14 is a personal view of the shutdown.)

What happened next within the scientific community happened within the psychotherapy and spiritual communities as well. The urge to discover and explore seems impervious to government control. Some scientists continued experimenting with these substances, though they could not publish—or for many, even reveal their experimentation to their colleagues. Over the years, more and more people, including scientists, engineers, writers, artists, and business leaders, have acknowledged the pivotal role psychedelics had played in their discoveries. Nevertheless, the established belief is still that creativity cannot be cajoled, corralled, or controlled—let alone amplified—with psychedelics used as "consciousness-alerting" substances. On the other hand, the new drugs of choice among the hard-driving young intellectual set are called "cognitive enhancers," like Alderall. Originally prescribed for people with learning disabilities to help them focus on school tasks, these drugs are being used off-label to stay awake longer, work more steadily, and get more accomplished.[1]

From time to time, however, some of this underground use surfaced. John Markoff, a science reporter for the *New York Times,* documented the pivotal influence of psychedelics in the creation of the personal computer in the 1960s and 1970s.[2] For example, Markoff wrote, "He [Steve Jobs] explained that taking LSD was one of the two or three most important things he'd done in his life."

A contemporary use of psychedelics is evident at the annual Burning Man Festival held in the Nevada desert. The novel constructions, made to be seen, ridden, inhabited, and/or destroyed, are a vibrant exhibition of creativity fueled at least in part by psychedelics. "I only take LSD at Burning Man," a young man told me. Only there did he feel there were no limitations to his experience. Burning Man, without privacy or protection in the usual sense, was for him the safest and most supportive situation.

Although a "Burner" might think that the methodology described in part 3 is both timid and constrained, it appears that an experienced guide, a safe and secure setting, and clear intentions are most likely to produce useful solutions.

In 2001, *Fortune* magazine ran an article by Michael Schrage imagining a facility on an island beyond the reach of American law, a haven where major figures in finance, government, philosophy, and science would converge for psychedelic sessions focused on their most pressing problems.[3] He cast it as a speculative fantasy, apparently unaware that such an establishment had once existed and that the kinds of results conjectured in the article had actually occurred. At the time the results were first reported, the expansion of the project seemed assured. To quote from the report: "The implications of the work are, we believe, much broader than this particular application. Indeed, the basic assumption underlying setting up the project, and not negated by any of our observations during the course of the research, is that, given appropriate conditions, the psychedelic agents can be employed to enhance any aspect of mental performance, in the sense of making it more operationally effective. While this research was restricted to intellectual and artistic activity, we believe the assumption holds true for any other mental, perceptual, or emotional process."[4]

These conclusions remain valid today.

9

BREAKTHROUGH RESEARCH

Selective Enhancement of Creative Capacities

WILLIS HARMAN, Ph.D., and
JAMES FADIMAN, Ph.D.

This chapter describes research terminated in 1966 when the U.S. Food and Drug Administration declared a moratorium on all psychedelic research. It is updated from an article originally published in 1966 in Psychological Reports.[1]

Amid much controversy over the place of psychedelic chemicals in contemporary culture, now we have quietly entered a third phase of research on their use.

The first phase, prior to the 1960s, typically identified these substances as psychotomimetic, and was based on a priori models of mental illness. Underestimating the effects that such preconceptions might have on the content and aftereffects of a subject's experience and almost totally unaware of the effects of expectations or the setting, researchers variously reported that psychedelic-induced states mimicked mental illness when given in a setting that provoked it. For instance, it illuminated Freudian theory when administered by a committed Freudian, evoked Jungian archetypes when administered by a longtime Jungian, substantiated the tenets of behavior therapy to a behaviorist by increasing suggestibility and modifiability, and demonstrated the soundness of the existential approach when given by someone who identified with that theory. As I wrote in my dissertation, "What is puzzling . . . is that all these investigators found that using psychedelics in their particular framework tended to validate that framework."[2]

The second phase—which occurred during the sixties and saw Humphry Osmond's neologism *psychedelic* adopted—allowed a session to run its natural course to minimize the influence of the therapist's or monitor's conceptions and interpretations. Research led to a variety of psychotherapeutic applications, as well as widespread—mainly illicit—use oriented to sensual, philosophical, and transcendental goals.

Out of this experimentation and clinical research, largely as a consequence of suggestive spontaneous occurrences, there was the suggestion that the results obtained selectively enhance different areas of performance. Thus began a third phase of psychedelic research that continues to this day. Whereas, in the first phase the participant's experiences tended to be controlled and delimited, even if inadvertently, by the experimenter's and the subject's preconceptions, and in the second phase to be more uncontrolled and wide-ranging in scope, the emphasis now was on the selection of specific kinds of psychedelic experience and of specific ways to produce and maintain them.

These experiments on cognitive enhancement went on in various countries, on both sides of the Iron Curtain. Since much of this work was done in defiance of existing laws governing use, publicly available information about results has been scant and scattered. What follows is a review of the results of one study I worked on, sponsored by the Institute for Psychedelic Research at San Francisco State University in which the objective was to enhance creative problem-solving ability.

Rationale Behind the Creative Problem-Solving Study

The literature on the effects of psychedelic agents on performance is inconclusive or contradictory. In some studies, learning was impaired during the drug session, in others it was enhanced. Similarly, contradictory results have been noted for color perception, recall and recognition, discrimination learning, concentration, symbolic thinking, and perceptual accuracy.[3]

In some cases of impairment, the drug was used as a stressor with the intention of simulating psychotic performance impairment. Performance enhancement during the drug experience has been sporadically reported in both experimental and clinical research, but not in general where a psychotomimetic orientation was dominant. Research in which improved performance was claimed subsequent to the drug experience has almost all been in clinical settings. The authors' prior experience in clinical research[4] had amply convinced us of the possibility of long-term performance enhancement using psychedelic agents in a safe, supportive setting. Though not deliberately sought, there were numerous spontaneous incidents of what appeared to be temporarily enhanced performance during the drug experience itself.

These observations led us to postulate the following:

- Any human function can be performed more effectively. We do not function at our full capacity.
- Psychedelics appear to temporarily inhibit censors that ordinarily limit what is available to conscious awareness. Participants may, for example, discover a latent ability to form colorful and complex imagery, to recall forgotten experiences of early childhood, or to generate meaningful symbolic presentations. By leading participants to expect enhancement of other types of performance—creative problem solving, learning manual or verbal skills, manipulating logical or mathematical symbols, acquiring sensory or extrasensory perception, memory, and recall—and by providing favorable preparatory and environmental conditions, it may be possible to improve any desired aspect of mental functioning.

As the following table indicates, commonly observed characteristics of the psychedelic experience indicate that performance may or may not be enhanced. In our research, we tried to provide an environment that would maximize those characteristics that tend to improve functioning, while minimizing those that might hinder any improvement.

TABLE 9.1. SOME REPORTED CHARACTERISTICS OF THE PSYCHEDELIC EXPERIENCE

Supporting Creativity	Hindering Creativity
Increased access to unconscious data	Diminished capacity for logical thought processes
More fluent free association; increased ability to play spontaneously with hypotheses, metaphors, paradoxes, transformations, relationships, for example	Reduced ability to consciously direct concentration
Heightened ability for visual imagery and fantasy	Inability to control imaginary and conceptual sequences
Relaxation and openness	Anxiety and agitation
Heightened sensory inputs	Constricted verbal and visual communication abilities
Heightened empathy with external processes, objects, and people	Tendency to focus on inner problems of a personal nature
Heightened aesthetic sensibility	Lessened ability to express aesthetic experiences
Enhanced "sense of truth"; ability to see through false solutions and phony data	Tendency to become absorbed in hallucinations and illusions
Lessened inhibition; reduced tendency to censor own ideas by premature negative judgment	Even the best solution dismissed as unimportant
Heightened motivation promoted by suggestion and the right set	Tendency to regard "this-worldly" tasks as trivial, and hence, little motivation

We chose to focus on creative problem solving for several reasons. One was its obvious utility, an important consideration at that juncture because of those who doubted that psychedelics were good for anything at all. Besides, many of the spontaneous occurrences we had observed were of this problem-solving kind. Finally, extensive research activity in the field of creativity had yielded a number of objective measures to use. The study attempted to shed light on three questions:

- Can the psychedelic experience enhance creative problem-solving ability, and if so, what is the concrete evidence of enhancement?
- Can this enhancement lead to concrete, valid, and feasible solutions assessable by the pragmatic criteria of modern industry and mainstream science?
- In working with creative individuals, would there be changes indicative of increased creativity continuing after the psychedelic intervention?

Participants

The participants were twenty-six men engaged in a variety of professional occupations: sixteen engineers, one engineer-physicist, two mathematicians, two architects, one psychologist, one furniture designer, one commercial artist, one sales manager, and one personnel manager. At the time of the study, there were few women in senior scientific positions, and none was found who wished to participate. Nineteen of the subjects had no previous experience with psychedelics. They were selected on the basis of the following criteria:

- The participant's occupation required problem-solving ability.
- The participant was psychologically stable, as determined by a psychiatric interview examination.
- The participant was motivated to discover, verify, and apply solutions within his current employment.

Six groups of four and one group of three met in the evening several days before the session.* The sequence of events to be followed was explained

---

*There were twenty-six people and twenty-seven individual sessions (one person had two sessions).

in detail. In this initial meeting, we sought to allay any apprehension and establish rapport and trust among the participants and the staff.

Participants were assured that they would experience few if any distractions such as visions or personal emotional states and that the experience could be directed as desired. Suggestions were given on how to promote mental flexibility. Included were the following:

- Try to identify with the central person, object, or process in the center of the problem. See how the problem looks from this vantage point.
- Try to "see" the solution—to visualize how various parts might work together, how a certain situation will work out.
- Scan rapidly through a large number of possible solutions, ideas, and data. The "right" solution will often appear with a sort of intuitive "knowing" that it is the answer. You will also find that you can be simultaneously aware of an uncommonly large number of ideas or pieces of data processes simultaneously.
- You will be able to step back from the problem and see it in a new perspective, in more basic terms. Since there is much less of yourself invested than in your prior trials, you will be able to abandon previously tried approaches and start afresh.
- Above all, don't be timid about asking for answers. If you want to see the solution in a three-dimensional image, or to project yourself forward in time, or to view some microscopic physical process or something not visible to the physical eye, or to reexperience some event out of the past, by all means do so. Ask. Don't let your questions be limited by your notion of what can or cannot be done.

Participants were given one hour of pencil-and-paper tests and told that they would take a similar battery during the session itself. To make sure that the problems to be worked on were appropriate for the purpose, each participant was asked to give a brief outline of the problem he had brought. [The first two sessions were so successful that members of subsequent groups were asked to bring several problems each.] By the end of the preparatory meeting, participants were generally eager and at ease.

They had been given a clear picture of what to expect and how to cope with any difficulties that might arise.

The day of the experimental session was spent as follows:

8:30. Arrival at session room

9:00. Psychedelic material taken (200 milligrams of mescaline), equivalent to 100 micrograms of LSD*

9:00–12:00. Music played while subjects relaxed with eyes closed

12:00–1:00. Psychological testing

1:00–5:00. Participants worked on problems

5:00–6:00. Discussion of experience; review of solutions

After this, participants were driven home; they were given a sedative to take if they had any difficulty sleeping. Many of them preferred to stay up half the night, working on insights and solutions discovered earlier in the day.

Within the next week, each subject wrote an account of his experience. About six weeks later, subjects were given questionnaires on how the effects of the session had affected their ongoing creative ability as well as how valid and acceptable the solutions conceived during the session seemed to them at that time.

Results: Subjective Reports

The literature on creativity includes analytical descriptions of the components of creative experience, the personal characteristics of creative individuals, and the distinguishing features of creative solutions. From the

---

*The research facility was licensed to use both LSD and mescaline. We used mescaline in this study because, for some reason, the U.S. Food and Drug Administration (FDA) was looking at our Sandoz LSD. Several months earlier, the FDA had asked us to not use mescaline until the mescaline in our possession had been sampled and tested for purity against the standard mescaline in the FDA office in Washington, D.C. Naturally we complied, but were not concerned since our mescaline was part of the same batch the government was testing it against. The FDA, in its blundering way, was trying to put the genie back in the bottle. Soon afterward, it stopped all research on psychedelics. That added to the explosive rise in illegal use that continues to this day.

participants' reports, it was possible to extract eleven types of improved functioning that occurred during the session.[5] (Those interested in the relationship of these aspects to current research and theory on creativity can refer to the detailed technical discussion in Harman, McKim, et al., 1966).

These ways, along with representative quotations from the subjects' reports, are as follows:

1. Low inhibition and anxiety

"There was no fear, no worry, no sense of reputation and competition, no envy, none of these things which in varying degrees have always been present in my work."

"A lowered sense of personal danger; I don't feel threatened anymore, and there is no feeling of my reputation being at stake."

"Although doing well on these problems would be fine, failure to get ahead on them would have been threatening. However, as it turned out, on this afternoon the normal blocks in the way of progress seemed to be absent."

2. Capacity to restructure problem in a larger context

"Looking at the same problem with [psychedelic] materials, I was able to consider it in a much more basic way, because I could form and keep in mind a much broader picture."

"I could handle two or three different ideas at the same time and keep track of each."

"Normally I would overlook many more trivial points for the sake of expediency, but under the drug, time seemed unimportant. I faced every possible questionable issue square in the face."

"Ability to start from the broadest general basis in the beginning."

"I returned to the original problem. . . . I tried, I think consciously, to think of the problem in its totality, rather than through the devices I had used before."

3. Enhanced fluency and flexibility of ideation

"I began to work fast, almost feverishly, to keep up with the flow of ideas."

"I began to draw . . . my senses could not keep up with my images . . . my hand was not fast enough . . . my eyes were not keen enough. . . . I was impatient to record the picture (it has not faded one particle). I worked at a pace I would not have thought I was capable of."

"I was very impressed with the ease with which ideas appeared (it was virtually as if the world is made of ideas, and so it is only necessary to examine any part of the world to get an idea). I also got the feeling that creativity is an active process in which you limit yourself and have an objective, so there is a focus about which ideas can cluster and relate."

"I dismissed the original idea entirely, and started to approach the graphic problem in a radically different way. That was when things started to happen. All kinds of different possibilities came to mind. . . ."

"And the feeling during this period of profuse production was one of joy and exuberance. . . . It was the pure fun of doing, inventing, creating, and playing."

4. Heightened capacity for visual imagery and fantasy

"Was able to move imaginary parts in relation to each other."

"It was the non-specific fantasy that triggered the idea."

"The next insight came as an image of an oyster shell, with the mother-of-pearl shining in different colors. I translated that in the idea of an interferometer—two layers separated by a gap equal to the wavelength it is desired to reflect."

"As soon as I began to visualize the problem, one possibility immediately occurred. A few problems with that concept occurred, which seemed to solve themselves rather quickly. . . . Visualizing the required cross section was instantaneous."

"Somewhere along in here, I began to see an image of the circuit. The gates themselves were little silver cones linked together by lines. I watched the circuit flipping through its paces. . . ."

"I began visualizing all the properties known to me that a photon possesses and attempted to make a model for a photon. . . . The photon was comprised of an electron and a positron cloud moving together in an intermeshed synchronized helical orbit. . . . This model was reduced for visualizing purposes to a black-and-white ball propagating in a screw-like fashion through space. I kept putting the model through all sorts of known tests."

5. Increased ability to concentrate

"Was able to shut out virtually all distracting influences."

"I was easily able to follow a train of thought to a conclusion where normally I would have been distracted many times."

"I was impressed with the intensity of concentration, the forcefulness and exuberance with which I could proceed toward the solution."

"I considered the process of photoconductivity. . . . I kept asking myself, 'What is light? and subsequently, 'What is a photon?' The latter question I repeated to myself several hundred times till it was being said automatically in synchronism with each breath. I probably never in my life pressured myself as intently with a question as I did this one."

"It is hard to estimate how long this problem might have taken without the psychedelic agent, but it was the type of problem that might never have been solved. It would have taken a great deal of effort and racking of the brains to arrive at what seemed to come more easily during the session."

6. Heightened empathy with external processes and objects

". . . the sense of the problem as a living thing that is growing toward its inherent solution."

"First I somehow considered being the needle and being bounced around in the groove."

"I spent a productive period . . . climbing down on my retina, walking around and thinking about certain problems relating to the mechanism of vision."

"Ability to grasp the problem in its entirety, to 'dive' into it without reservations, almost like becoming the problem."

"Awareness of the problem itself rather than the 'I' that is trying to solve it."

7. Heightened empathy with people

"It was also felt that group performance was affected in . . . subtle ways. This may be evidence that some sort of group action was going on all the time."

"Only at intervals did I become aware of the music. Sometimes, when

I felt the other guys listening to it, it was a physical feeling of them listening to it."

"Sometimes we even had the feeling of having the same thoughts or ideas."

8. Subconscious data more accessible

". . . brought about almost total recall of a course that I had had in thermodynamics; something that I had never given any thought about in years."

"I was in my early teens and wandering through the gardens where I actually grew up. I felt all my prior emotions in relation to my surroundings."

9. Association of dissimilar ideas

"I had earlier devised an arrangement for beam steering on the two-mile accelerator which reduced the amount of hardware necessary by a factor of two. . . . Two weeks ago it was pointed out to me that this scheme would steer the beam into the wall and therefore was unacceptable. During the session, I looked at the schematic and asked myself how could we retain the factor of two but avoid steering into the wall. Again a flash of inspiration, in which I thought of the word 'alternate.' I followed this to its logical conclusion, which was to alternate polarities sector by sector so the steering bias would not add but cancel. I was extremely impressed with this solution and the way it came to me."

"Most of the insights come by association."

"It was the last idea that I thought was remarkable because of the way in which it developed. This idea was the result of a fantasy that occurred during Wagner. . . . [The participant had earlier listened to Wagner's 'Ride of the Valkyries.'] I put down a line which seemed to embody this. . . . I later made the handle which my sketches suggested and it had exactly the quality I was looking for. . . . I was very amused at the ease with which all of this was done."

10. Heightened motivation to obtain closure

"Had tremendous desire to obtain an elegant solution (the most for the least)."

"All known constraints about the problem were simultaneously imposed as I hunted for possible solutions. It was like an analog computer whose output could not deviate from what was desired and whose input was continually perturbed with the inclination toward achieving the output."

"It was almost an awareness of the 'degree of perfection' of whatever I was doing."

"In what seemed like ten minutes, I had completed the problem, having what I considered (and still consider) a classic solution."

II. Visualizing the completed solution

"I looked at the paper I was to draw on. I was completely blank. I knew that I would work with a property three hundred feet square. I drew the property lines (at a scale of one inch to forty feet), and I looked at the outlines. I was blank. . . . Suddenly I saw the finished project. [The project was a shopping center specializing in arts and crafts.] I did some quick calculations . . . it would fit on the property and not only that . . . it would meet the cost and income requirements . . . it would park enough cars . . . it met all the requirements. It was contemporary architecture with the richness of a cultural heritage . . . it used history and experience but did not copy it."

"I visualized the result I wanted and subsequently brought the variables into play which could bring that result about. I had great visual (mental) perceptibility; I could imagine what was wanted, needed, or not possible with almost no effort. I was amazed at my idealism, my visual perception, and the rapidity with which I could operate."

Results: Subjective Ratings

As mentioned above, several weeks after the experimental session, all participants were asked to complete a brief questionnaire. They rated their experience with respect to nine characteristics relevant to enhanced functioning. Items were rated on a five-point scale from "Marked Enhancement" (+2) through "No Change" (0) to "Marked Impairment" (-2).

The data in Table 9.2 substantiates the hypothesis of enhancement of both verbal and nonverbal skills.

TABLE 9.2. MEAN SUBJECTIVE RATINGS* OF FACTORS RELATED TO ENHANCED FUNCTIONING

Factors	Mean Score	Standard Deviation
1. Lowering of defenses, reduction of inhibitions and anxiety	+1.7	0.64
2. Ability to see the problem in the broadest terms	+1.4	0.58
3. Enhanced fluency of ideation	+1.6	0.69
4. Heightened capacity for visual imagery and fantasy	+1.0	0.72
5. Increased ability to concentrate	+1.2	1.03
6. Heightened empathy with external processes and objects	+0.8	0.97
7. Heightened empathy with other people	+1.4	0.81
8. Data from unconscious more accessible	+0.8	0.87
9. Enhanced sense of knowing when the right solution appears	+1.0	0.70

*All ratings refer to behavior during the session.

Results: Creativity Tests

Test–retest scores on some of the measures used showed dramatic changes from the pre-meeting to the psychedelic session. Most apparent were enhanced abilities to recognize patterns, minimize and isolate visual distractions, and maintain visual memory despite changes of form and color. Specific tests used included the Purdue Creativity Test, the Miller Object Visualization Test, and the Witkin Embedded Figures Test. The scores on the Witken have been reported to be stable under a variety of experimental interventions, including stress, training, sensory isolation, hypnosis, and the influence of a variety of drugs.[6] With these twenty-seven subject-sessions, enhancement was consistent ($p < .01$), and in some cases improvements were as great as 200 percent.[7]

Long-Term Results

The practical value of the solutions obtained is one way to determine if the subjective reports of accomplishments might be temporary euphoria. The nature of these solutions covered a broad spectrum, including:

- A new approach to the design of a vibratory microtome
- A commercial building design, accepted by the client
- Space-probe experiments devised to measure solar properties
- Design of a linear electron accelerator beam-steering device
- An engineering improvement to a magnetic tape recorder
- A chair design modeled and accepted by the manufacturer
- A letterhead design approved by the customer
- A mathematical theorem regarding NOR-gate circuits
- Completion of a furniture-line design
- A new conceptual model of a photon found to be useful
- A design of a private dwelling approved by the client

Table 9.3 summarizes the initial results of applying the solutions in the subjects' industrial and academic settings. (This data was obtained by questionnaires and follow-up interviews six to eight weeks after the session.)

TABLE 9.3. APPLICATION OF SOLUTIONS OBTAINED IN EXPERIMENTAL SESSIONS

New avenues for investigation opened	20
Working model completed	2
Developmental model to test solution authorized	1
Solution accepted for construction or production	6
Partial solutions being developed further or being applied	10
No further activity since session	1
No solution obtained	4
Total problems attempted (many subjects attempted more than one problem)	**44**

A quotation from a follow-up report illustrates the usefulness and validity of the session-day solutions: "In the area of ionospheric source location and layer tilt analysis, I was able in the weeks following the session to build on the ideas generated to the extent of working out the mathematics of the schemes proposed, and of making them more definite. The steps made in the session were the correct ones to start with . . . the ideas considered and developed in the session appear as important steps, and the period of the session was the single most productive period of work on this problem I have had in the several months either preceding or following the session."

Many subjects in the follow-up interviews reported changes in their working behaviors consistent with the enhancement experienced during the session itself. Table 9.4 summarizes the responses to a questionnaire dealing with changes in work effectiveness several months after the session.

TABLE 9.4. WORK PERFORMANCE SINCE SESSION

(Sixteen Participants)

Key: −2 = marked impairment; −1 = significant impairment; 0 = no change;
+1 = significant enhancement; +2 = marked enhancement

	−2	−1	0	+1	+2
Ability to solve problems	0	0	8	8	0
Ability to relate effectively to others	0	0	8	5	3
Attitude toward job	0	0	7	8	1
Productivity	0	0	9	5	2
Ability to communicate	0	0	10	5	1
Response to pressure	0	0	7	8	1

As can be seen, about half the respondents were still noticing some change in their performance level several months after the experimental session. These results are particularly interesting in view of the relatively low dose administered and the fact that no suggestion was ever made that continuing changes of this nature were expected. Participants were led to anticipate enhanced performance levels and a high degree of motivation.

All of this was in a sheltered and non-critical atmosphere, but there was no suggestion that they could expect long-term performance changes or permanent benefit. Yet a certain amount of such change seems to have occurred.

One implication is clear: we are dealing with substances and experiments that have long-term effects; it would be foolhardy and irresponsible to treat this kind of research as if it were isolated from the fabric of the subjects' lives. In addition, the fact that not a single subject suffered any loss of interest or capacity in his normal work life is in sharp contradistinction to the fears still expressed in the popular and medical literature that taking a psychedelic would lead to a slacking off of motivation and involvement in cultural or scientific pursuits.

Follow-Up

Several of the participants in this original study were contacted recently and, although long past retirement age, they were self-employed in their chosen fields and extremely successful.

Comments and Speculations

The need for controlled hypothesis testing, including double-blind placebo studies, in this perplexing area of biochemical facilitation of mental functioning is a common plea and rightly so. But there is an equal need to continue the exploratory research that aims at conceptual models and hypothesis construction. In the research described above, two-thirds of the participants had no prior psychedelic experience. While there are clear methodological virtues in using untrained subjects, when the central question is not one of pharmacological effect, but the degree to which certain mental faculties can be facilitated, the greater a person's experience, the more we are likely to learn. Thus, further investigations might benefit from having the same subject have a series of sessions.

As to the selection of participants, clinical studies indicate that subjects who are more stable and productive beforehand tend to "benefit considerably from the psychedelic experience along the lines of self-actualization, richer creative experience, and enhancement of special abilities and aptitudes."[8] The subjects chosen for this study were known to be creative. In general, we would expect this kind of psychedelic session to be more fruitful with gifted individuals.

In contrast with reports of other researchers, we experienced little difficulty in getting subjects to work on psychological tests. Many studies seem to point to a temporary debilitating effect of psychedelics on higher cortical processes. It seems that variables that affect results in such studies need to include attention to attitude and motivation, as well as ability. We found that discussing this with subjects in the preparatory meeting eliminated any tendency in the experimental session to shrug off tests as meaningless or to resist them as disconcerting. By establishing an anticipation of improved performance, we seemed to bring it about.

These findings, if substantiated by additional research, have obvious applications in industry, professional practice, and research. The procedure could play a role similar to consultants, brainstorming, Synectics, and other methods now used to augment and "unstick" the creative process. A quotation from one of our subject's reports illustrates this potential: "I decided to drop my old line of thinking and give it a new try. The 'mystery' of this easy dismissal and forgetting did not strike me until later in the afternoon, because I had many times before this session indulged in this line of thinking and managed to work the whole thing into an airtight deadlock, and I had been unable to break, much less dismiss, this deadlock. The miracle is that it came so easy and natural."

An additional application would be the use of the psychedelics, correctly administered, to upgrade the performance level of already effective personnel. Of all the results, the most significant, in our estimation, has been the new knowledge gained of the higher processes of the human mind, the framing of new and more productive research questions, and the effect on our understanding—of what we can be and what vast potentialities we have still only begun to tap.

10
FACILITATION FOR ENHANCED PROBLEM SOLVING

The material below is not as fully detailed as the instructions and consider-ations for entheogenic uses detailed in chapters 1, 2, and 19. The material there was designed to fill a void in the information available to people who were going to be using psychedelics anyway. Here full guidelines are not appropriate. No one should feel that reading this qualifies him or her to facilitate a similar group event. One group with a government clearance to use LSD for creativ-ity is considering the approach outlined below; however, they understand that they will need consultation and training before they can proceed. [Follow-up note: They chose to run their study as if they were testing a pharmaceutical, did it in a laboratory setting, gave a test battery to subjects during their expe-rience, and had such uninteresting results that they chose not to publish.]

In order to maximize the benefits of using low-dose psychedelics for cre-ative breakthroughs as described in the prior chapter, the following six areas are important.

Set: expectations and pre-session meetings
Setting: physical atmosphere
Substance: kind and dose
Sitter: facilitator

Session: time spent with facilitator
Support: post-session work environment

Set

While all of the above factors are important, set is the most critical for problem solving. When psychedelics are taken for other purposes, people gravitate toward internal complexity, visual and sensory enhancements and distortions, and emotional intensity. To help participants achieve significant progress on their own intellectual problems, establishing the set requires a deliberate and ordered ambience.

The first and perhaps the determining question is, does the participant care enough about the problem, area of research, or intellectual issue to be engrossed in it, and is he or she emotionally involved? One criterion is to determine if the person has already put out considerable effort toward its solution or resolution. The more the problem matters, the more likely the session will be successful.

People who are so involved with the problem that its solution is vital to their well-being are more likely to do well. The issue could be delighting them or tormenting them. In either case, solving it matters deeply. The person should not be too enamored of rational thought. They should, at least understand—even if not through their own experience—that reason is only one tool among many.

If the intention is weak, then a person should be advised that this kind of focused experience is not right at this time. If he or she has the necessary motivation, the follow-up question is, has he or she had psychedelic experiences before?

At the time of our original research, it was not difficult to find many scientists with careers of ten to thirty years behind them who had never been in an altered state more challenging than one brought on by fatigue, coffee, or alcohol. Today, scientists and other professionals are more likely to have had prior experiences with psychedelics, if little or no experience with guidance. The upside of this change is that a facilitator can explain the dynamics of the session more easily, especially how to stay with a chosen project during the working hours of the session.

The facilitator should be familiar with those factors described in detail in chapter 9 that inhibit or support creative problem solving, to be able to answer such questions as "Can I stay focused on my problems if I tap into my divine nature and wish to stay with that?" A possible answer might be that perhaps the participant's divine nature brought him to psychedelics to make progress on the problems.

If participants have had considerable psychedelic experience, the facilitator should establish the difference between this and prior sessions to underscore that the participants can maintain sustained attention on professional rather than personal concerns.

Pre-session Meetings

The purposes of pre-session meetings are:

- To intensify the focus on problems to be worked on as well as to evaluate their suitability. In the session itself, the "aha" experience may come early, and it becomes clear that the rest of the solution can be worked out in ordinary consciousness. A second problem and a third should be at the ready.

- In working with a group, to acquaint group members with one another and with each other's goals, not so that they can help each other, but to improve the concinnity for all. It has not proved difficult to attain harmony during the resting morning hours, which is then maintained for the duration of the session.

- To let participants know that their experience may be one of discovery and confirmation rather than the welling up of original thoughts. Someone who has already grappled with a problem and has the expertise, technical background, vocabulary, and experience to solve that kind of problem may recognize that he or she had all the necessary elements when a solution presents itself.

- To explain the feeling of "rightness." Experience with successful group problem-solving sessions, even without psychedelics, indicates that participants often have a keen awareness of being "on the right track." The feeling emerges well before they have a clear idea of a solution. There is a feeling of rightness, of "getting in the groove," of "going with the flow." It is sometimes experienced as if the group or the individual mind has penetrated to layers of consciousness where the answers are kept.

Another purpose of preliminary meetings is to generate pleasure and excitement at the prospect of an extraordinary opportunity. Facilitators should be familiar with the successes described in chapters 11 and 13 as well as, for example, Francis Crick's discovery of the DNA structure while using LSD.

With one or more pre-meetings, the session itself should run smoothly. The chances are very small that any single member of a group will drift away from the problems, and in any case, should this occur, it should not disturb the others.

Number of Participants

Up to four people can be accommodated without lowering the level of individual success. For any group session, at least two facilitators should be present. Larger groups can be accommodated, but only if there are enough facilitators and ample spaces so that individuals can work away from the group if they choose to. The larger the group, however, the more likely it is that a single participant can disrupt the overall tone.

Setting

The best physical setting is probably a living room with enough floor or couch space for each member of the group to lie down. The setting should be comfortable, with no medical and laboratory overtones. Desks or lap desks to help the participants make notes or sketches may be useful. No computers, cell phones, or the like. If there is only one participant, an audio recording may be made. However, for many participants, speaking about what they are thinking seems to slow down and constrict creative thought. Even the most analytic types usually find themselves working with visual events, metaphorical representations of their problems, or visions of physical objects, all of which they can manipulate faster than they can record what they observe.

Substance

While this section is about using LSD, as has been noted, mescaline and morning glory seeds as well as psilocybin and psilocybin-containing mushrooms are in the same family, although each has a different active molecule and should be dosed accordingly.

Our original study used mescaline and LSD interchangeably, depending on which government agency was conducting an investigation or audit of which drug at our facility. The fact that our initial investigations used mescaline had no bearing on the results. Other experiments (unpublished because they were done after the research ban) showed that LSD is equally effective. Morning glory seeds are a last choice because they can cause nausea in some individuals.

Dosage

For participants with no prior experience but who are sufficiently motivated, 100 micrograms of LSD is an optimal dose. For participants with considerable prior experience, 50 micrograms is probably enough. If a participant is not anxious but feels uncomfortable or unable to focus and relax into the music, another 50 micrograms may be given an hour or so after the initial dose.

Sitter

The session director is a facilitator, not a guide in the sense that the term has been used in this book up until now. To be credible and knowledgeable and capable of running a session, a facilitator may be a scientist or engineer, should have some general psychedelic experience, and have been a participant in one or more sessions devoted to creative problem solving. Everyone who will be a facilitator should also be at any pre-session meetings of the group.

The facilitator's responsibility is to keep the group focused. If during the morning, a participant is weeping or agitated, a facilitator may reassure the person by holding his or her hand, but should not discuss or interpret what is being experienced, if possible. The goal is to help the participant back into a state of attentive relaxation.

As with sacred and psychotherapeutic sessions, the facilitator is present to make people feel safe and cared for and to deal with any concerns or confusion that arise rather than acting as a guide, since the participants will be working on different problems using different strategies.

Session

As the LSD effects begin to be noticed, participants should be encouraged to lie down, put on eyeshades, and listen to music. The kind of music should be agreed on beforehand. Solo instruments are good; Bach or Indian ragas are fine. Highly emotional music and vocal music should be avoided. Participants should be allowed to lie quietly, listening to the music, for up to three hours or until they show interest in sitting up, reflecting on their morning journey, or turning to their chosen problems.

There should be finger food available for lunch and snacks available throughout the afternoon. A lunch break is not necessary because many participants will have no interest in food. Facilitators, however, should eat something since any feelings of hunger may be picked up by the participants and may be a possible distraction.

When people sit up and take off their eyeshades, they should be reminded that it is now time to work on their problems, which may need to be restated to them. There should be no more music unless it is requested by a participant. If requested, it should be kept at a very low volume.

Participants may choose to sit or lie down, to work with eyes closed or open, or to make notes or sketches. Every person finds his or her own way. The facilitator's job for the next few hours will be like that of a good airline steward or a waiter in a four-star restaurant: attentive to the participants' needs, but not obtrusive. Some participants may ask for paper and pens or other aids, ask for a snack, or ask the facilitator to make note of an idea. Others will not want to be intruded upon. Discourage conversation. Remind people that they are there to work on their own projects.

After a few hours, some participants may begin to flag. They may act like children who wish that class would be over. If this happens, check if they need a break or whether or not they actually feel finished. It can be beneficial to have access to another room where a participant can relax, talk with a facilitator, or just be by him- or herself. If someone wishes to take a walk, that person should be accompanied.

After a break of ten to fifteen minutes, it is good practice to suggest to participants who are flagging that there is a second wind to these sessions and that they might take one more look at their problems. If they agree, they will almost always see a different approach or go on to a second problem or take off in a new and unexpected direction. As before, the facilitator should be attentive and supportive but not in the way.

Near the end of the afternoon, let participants talk with each other about the day's experiences. These conversations often spur new ideas, so be sure they have their notes or sketchpads beside them.

The group may have chosen to have dinner together or to be taken home by relatives or friends. If they are to eat together, takeout is best because they are still in a state where the chatter and bright lights of a restaurant will be distracting.

Once at home, some participants will feel finished and just enjoy the state they are in, but many will be up late, even all night, continuing to work on solutions exposed but not fully explored during the session.

It seems to be the case in these low-dose sessions that what was thought about, the steps involved, the mind-experiences along the way, the results and the alternative paths opened up are all retained with comparative ease. However, it is a good idea to suggest that each person write up as full a report as he or she can in the first few days following the session. Most people find that even with little sleep their energy remains high all the next day. Others will be deeply tired.

For some, the cognitive shifts last far beyond the session. Even after the problems they picked are completed, their capacity for problem solving remains enhanced. It is as if they found an extra gear on their mental bicycles and can go farther with the same amount of pedal power.

Support

Since the session is focused on external interests, part of the participants' work world, there is usually adequate support in the workplace to explore, express, and develop their solutions.

In situations where it is not okay to say what they have done, a person can say, "I spent a few days with this problem and made real progress." Few people will inquire further, especially if the new work is of interest or value to the company.

It is good to check in with each participant within a few days of the session to answer any questions and to encourage participants to reflect on important aspects of their experience. In any case, one should remain on tap for questions or concerns.

11

CASE STUDIES
Two Architects and Six Professionals

As useful as a formal research report like chapter 9 is, with its lists, table, and sample moments, it doesn't give the flavor of what it is like to be working on one's chosen problem, in the company of other professionals, aided by the support staff and fueled by a low dose of a psychedelic.

This chapter has both short and long excerpts written relatively soon after the sessions described in chapter 9. The first section was written by two architects. The second section contains reports by other professionals, including several who wrote rather daunting reports of their own creative process.

I have been approached by one foundation asking how to reinstate this kind of work. The answer at this point is to make the results more available. Then the normal desire of natural problem solvers to work more effectively can lead them to seek out these methods. In addition, corporations and governments will see that those who allow or encourage higher levels of creativity will have more and better results than those who don't.

Other than the usual caveats about careful participant selection and the necessary considerations of set, setting, substance, and trained guides, very little prevents us from supporting work—like the examples given in this chapter—so that it can occur more often.

Two Architects

We were very fortunate in having two successful architects participate in our study. While they worked in their own way, they both felt that their visualization capacities were enhanced during the session and that their design solutions were not greatly different from their usual work. The difference, as each noted, was having more freedom and reaching the eventual end design far more swiftly. While one of the architects we worked with had had a powerful psychedelic experience several years earlier, his capacity to focus and stay focused was no different from the participant with no prior exposure.

Henrik Bull: Architect Number One

Henrik Bull wrote up his observations and reflections some weeks after his session.

My experience during the session was an unbelievable increase in the ability to concentrate and make decisions. It was impossible to procrastinate. Cobwebs, blocks, and binds disappeared. Anything was possible, but I was working on real and rather tight problems. The designs were freer, but probably more from the standpoint of removing blocks in the consideration of what the client might accept. Three designs were outlined in the three hours. All were accepted by the clients.

The two houses that are referred to are now complete, and I feel are very successful. They are more free than my usual work, but not completely untypical. The clients would be horrified if they knew the history of the conceptual design. . . . Every person should have the experience to see what potential lies within himself.

There is definitely an enhancement of the ability to visualize, but my experience was that I became a better Henrik Bull and was not converted to an instant Gaudí.

The remainder of this section is from the report Bull submitted shortly after his session.

Until hearing J.K.'s description of his experiences under psychedelic drugs, I knew practically nothing about them. I had never read any articles or books, or participated in any discussions on the subject. I was fascinated with his experience in this study and responded with enthusiasm when he suggested that there might be an opening in the next week for me.

I had felt for a long time that my life was plagued with necessary, but relatively unimportant, detail work, which was competing with the design work, and both were suffering. Beyond that, I felt that my design efforts were often repeating old ideas and should be freer in spirit. I hoped that they might bring about some real change in my attitudes. This certainly happened beyond my wildest hopes.

The morning session is difficult to describe—as any dream is. Ordinary dreams are often difficult to remember. In this case my memory is vivid, but everyday words cannot convey fantastic thoughts.

My first impression was of the extreme clarity and beauty of the music. The instruments were not only stereophonic, but also existed at a particular point in space. This point would even move about in some cases. I had never heard music in this manner before. Soprano voices (which I had never before enjoyed) became fantastically beautiful.

Soon visions began to appear, not unrelated to ordinary dream patterns. There seemed to be a constant changing of varicolored and handsome fabrics of all kinds.

Next, the visions became more abstract and occupied the whole head. I was observing the scenes, but was conscious that there were no eyes, no ears, and no brain.

The head soon became the universe, infinitely expansible or contractible. The visions continued uninterrupted and were influenced in content by the music. This universe was sustained by that which was below, and that which was below had been my body. There had been fingers and toes on that body, and I felt it might be interesting to find out if I could communicate with these elements. I tried to move a finger; it touched another finger, and I felt it. Therefore I had fingers still. Having proved that, there was no necessity to find out about toes. This was my last contact with my former body.

From that point on there was no vision or thought which related to the real world.

There were no absolutes.

There were no specifics.

There were no dimensions.

There were no mistakes.

There were no people.

Do not ask questions!

This is truly a wonderful world of infinitely variable colors, forms, music. (The last had come from the other world, but improved.)

When the music stopped and we were told to get up, I really thought the whole morning had been very funny and I laughed out loud for quite a while. I had been anxious that I might be nasty to anyone who would shut off such a fine world. However, the world was still fine—just different.

I was looking forward to the opportunity to attempt some of the professional creative problems which we had been told to bring. There were four of these, ranging from an extremely complex state college building with a program of eighty-two pages to a rather simple vacation house.

My first decision was which problem to attack. I decided immediately to avoid the complex problem, because even though I felt very sharp, I knew it would be impossible to come to a conclusion or even to make considerable progress in three hours. This proved to be a wise decision.

The simplest problem (but possibly the one with the most potential interest) was attacked first. Almost immediately several relationships that had escaped my attention became apparent, and a solution to the spatial relationships followed soon after. I avoided looking at a watch throughout the session, but I would guess that twenty minutes elapsed. Normally, I would stew and fret for weeks before coming to such a solution. Don't misunderstand me; on a simple problem, the period at the end which is truly productive is often quite short under normal circumstances, but in any case a matter of hours.

My next dilemma was whether or not to continue developing the design and make an effective drawing of it. I realized that I was thinking better and would draw better than usual. My decision was that if I drew better than normal, I still would not be drawing well, and should stick to those things I was good at. I have never had much trouble developing a consistent design after the initial conception.

I decided to stay on this level of conceptual thinking and only make shorthand notes to myself to follow up later. This was a most important decision.

I did not know whether or not I would remember the unanswered questions later, and sorely resented the time it took to make notes to myself. My hand did not move any faster than usual and I became very impatient with it. I even resented the time it took to reach for a sharp pencil. My position was half-sitting, half-kneeling on the floor, leaning over the drawing board. Quite literally, I had only a head to think and a hand to make sketches and notes. The body was (again) unimportant. When the session was over and I got up, it was really quite painful because of the awkward position I had been in for three hours.

The first problem completed, I felt very exhilarated and could not wait to get on to the next.

This problem was basically a site problem, locating a number of condominium houses on a very beautiful piece of property. The decisions came very quickly and I outlined a solution, which pleased me in a very short time. In passing, I investigated the economic yield to my client for several similar solutions and decided on what I felt was the best one. Why not do a typical floor plan for one of the units? This too was accomplished without the usual number of false starts.

At this point I said to myself, "It would not be fair to Barney not to give his house one more try." This client had been very difficult, but also challenging. I had presented him several different preliminary schemes. All had various faults in his mind, but he would not give me any specific complaints. The only scheme which excited him was also too much money. But he did not lose faith in me—which is quite unusual.

This time my approach to the problem was unrelated to all previous attempts, and I looked at the challenging site in a new way. I really believe the solution that resulted in a few minutes is better than any of those that preceded it. This was a job that had taken several hundred hours of time, and represented a great monetary loss for the office. Why had I never seen this solution before?

I should emphasize that the solution could have happened before. It belongs to the same family as my other work. The only real difference was that the solution that I felt right about appeared in almost no time at all. At this point in the session, we were told there would only be a few more minutes to work on our problems. Having disposed of the other problems, I decided to take a fresh but superficial look at the state college problem. I made some quick notes and calculations, which resulted in a rough sketch for a different approach to the ground floor.

During the rest of the evening I felt very stimulated, something like being slightly high on alcohol. This was sustained for several hours. After my friends went to bed, I listened to their records until about 4:00 a.m. The visions of the morning session were missing, but the clarity of the music was the same.

The day had started at six in the morning and ended twenty-two hours later. It was probably the shortest and most enjoyable day in my life.

When I showed this to my partner and to the men in the office the next morning, they were very enthusiastic. Despite this, it was generally agreed that the new approach was too complicated to solve completely before a rather pressing deadline. We also agreed that it would be worth looking into later to see if it was in fact a better solution.

Eric Clough: Architect Number Two

A 1966 article in Progressive Architecture, *"LSD: A Design Tool?"* stated that "a number of architects [including Eric Clough, see below] have added to the extensive evidence for the drugs' use as an instrument for enhancing perception, for training in visualization." The report stated that, under the psychedelic effect of the drugs, visual and auditory acuity are 'revolutionized'. . . . The consensus among the architects interviewed . . . seems to be that LSD, when administered under carefully controlled conditions, does enhance creativity to the extent that it vastly speeds up problem solving, aids in visualizing three-dimensionally, and generally heightens perceptivity."[1]*

Clough's report shows how the highly trained mind and eye of an architect can effectively and purposefully utilize the heightened focusing of LSD. "I learned that whatever I was able to do that day was not because of the drug, but because the drug allowed me to function in a way that I was capable all along of functioning, without the usual frictions we encounter."

Clough had been part of an earlier LSD study. This is an excerpt from his report of the peak of that session.

I could hear and feel the heartbeat of my guide and it was me and I was it. The room breathed and it was I. My eyes opened and we shimmered in shining spectrum.

We (the tree of life and I, as one) grew and grew and formed a canopy of the universe. I saw (or was) the cosmos and it came together into a pinpoint of all the light and energy there is and burst and flooded the universe with twinkling stars again.

I saw a pile of shit mounded high and steaming. A fly walked through the steam. A piece of shit clung to his leg and I saw (and felt) that I was that little piece of dung. We exploded into particles of shining dust and merged with the cosmos.

I withdrew for a moment and thought about this rare phenomenon. Again laughter tumbled from the depths of my being. I was trying to do the impossible, to stand back and intellectualize about the most integral thought I had ever experienced. . . . Being transcending the sum of its parts. . . .

The remainder of this section is from Clough's report of the creativity session.

Two and one half years later I received a call from the International Foundation for Advanced Study. I was invited to take part in a specific experiment: the study of creativity while under the influence of a psychedelic agent. My field, architecture, was one they wanted to include in the study. . . .

We were instructed to choose a particular project and one or two alternates that we were currently working on, to give it some general thought prior to the day, but not to get too involved in it, so that we would have it on our minds but not arrive at the session with preconceived solutions. Preferably this would be a problem that we had not been able to find a solution for or that had some complexity and would require a considerable amount of our professional skill.

The plan was to have four participants in each full-day session. Each participant was from a different field of endeavor and would work on his own project, even though all would be in the same room. Interaction and discussion was permissible but not required.

The day came, and we four assembled in the session room and with little further preliminaries ingested mescaline. Our guides arranged us comfortably on the floor with our own sleeping bags, placed eyeshades over our eyes and stereophonic earphones over our ears, and started a tape of beautifully selected classical music.

After Clough described how he felt during the hours of music and relation, he continued.

I took off my headphones and slowly removed my eyeshades. A moment or two later one of our guides knelt at my side. I smiled at him and reached out to take his hand. We looked at each other (deep eye contact) for an eternal moment, and I closed my eyes again.

I saw that the personality of man is like layer upon layer of glass. The specific vision was of irregular but cleanly geometric pieces, each behind the other into infinity. Each piece of glass was attached on pivots at the top and bottom. At any place, if any piece were turned slightly it would reflect an external picture and, like a mirror, block any further vision inside. I knew, with deep regret, that most of us have many pieces turned askew.

For some time more I saw other mental images of similar kinds, all having to do with man's inability to mesh cleanly at all levels of functioning.

I sat up. It was 11 a.m. We had been instructed that we would be aroused at noon. I sat quietly and waited until the other subjects were brought back for lunch.

We ate lightly: fruit, cheese, a small glass of wine, and some coffee. We talked about our morning. Our experiences were not the same but we felt that we had shared something rather important. For that time we were close friends.

I picked up my sketchpad and some colored felt-tip pens and made myself comfortable on the floor in one corner of the room. I opened the pad, picked up a felt-tip pen and was ready to work . . . but I was a complete blank. Usually when I'm considering a problem, my head is full of pictures that I look at and discard or look at closer and elaborate on. I rarely draw anything until I have a pretty complete concept in my mental image. I had had a number of schemes for the project and had been looking at the mental picture of one on the way to the Foundation earlier that morning. Now there was nothing.

(I had better digress for a moment and describe the project in question: A client had retained me to make studies for an arts and cultural center near one of the San Francisco Bay area universities. The site had been tentatively selected—a flat, square, three-acre parcel. This was to provide artists and craftsmen with workshops and retail sales areas in an environment that would be conducive to sales and would be a wide cultural influence on the community. It would have a coffeehouse, a theater for plays, open lectures and forums, and galleries for artists who did not have their shops in the complex. It would probably house a hip bookstore, too.)

I still knew the dimensions of the site and slowly drew the approximate borders on the blank page. Still there was nothing in my head. The morning had somehow erased everything having to do with the purpose of the creativity session.

I closed my eyes. I did not try to think. I waited, but not in anticipation of anything—much as I had in the later part of the morning.

Within minutes it flashed to complete life. I could see the completed center. The trees were grown, cars were parked in the parking area, fountains splashed running water, and people walked through the building and the gardens. I could walk through, too.

I did, slowly. I looked at the details of the structure, I studied the construction, I looked at the types of plants growing there, and I watched the craftsmen at work. The colors were rich but subdued, in harmony with the paintings displayed in the shops and along the boardwalks.

I began to draw. In a few minutes, the basic plot and building arrangement were sketched on the pad. I laid out the parking lot and checked the number of spaces with the estimated need. It worked. I quickly calculated the probable cost of the project and checked it with the projected leasehold income. The economics were feasible, too.

During the next hour and a half I drew as rapidly as I could. The drawings were sketchy but captured the essence of the vision I had in my head, and many specific details were recorded on paper.

I stopped working. It was not yet three in the afternoon. We still had two hours allowed for work. I designed a couple of houses in my head and sketched a little. I played with a garden pavilion and some fountain designs, and at three-thirty I stopped for the day. I had done the equivalent of from one to two weeks' work. (I'll qualify this last statement: in a week I could have had many more sketches completed and some scale drawings, too, but the feeling I had was that I actually wouldn't have accomplished any more than I had that afternoon. . . .)

I showed the sketches to the client a few days later, and they were approved, complete. Three weeks later, I began to prepare working drawings of the project, the property plan first. I put my sketchpad (closed) on the desk beside me and began the scale layout. A few hours later the first dimensioned sheet was done, and then I compared it with the originals. It was almost exactly the same. I had, without scaling the original sketches, laid out three acres of buildings, parking, outdoor theater, walks, patios, and so on in their exact dimensions and had kept it in my head as clearly as it had been when I walked through it. . . .

I have tried here to describe exactly what happened and no more. Much is being learned.

Six Professionals

Contained in this section are representative individual problem-solving experiences that illustrate some of the modes of creativity considered in chapter 9.

Commercial Artist

Problem: *Design of a letterhead, after several presentation sketches had been rejected by the client.*

I decided to drop (my old) line of thinking and to give it a new try. The "mystery" of this easy dismissal and forgetting did not strike me until later in the afternoon because I had many times before this session indulged in this line of thinking and had managed to work up the whole thing into an airtight deadlock, which I had been unable to break, much less dismiss. The miracle is that it came so easily and naturally.

I decided to go ahead with it, without worrying about what would come of it or whether anybody would like it or not. I started by modifying the original idea of the presentation sketch a little. After a couple of those, I dismissed the original idea entirely and started to approach the graphic problem radically differently. That's when things began to happen. All kinds of different possibilities began to come to mind, and I started to quickly sketch them out on the blank letter-size sheets that I had brought with me for that purpose. Each new sketch would suggest other possibilities and new ideas. I began to work quickly, almost feverishly, to keep up with the flow of ideas. And the feeling during this profuse production was one of joy and exuberance: I had a ball! It was the pure fun of doing, inventing, creating, and playing. There was no fear, no worry, no sense of reputation and competition, no envy, none of those things which in varying degrees have always been present in my work. There was just the joy of doing.

This person became so delighted with his heightened capacity for idea production that he chose to defer idea selection until the next day, when he selected and developed for presentation twelve of the twenty-six original conceptions. One of those was later accepted by the client.

Engineer

Problem: *The formation of a visible image corresponding to the heat distribution of an object such as the human body. (The application is in medi-*

cal diagnosis since diseased tissue tends to have a higher temperature than healthy tissue.)

I "asked my unconscious" to supply ideas. The insight came as an image of an oyster shell, with the mother-of-pearl shining in different colors. I translated that in the idea of an interferometer—two layers separated by a gap equal to the wavelength it is desired to reflect—which is the principle of the mother-of-pearl where a change in heat would cause a microscopic displacement, clearly observable by the color of the reflected light. The remaining problem was therefore to change thermal energy into mechanical displacement.

Another insight at this point was that the most efficient way to do this was by an expansion of gas because that was superior to any other operation that could be performed on solids. I then visualized this as two thin film layers, formed by vacuum evaporation, spaced about the wavelength of yellow light. Many pneumatic cells (of the shape of a long, thin cylinder) could be formed, say in a 200×200 array (with the parallel thin films located at one end). If the thermal image is projected on this array, the temperature reached by each cell will determine the pressure of the gas and the consequent elastic deformation of the thin films toward reestablishing ambient pressure. If the array is lighted by white light, each individual cell will reflect light of a color which is a function of the temperature of the source object. . . .

Many other insights were related to the actual fabrication process, method of testing, and other applications. It is significant that a high number of associated ideas came into my mind the next day.

Furniture Designer

I had two specific problems, both in furniture design. The primary problem was to find a method for making an integral drawer-pull design that complemented an existing group of furniture that I had designed a few years ago. This group was successful both in design and in sales. I needed a solution that combined the same kind of good looks with economy in production.

Case goods, that is, cabinets and chests of drawers, are basically boxes distinguished primarily by surface and edge treatments. Case goods always seem to look best when the design seems to be a natural outgrowth of the materials used. I try to avoid "applied" design elements. I'd already designed a line or series of case goods that embodied these elements, but it seemed to lack a certain spark which both the manufacturer and I felt was needed. I had gone over and over this problem trying new tacks, but nothing seemed to come of it. I really didn't expect to be able to do anything new since my feeling was that all possibilities were exhausted. What actually happened was a complete surprise.

I found that as soon as I began to visualize the problem, one possibility immediately occurred. A few problems with that concept also occurred, but these seemed to solve themselves rather quickly. This was quickly followed by another idea based on this first thought but with a variation that gave it another look. Visualizing the required cross section was instantaneous.

I thought that my last idea was the most remarkable one because of the way in which it developed. This idea was the result of a fantasy that occurred while listening to music composed by Wagner. I knew that there was a classic quality in some of the shapes that I saw during this period, so I put down the line that seemed to embody this characteristic. (This evolved in a series of rapid sketches to a completed drawer-pull.) I've made this handle, and it has exactly the quality that I've been looking for. All this time I kept being very amused at the ease with which all of this was done. It was so easy to do that I felt no necessary impetus to do more since I felt I could do a lot more of them at a later date. However, it was the nonspecific fantasy that triggered the idea that led to this result.

I went on to tackle a headboard problem for another manufacturer, which was also quickly solved. This solution had to be rejected the next day because of some cost factors that I was not aware of during the design time, but I had no difficulty coming up with another solution that had never occurred to me before.

I then decided to do something that always takes a lot of time. Doing a good dining chair that is both elegant and inexpensive is very difficult. Chairs are always seen as sculpture and seldom in pure profile. Chairs also require a discipline in shape and structure unnecessary in other furniture: discipline in shape because of the human anatomy and in structure because of the hard usage it gets. I had not been able to do an original design for some time. Very rapidly I ascertained what the basic structure should be; the basic details quickly followed. I did no refining, because this kind of thing is best done in three dimensions, although I could visualize the finished product. I decided that I had the chair and then went on to think of a type that I'd never done before. This one too seemed to present no difficulty. Even when I look at this today it all seems so obvious.

The drawer-pull was reduced to a model in one week's time and has been accepted by the manufacturer-client. One of the chair designs was modeled satisfactorily on the second try, with no radical changes from the original concept. Previously, chair designs had required on the order of two months and ten trial modelings to complete.

Theoretical Engineer

The problem I took in was a problem in combinatorial analysis, which has plagued a number of people, including myself. The problem is to prove, or disprove by counter example, the following conjecture:

We consider logical circuits that are constructed entirely of NOR gates. (A NOR gate is an element that produces an output if and only if none of the input has a signal on it.) Such circuits can be designed to go through cycles. That is, we start the circuit operating with some set of inputs to the various gates. As time advances, some gates that were off switch on and vice versa. Since the number of possible states of the circuit is finite, either the circuit must eventually reach a stable state, when no further action occurs, or it must reach a state previously reached and then proceed through the same sequence of states as it did before. This last sequence is called a cycle.

We call a cycle "totally sequential" if every time the circuit switches state, it does so by the change in the output of just one gate. (The importance of this is that it leaves no ambiguity as to what the circuit does. If two gates must switch in going from one state to the next, it may make a difference which gate switches first.)

The hypothesis is that, in a NOR gate circuit, the longest totally sequential cycle that can occur involves $2n$ states, where n is the number of NOR gates in the circuit.

At the close of the session, I thought I had a proof of this theorem. Working on it that night, I saw some additional complications but still thought that I could prove it. The next day, I found some additional possibilities. The theorem, so far, therefore remains unproven.

The approach that I discovered in the session remains a very valuable one and one that is new both to me and to others in the lab who have worked on the problem. For example, it immediately knocked out another conjecture that had been made regarding such circuits, namely that is impossible to get a sequential tail on a sequential cycle of NOR gates. Using this approach, it became obvious how to set up a counterexample to this conjecture.

I still have hope that the approach will lead, eventually, to a proof of the original conjecture—or to a counterexample.

Also, it may lead to a method of synthesis of such circuits to generate specified cycles.

Hence, the results seem to be quite valuable, even though the original purpose was not achieved.

My previous attacks on this problem had been mostly by matrix algebraic methods. When, in the session, I started studying the problem, I still tried to use these methods. I could not really see how to use the powers of the psychedelic state to advantage here. I could visualize a matrix and make a given row look all bright and shiny, and so stand out. And I could see, and aesthetically appreciate, patterns in the distribution of entries in the matrix. But it seemed fundamentally futile to try and do the detailed manipulations required to pull any other information out of the matrix.

Somewhere along in here, I began to see an image of the circuit. The gates themselves were little silver cones linked together by lines. I watched this circuit flipping through its paces. First, they were all strung out in a line, with each one triggering the next one. If the line closes and no other change occurs, then you automatically get a $2n$ cycle. So you must block this cycle. But having blocked it, then you must provide an auxiliary circuit to keep the operation going. The problem is, how can you do this without losing the property of being totally sequential?

At this point, I came back to the external world and tried to handle the thing in the purely analytic or logical mode. At that point, I thought I could show that you were driven inevitably into non-sequential operation eventually. The difficulty is to see all the possibilities that there are and to trace down each of them. In the session and afterward, I still had not found all the alternate possibilities. Hence, the proof foundered. But the central thought of picking out a main sequence that would run by itself as a $2n$ cycle if the blocks were removed and of subsidiary sequences to bypass the blocks is, I think, a valuable one.

After this engineer returned to his working group and shared his experience with them, several others in the group requested to become and were accepted as experimental subjects, working on the same general problem.

Manager, Product Planning

I have been assigned the task of defining and initiating a new family of recording products. They use a similar modulation scheme, but cover quite a range of applications, performances, and costs. I had just completed an extensive market research trip and had developed a table or matrix of interrelationships in which I had attempted to display the type of system, level of performance, and some estimate of practicality and schedule. It was quite a task since so many variables are involved and was further complicated by a considerable workload and unsympathetic attitudes in the area of Engineering where it would have to be executed.

After some struggle, I discovered a kind of relaxation, letting the problem talk to me. I detached from having to perform and let a different mode of viewing the data take over. I was quite able to cast out complexifying notions and get to the heart of the matter. A new matrix presented itself, one that was immensely simplified and one that would be much simpler to communicate. It became more apparent as I worked around this array that it would probably capture most of the market for which it was intended and would present the simplest sales task. It became apparent that part of the previous trouble had been caused by unnecessary perfectionism and a kind of greed.

I was next able to make a trial run in my inner "stage" as to how to get to act. The relationships between key individuals literally jumped out at me. Their hang-ups and the effect of them on acceptance and performance of the development task became quite clear. I tried different approaches in my mind and then realized that the solution had been easily overlooked. I had to change, and then they would be more likely to respond. It became unnecessary to plot, only to develop the right attitude. This attitude has to do with the confidence that comes from study and data and the acceptance (of others) that comes from understanding, sympathy, and tolerance.

The results of this have not been spectacular, but formidable. People are moving. The most antagonistic have become much more open and friendly. The amount of energy required of me has noticeably decreased. My boss has remarked more than once of a notable change in my mode of functioning. Measurable progress on the product array has been there, but has been marred a little by reorganization.

In summary, the experiment produced not so much a giant brainstorm or breakthrough in the usual connotation of creativity, but a very practical result.

Engineer

Irwin Wunderman was an engineer associated with a major California electronics laboratory. The fluid energies of his experience were channeled into a highly abstract model-building process. His observations about his own mind, recalled some weeks later, are unusual in the way he recalled them and the way he reported them.

Reactions during initial three-hour period:

1. Gradual awareness of reduced inputs from tactual senses. Numbness in extremities, which could be overcome by deciding to move and executing same.
2. Feeling of trying to minimize extraneous inputs concerned with contemporary surroundings. Noted that I allowed my body to gradually relax to its "lowest energy" position. Suggest this occurs to other individuals.

3. Was keenly desirous to remember all sensations and report them to the Foundation.
4. Many relatively simple observations, which I analyzed and subsequently understood, appeared as more significant revelations at the time than they really were. For example, when the hymnlike music came on, I realized the religious significance of the pictures on the walls. It appeared that this was a basic understanding I had not comprehended before, yet it seems quite obvious looking back.
5. The central theme of my thoughts was:
   a. Worldly inputs were gradually decreasing.
   b. My nose, ears, and eyes still retained moderate to high sensibilities, but the inputs were not "automatically" communicated to me unless I thought about them.
   c. My mental capabilities were relatively unaffected, but due to reduced normal inputs, my mind seemed to wander into various thoughts.
   d. I realized that in the limit all contemporary stimuli would be cut off (or desensitized) so that I could devote my entire thought processes to things remote from current reality. I tried to minimize disturbing inputs and maximize the conditions of the new circumstances, thereby permitting my thoughts to drift.
   e. I imagined that all local inputs were cut off; only my mind, the music, and the universe were present.
   f. I tried to mentally move my mind around the universe and explore what could be seen with the ability of this new tool.
   g. The universe was totally black and, to distinguish it in my mind, was a tiny white speck about which everything was radially symmetrical.
   h. I placed the music within this universe, and it was either pervading everywhere or emanating from another speck, which was also radially symmetrical.
   i. I was aware that all my thoughts were not dreams in that I had control, and applied logic; it was like thinking to myself under the influence of a trancelike drug.

j. My conclusions, after attempting to let my mind drift around the universe, were that without the perceptual senses, I would not be able to perceive and everything would be blackness.

k. I concluded that an introspective view of my mind would be more appropriate and revealing under the circumstances.

l. I questioned the method of locomotion used to allow my mind to propel in the preceding thought (j). I could not envision any propulsion mechanism and noted that I simply imagined it to drift through space.

m. In looking at my mind, I was aware that the outside antagonistic world, which normally provides the interplay for my thoughts, was no longer present. I was aware that the effect of the drug was to provide a great "self-consistency" about my thoughts and that to be objective under its influence, I had better give self-scrutiny to that which I might consider valid.

[*Editor's note:* Points 6 and 7 have been intentionally omitted by the author.]

8. In assessing how the music sounded and how my other inputs were affected, it seemed as though the best simple description was "having passed through a mellowness filter."

9. I was aware that I had not seen any vivid colors nor had any hallucinations and had tried hard to imagine things in color. (My involuntary thoughts were in black or white.) I could not make apparent anything but normal color perception.

[*Editor's note:* Points 10 through 19 have been intentionally omitted by the author.]

20. Considered a problem in which I visualized the result I wanted and subsequently brought the variables into play that could bring that result about. I had great visual (mental) perceptibility; I could imagine what was wanted, needed, or not possible with almost no effort. In what seemed like ten minutes, I had completed the

problem, having what I considered (and still consider) a classic solution. However, I gerrymandered the boundaries of the problem somewhat to make this solution possible. I decided to be more pragmatic about the problem and insist that the real constraint of practicality be imposed. I found that I was much less willing to consider that. I had solved one with optimum efficiency, was unwilling to compromise—Q.E.D. I was amazed at my idealism, my visual perception, and the rapidity with which I could operate.

21. Scrutinized the modus operandi with which I attacked the problem. Realized that my mind was working like a computer, and although I could not visualize the "local-level" operation, all known constraints about the problem were simultaneously imposed as I hunted for possible solutions.

22. I was impressed with the intensity of concentration, the forcefulness and exuberance with which I could proceed toward the problem.

23. I then left the room with one of the guides and discussed the results to that point. He suggested I return to the original problem and see what could be done.

24. I went back and considered the process of photoconductivity. I found I was unable to visualize what happened when light was absorbed in a photoconductor. I kept asking myself, "What is light?" and subsequently, "What is a photon?" The latter question I repeated to myself several hundred times till it was being said automatically in synchronism with each breath. I probably never in my life pressured myself as intently with a question as I did with this one. I began visualizing all the properties known to me that a photon possesses and attempted to make a model for a photon. The process took a long time and was exasperating, but I gradually built up a model of a photon, which satisfied the constraints I knew. The photon comprised an electron and a positron (positive electron) cloud moving together in an intermeshed synchronized helical orbit. The positron had a negative mass equal in magnitude to an electron.

This model was reduced for visualization purposes to a black-and-white ball propagating in a screwlike fashion through space. I kept putting the model through all sorts of known tests: instantaneous E-field requirements, diffraction gratings, dielectric refractors, generating photons in incandescing bodies, absorbing them in solids and in a reverse biased photodiode, for instance. Each test modified it or left it unaltered, until I had put it through all the tests I could think of.

I thought of the ridiculousness of the situation. The model was very crude; I had not set out to find a model for a photon; it had been exceedingly difficult to derive and ended up superficially simple and not very much in tune with what I had previously considered a photon to be. I felt almost ashamed to reveal it and asked myself what good it was even if it satisfied the various tests. My reasoning and my answer only served to drive me harder. If this model satisfied all constraints known to me about a photon, it was as real as anything else I knew. Sure, I realized black-and-white balls rotating through space were a simplified picture, but if they satisfied all the constraints, that was the model to use. This was no different than anything else in reality. The model was right for the application, regardless of what the rest of the world or I thought of it personally.

This latter rationalization was particularly important to me at the time. Even now, I consider it a significant argument against deterring inhibitions for conceptualizing something that is abstract but self-consistent.

After many hours of developing the model (and many attempts at applying it to a photoconductor only to be rejected by my mind), I began to consider it satisfactory. Now I had to go through the same process for a semiconductor. I developed a valence-and-conduction-band picture with positrons and electrons as the entities of importance (analogous to conventional holes and electrons). I added impurity states for acceptors and donors in the same framework and was busy putting my model for the semiconductors through various tests when I was engaged in the external discussion.

I considered my method of working at various stages.

25. In treating the problem to this point, one factor was obvious: I

had not made one single assumption that I did not force myself to prove if there was any question of doubt. Normally, I would overlook many more trivial points for the sake of expediency, but under the drug, time seemed unimportant. I faced every possibly questionable issue square in the face. Indeed, I was continually searching for errors, fallacies, and so on.

26. A second noteworthy observation: I would not have believed what transpired had it not really occurred to me. Good, bad, or indifferent, the results were beyond my expectations.

27. After the group discussion, we were driven home. I spent almost an hour relating the events of the day to the family. I then lay down in bed and continued working on the problem.

28. The development of the semiconductor model was completed with much effort, and I finally put the photon model to the test by absorbing it in a photoconductor.

29. I worked until four in the morning and was highly motivated to continue, but I was limited by a very severe headache that developed. I had a hard time not thinking about it, however, in that I kept drifting back to where I left off.

30. Several conclusions about the photoconductor model were resolved that evening.
    a. Basically the model is correct, but one cannot ascertain all the desired characteristics of the photoconductor without bringing in additional phenomena to the reaction kinetics I considered.
    b. An exciton population (of electrons and holes) comprises the majority of the photoexcited carriers. These carriers do not participate directly in the conductivity mechanism but dominate the recombination processes. Accordingly, this population is difficult to measure, although it is very important in determining observed results. I feel that this point is perhaps the only real contribution made under the drug toward the model's development, and the possibility of this being so was recognized before. However, the assurance of this point is now far more apparent.

31. There are other conclusions about the effect of the drug that are noteworthy:

a. I felt that nothing was done under the influence of the drug that could not have been done without it, but in several orders of magnitude more time. (There is some reservation about this statement with regard to the development of the model for the photon. I may never have been motivated to go through all the effort for something of such abstract value.)

b. I have not found any flaws to date in the concepts derived under the influence of the drug. . . . Perhaps an important observation is that the drug appears to maintain motivation to pursue what is aesthetically intriguing to a point far beyond what I would normally do. . . . At all times, I had complete control of my faculties. I saw no unrealities atypical of those I can and do imagine at various times.

c. I feel that there has been a general improvement, maintained to date, in my:

- Ability to concentrate on specific problems.
- Motivation toward my short- and long-range goals in life (drive).
- Visual perceptibility of problems.
- Tolerance toward what I consider incompetence and viewpoints significantly different from mine.
- Ability to work without getting tired. For example, I have sat down and written this in just a few consecutive hours.
- A general reduction of inhibitions where society has established codes contrary to my basic personal philosophy. For example, I would normally feel embarrassed about discussing with my peers such a model of a photon, derived under such extraordinary circumstances and so superficial in appearance.

The technical aspects of Wunderman's experience led to the development of a rigorous theoretical model that he described in a paper titled "A Kinetic Theory of Photoconductivity Decay Processes."

GROUP PROBLEM-
SOLVING SESSIONS

WILLIS HARMAN, Ph.D.

This unpublished report describes two experimental sessions our group ran in the weeks before the more successful sessions reported on in chapter 9. Willis Harman and I were members of the first group included here; therefore, I have added personal observations to this report of his, where appropriate, in italics. As you will see, these sessions were only moderately successful and highlighted various problems we experienced in working this way. This is the nitty-gritty of science that usually is not published. It is what I call "search." It is what happens when you are not sure what you are doing or what you are hoping to find. "Research," which is what usually gets published, is about what comes later, after you know a lot more about your subject. In this case, however, because there is so little published about this kind of group work and because lots of people still do it informally, it seems useful and instructive to present this first round of our studies as well.

This is a summary report of two group problem-solving sessions held to test the degree of enhancement in problem solving that might result from low-dose, facilitated group sessions. The first group was fairly diversified in background, consisting of four people with professional experience in electrical engineering, engineering design, engineering management, and psychology. All four had at least two previous LSD sessions. The dose was 50 micrograms of LSD, preceded by energizers. (The primary problem area was the development of new children's toys.)

The second group consisted of four research engineers, three with electrical backgrounds and one with a mechanical background. None had any previous experience with psychedelics. The dose was 100 milligrams of mescaline, preceded by energizers. The primary problem area was an improved phonograph pickup cartridge.

These two experiences suggest a number of tentative conclusions. On both occasions, some group members felt there was enhancement of their individual creative abilities some of the time. In both sessions, it was generally felt that the group communication and ability to work together were improved, during a portion of the session. In both cases, there was one member of the group who felt no noticeable enhancement of his abilities. While creative ability seemed to be somewhat released, there appeared to be impairment of some more routine abilities, such as solving simple arithmetic calculations, which appeared in connection with the assigned problems. In both cases, there was carryover into following days—individual members receiving new ideas relating to the problems or following up on particularly interesting ideas that had come up during the session. In a more realistic situation, this would probably have resulted in the refining and probably the creation of prototypes of the new concepts.

In both of these sessions, the group was relatively unproductive when it shifted to a second problem area, which had also been chosen beforehand. This was apparently in part due to lower motivation (although the second problems had seemed interesting when chosen) and in part due to the group members being tired. Possibly another contributing factor was that in both cases, the second problem was less specific and concrete, more abstract, and, in general, less suited to this kind of group approach.

The spirit of fantasy, freedom, freewheeling, and spontaneous play seemed to liberate the creative energy of both groups. An additional person acting as observer (who did not take a drug) was able to help the group members stay centered on the problem (while allowing profitable digressions), to pick up suggestions that the group passed over and might not otherwise have returned to, and to aid in moving on when a particular attack appeared to be unproductive. Large sketchpads, provided in the second session, were found to be very helpful in the communication of visualized devices and processes.

One incidental observation from the second session, wherein three of the four participants had been born and educated in foreign countries, was that there was some tendency to revert to thinking in the person's original language rather than in the acquired language (English).

One complicating factor turned out to be the increased sensitivity to the feelings of other members of the group. In the first session, considerable attention was directed toward one group member who experienced difficulty in moving with the group and consequently felt rather "out of it." In the second session, one member deliberately held back when he sensed that his somewhat disproportionately enthusiastic contribution resulted in a barrier between the others and him. The overall impression was that feelings assumed a greater than usual importance and were likely to constitute an unplanned agenda.

Session Number One

The first three hours of the first session were spent in individually listening to music, light conversation, and a group introspective examination of one member's anxiety and blocking of mind-expansion. (In retrospect, the group generally agreed that putting a member "on the spot" when he is unable to participate is poor practice. The individual needs the freedom to be silent, blocked, anxious, and so on without feeling judged by the rest of the group.)

Following this preparation period, the group was reminded of the agreed-upon problem: the creation of new and commercially profitable toys, games, and playground equipment. Proposals emerged that the toys should be educational in the sense of encouraging discovery, promoting wonder, and evoking a sense of accomplishment. Member D suggested that mothers would appreciate a toy that would require no supervision of the child playing it, and thus the mother would be uninterrupted in her household tasks. Member B noted that TV does this, but with questionable value to the child and proposed a game-you-play-with the-TV, perhaps with the possibility of accidental or spontaneous discovery.

Member D was intrigued with the commercial possibilities of a game that would have to be purchased (at the local supermarket perhaps) in order to watch and participate in a TV program. Member A suggested the possibility of "awareness kits" to go with special programs about botany and other areas of science. This caught on, and various suggestions were made regarding the potential use of easily available materials such as flowers and vegetables, the contents of a "botany kit" (e.g., microscope, microtome, specimens), the desirability of showing life processes in action, and so on. Member D suggested the example of a program on a rose, perhaps looking at it from the standpoints of a botanist, a biologist, a poet, and so on, with the suggested aim of heightening perceptual awareness. Member B wondered what you could do with a quick-growing fungus or another organism for the child to experiment with, possibly accompanied by stop-action films of a rose's growth cycle, for instance. The group decided, at this point, that this idea had been carried far enough for the moment; a botanist might be brought in later to carry it on further.

Member B suggested that the group consider a toy to develop a sense of wonder regarding one's own body, and something requiring muscular coordination and promoting a sense of balance appealed to the group. Some way of simulating surfing in the backyard was suggested, but this sounded pretty expensive. The attractive features of a trampoline were noted; it requires balance and muscular coordination, is noncoercive, and allows for a variety of possibilities, including the chance of a "hilarious accident." A board suspended over a soft surface was suggested. Member A recalled watching lumberjacks' logrolling contests as a child and suggested a backyard version of this.

One version which evolved was a cylindrical log mounted at the ends using bearings supported by coil springs, allowing the log to rotate freely but also to buck and sway. The log would need to be surrounded by some sort of soft cushion to break the child's fall; one suggested variant was to use air-filled mattresses with "poopers" between sections so that the fall would result in a rude noise. Another version, for swimming pools, was a hollow log with a roughened surface, equipped with internal baffles, and partially filled with fluid to make it a little less "quick" and easier for the child to stay on top of.

The group decided to shift to a rainy-day toy, which would occupy a small child for a long period of time. Member A recalled a simple toy that a friend had made for his small child, consisting of four lights and four switches. Various suggestions from group members caused this to evolve into the idea of a set of lights and a set of switches, with a plug-in board in the back for wiring up the lights and switches in different ways. One game would consist of randomly selecting a circuit arrangement and then experimentally finding switch settings, which would result in all the lights being lit. This toy had the possibility of simple versions for very young children and more elaborate and challenging ones for adults.

One member suggested that electric railroads seem to be a type of toy with unusual fascination, particularly for boys. There was some discussion of what characteristics seemed to account for this, and some attempt to think of other toys that possessed these same characteristics.

Since this didn't seem to be immediately productive, one member proposed consideration of some toy to promote aesthetic sensibility, but one that would be somewhat more structured than simply a supply of art materials or modeling clay, for instance. Member B suggested working on the visual awareness of space, and this ultimately resulted in the suggestion of a "build-your-own-cave" kit. The question was raised as to whether the building materials of chairs, tables, and blankets could be improved upon. It was suggested that children prefer blankets to hard, cold panels of fiberboard or cardboard. This led to a discussion of the sense of touch, and toys that would develop tactile awareness. Member B proposed a game that would be played with tactual inputs only: different kinds of textures, or whimsical blindfolds to eliminate visual impressions, or inexpensive vacuum-formed cards with tactual coding.

The group then decided to switch to the second problem area, which was the question, what social problems are likely to be most demanding of solutions during the next decade? It was proposed that the group imagine itself appointed by the executive branch to study national goals. As a starting point, the question "What is society for?" was put forth for consideration.

Survival, psychological security, and various other answers were discussed. Member C and others stressed problems of continuing expansion of ourselves through advancing technology and the social effects of this—remoteness from natural and life processes, submergence of feeling responses by the need to be rational, work losing meaning, and the dehumanizing effect of mass production methods, among others. A central problem seemed to be spiritual poverty, lack of meaning, and loss of contact with basic life processes. At this point, various remarks were made to the effect that there was little group thinking going on; more expressions of various individual points of view were being put forth instead. It was apparent that the group wasn't "swinging" as they had been with the toy problem, and they felt a need for working with something a little more specific.

Member C proposed city planning as a more specific aspect of the general problem. The group agreed to imagine having the assignment of planning for the Bay area, although two members expressed difficulty in feeling motivated about solving the city-planning problem. Various aspects were discussed, including conservation of hills and forestlands, bringing nature into the communities, European-type communities with social centers, transportation, and the feasibility of central planning. Member D withdrew from the group, frustrated by the group's inability to function smoothly together on this problem. He returned shortly afterward, but meanwhile the group had generally agreed they had "run down." The active time on the assigned problem had been in the neighborhood of three hours, and informal discussion continued for several hours afterward.

Left out of this report was time spent on another toy that arose from the discussion about the need to create something to increase physical skill and awareness. We came up with the idea of a tiny paper float that could be dropped into a toilet so that a small boy might aim for it with his stream of urine. While at the time, we were delighted with the idea of a line of one-use-only "pee-pee toys," they never made it into the original report. We also saw in the overall group effort that unless people had a real stake in the outcome, it was easy to be clever and brainstorm but harder to bore down to the next level of solution, where the practical considerations need to be as involving as the idea-making.

Session Number Two

Warning: *This session was much more technical and may be hard to follow. Even worse, the first problem—ways to improve on the phonograph cartridges and needles—has now been solved. For those of you unfamiliar with that technology, the problem with a needle and a phonograph record is that each time the record is played, the needle and the grooves in the record are both worn down. If you follow the suggested solutions, however, you can see that the later invention of the CD, which is read by a laser beam, was foreshadowed in various ways in this session.*

The second problem, designing an analog storage device, is no easier for the nontechnical to follow. This session, as did the prior one, underscored the kinds of intention and preparation necessary for success. In addition, as you will see, as the problems became more general, interest flagged.

The first hour after administration of the psychedelic agent was spent in informal conversation, and the next hour and three-quarters in listening to music without conversation. Toward the end of this period, some distortion entered the sound system, which was generally disturbing.

The first assigned problem was the design of an improved phonograph pickup cartridge that produced less distortion and reduced record wear. Member H reported that during the last portion of the music (after the distortion started), he had vividly imagined himself to be the needle being jounced back and forth by the undulations of the groove face, and he found this most distressing. He discovered that he felt much better floating along above the groove and sensing the surface variations in some way—somewhat like an airplane mapping the terrain with an echo sounder.

Member G suggested using a concentrated light or ultrasonic beam for sensing. This was developed at some length in the ensuing discussion. There appeared to be two parts to the problem: getting the "space platform" to track the groove and picking up the information from the two stereo channels impressed on the sides of the groove. Possibly the difference between the two information signals could be smoothed and used for tracking. Various ways were proposed for obtaining the information signal from the reflected beam, including sensing the amplitude, phase shift, Doppler shift, phase or amplitude modulation of the carrier, or the amplitude or delay of pulses. It was realized that several of these might work, but comparison of them required analysis of a sort best carried on outside this group session.

Member E raised the question of how important it really was to eliminate the needle completely. Record wear is a problem, but it can be reduced by touching the grooves more lightly. Member G proposed having the pickup arm float on an air cushion (using a stream of air directed downward from the cartridge). This would allow some weight to be put on the record, to ensure good mechanical contact, without actually touching it. A very lightweight needle could follow the variations with minimal mechanical force on the groove sides. Various methods, such as using magnetic coils or light beams, were considered for obtaining the information from the needle while still keeping the mass of the moving part extremely low. One proposal was to use a hollow needle, held off the groove by a small stream of air forced down its center, so that even the needle would not need to actually touch the groove sides as it followed the surface variations.

An alternative proposal was injected at that point, to go back to a straight mechanical system but provide two lightweight needles in a cartridge suspended just above the record surface. The first needle, riding ahead of the pickup needle like a guide truck on a locomotive, would provide, through pickup coils, a signal for a servo system to move the cartridge holder. The second needle, following behind in the groove, would pick up the two information signals. (The possibility of combining these functions in one needle was noted.)

Member H remarked that capacitive pickup might be considered and recalled again how uncomfortable he had felt as a phonograph needle. "When *would* you feel comfortable in the groove?" asked Member F. Member E now reported imagining himself hanging from the "space platform," one foot on each side of the groove, as if on a skateboard, following the groove surface. "It's sensational! Like riding two horses in a circus," he said. "The groove looks pretty big. The problem is how to do it and have it be fun." Member H noted that the main thing he didn't like, as a needle, was the unexpectedness with which bumps and undulations in the groove surface would hit him. Member F said that if you were riding above the groove, you could see ahead and anticipate changes. This approach was dropped without further exploration.

There were a few further suggestions along the lines of employing separate pickups for the two channels in place of sensing the two quadrature components of motion in one needle. But discussion seemed to be at a lull, and the observer proposed shifting to the second problem. (Time spent on the first problem was nearly two hours.)

The second problem was to design an element for the storage of analog (i.e., continuous, as contrasted with digital) information. Examples were a capacitor and electrolytic plating for storing information proportional to electric charge. Low driving power, small size, of reasonable expense, a nondestructive readout, and erasability were given as desirable characteristics; linearity also was included, although that was less important.

Member F asked how analog information is stored in nature. Member G noted that genetic information is in digital form. Member H suggested something along the lines of "freezing" ions, like the orientation of polarizable ions in an electret. Various possibilities along the lines of the operation of a vidicon TV transmitting tube were considered.

Member G described a cell with electrodes at each end, filled with a transparent material in which opaque ionized particles had limited freedom to move. A voltage applied to the electrodes would cause the particles to move toward one end, affecting the light transmission as sensed by a photocell.

Various other proposals were made of other physical phenomena to look into, including rotation of a magnetic field or magnetic particles in a field; shifting of domain walls in a magnetic material; and a hole whose diameter depended upon the amplitude of the signal, which was sensed by the amount of light shining through. The observer was unable to stay out of it at this point and suggested frequency as a convenient analog quantity; possibly a conditionally stable nonlinear circuit could be arranged that would start and continue oscillations at the frequency of a signal pulse input. Shortly after this, the session was declared ended. (The total time spent on the two problems was about three and one-half hours.)

The group members, none of whom had previous experience with psychedelics, varied in their opinions regarding the amount of enhancement they felt. Member E felt that his level of creativity never rose above his usual norm. During the early part of the session, he felt that "if anything, I was operating at a level lower than par . . . later on, I felt that I was functioning up to my usual standard." At the other extreme was Member G, who reported that he felt he was able to work unusually well with the group. "Ideas came up with a speed that was breathtaking. . . . I was very pleased that I could think much faster than H. Normally this is not the case."

Future Experiments Contemplated

The present feeling is that this approach to creative group problem solving has considerable promise but some unanticipated problems. Unresolved is the question of to what extent (in either a positive or a negative sense) a preceding large-dose psychedelic experience is likely to affect performance in the small-dose problem-solving sessions. (All four of the participants in Session Two plan to have large-dose experiences within the next few months, after which another small-dose, problem-solving session is planned for comparison.) Further development is required of the art of optimizing effective use of the few hours of peak creativity.

When this report was written, given the results, none of us could imagine that the government would stop this line of research. The anticipated later session with the same four people in Session Two did not happen. One reason was because we decided that this kind of session had proved that intellectual work at a high level was possible, but that by focusing on individuals with a strong desire to solve their own technical problems, we could expect (and we found this to be true) more impressive and reportable results.

A final historical note: The two groups reported here were not the first groups we ran. The first group to test if a psychedelic could be used to focus on conventional scientific problems was our own team. The problem we gave ourselves was to design an experimental protocol to test the hypothesis. In other words, four of us developed the study reported on in these chapters after having taken a psychedelic. One result was that because we were so intent to see if it could work, the variable of how much one cared about a problem, which later became a central criterion of success, never arose.

I had one insight that evening that forever colored my view of the effects of these substances on consciousness, especially for creativity. I observed that the so-called perceptual constancies were not overriding my actual visual perceptions. A visual constancy is the capacity of the brain to retain an image as unchanging despite the fact that the actual representation is changing. For example, if a man opens a door and enters a long room with you sitting at the other end, what you see visually is a tiny, tiny person who grows rapidly in size as he approaches you. However, what your mind turns that into is that the person seems to be the same size as he approaches. This reorganization of perception is ongoing. If you sit quietly and look at a post, it stays steady, even though someone observing your eyes would see constant small shifting motions, what we call "sparkle" when we see it in another's eyes.

As I observed my own constancies relaxing during that evening, I realized that if such a fundamental filtering and reordering process, which is basic to human survival, could be set aside, then it seems reasonable to assume that the filters we keep around our thoughts (e.g., beliefs, attitudes, prejudices, inhibitions, compulsions, language, cultural constrictions) could also be set aside and that new and original configurations could not only form, but would be less likely to be rejected. It may be that many of the methods used to stimulate or increase creativity actually are ways to reduce "non-creativity" instead and that normal awareness is far more fluid and flexible and innovative that it is given credit for.

THE *LOOK* MAGAZINE EXPERIMENT

Designing the California Issue

GEORGE LEONARD

This chapter is excerpted from George Leonard's 1988 book, Walking on the Edge of the World.[1] *In 1966 George was a senior editor at* Look *magazine and the events he describes represent the most successful of the group problem-solving experiments. In many ways, it is a model for what we thought might be possible: people letting go of their attachment to their own ideas and letting a natural evolution of ideas occur.*

The question I'm most often asked about this way of using psychedelics is whether the creative upsurge lasts. The latter part of this chapter includes descriptions of the high-energy aftereffects that Leonard experienced in the weeks following the session.

The LSD genie was out of the bottle, and the authorities were becoming increasingly alarmed. That young people were dropping acid and then going to a dance hall or an amusement park pretty well destroyed the concept, which I had shared, of LSD as strictly a sacramental drug.

One morning Jim Fadiman, a psychological researcher for the International Foundation for Advanced Study, phoned and asked if I had a specific creative problem that I was working on; if so, he would like Paul Fusco [*Look* photographer] and me to participate in an experiment on creative problem solving with psychedelics. Well . . . there were the picture portfolios that would go along with the opening and closing essays for the California issue. "That should do it," he said. . . .

However, I was not eager to take that trip. "You can ask Mike* if you wish," Fadiman said, perhaps sensing my reluctance. "He's a pretty good creative problem solver."

On the night before the experiment, we met at the foundation's suite of offices and conference rooms not far from Stanford University, [where we were briefed] on the research project and our part in it.

We spent the night in a nearby motel and reported for the session at 7:30 in the morning. After another briefing, [we were offered] miniature silver cups on a small silver tray. The cups held small white pills. We trippers toasted each other with the cups and threw the pills down. We were then led into a room with couches and cushions. We were fitted with stereo headsets and then lay on a carpeted floor that was itself like a cushion.

For the next four hours, we listened to a program of music taped for this session: flute sonatas by Bach, Rimsky-Korsakov's *Scheherazade,* a series of Indian ragas. When the Indian music came on, I experienced the dark sinuosity of the sitar as the interconnectedness of everything in the universe and the constant drone of the tamboura as the Essential Ground from which the endless weaving rose. My own independent existence became a mere spark among an infinitude of similar sparks, or not even that, but simply a sort of generalized awareness entirely independent of time and place.

Then—suddenly, unexpectedly—a brilliant major chord, a series of ascending major triads, the full-throated sound of a church organ: a Handel organ concerto! And there I was in a great Gothic cathedral with golden sunlight streaming in through golden stained-glass windows. All the darkness, all the sinuosity was gone in the wink of an eye, and there was only this clarity, this golden light. . . .

---

*Mike Murphy was the owner and director of Esalen. George Leonard later became the vice president of Esalen.

When the music ended, we took what seemed a long time to stretch, sit up, and get ready to work. Mike had already made a few notes. Paul and I got our notepads and layout sheets, and we were ready to begin.

In the few minutes before we started talking, I had already visualized the whole layout: three two-page spreads of color pictures, with only one or two very large pictures on each spread. The first spread expressed the theme "All men are brothers" and consisted of one large picture, almost monochromatic, of black and white people. The second spread had the future as a theme. On the left side was a huge fire consuming swastikas, guns, bombs, and missiles, while on the right, in dark plum tones, was a picture of all races living in harmony. The theme of the final spread was "The joy of now." On the left was a beautiful young woman, nude, in a bed of greenery and golden flowers. On the right was a crucifix superimposed on an indistinct face that represented death, with golden light streaming from behind it. Joy and death seemed somehow to go together, in either a contrasting or a complementary relationship.

My colleagues greeted this vision with something less than enthusiasm. It gradually dawned on me that it was pretty bad, which only made me defend it more vigorously. Paul said that the pictures had to stay in human terms, not symbolic ones, and especially not those clichés I had suggested. I yielded; my premature solution was not just bad, it was terrible.

Mike came up with home as a metaphor. He pointed out that America has never really found a home. The only home is in God, but by not realizing that, Americans are forever trapped in a polarity between comfort and security on the one hand and adventure and expansiveness on the other. We can never find either until we realize that home is God. Good enough, but what pictures did that suggest? Paul saw the concept of home less in God than in family. At least you could take pictures of a family.

Our conversation began moving in wider and wider circles: to the adventure and expansiveness of the space program; to the pill, which was making the birth of a child a moral choice; to the overwhelming power of technology, which was potentially making almost every choice a moral one; to the possibility of a police state in reaction to the explosive changes in mores and morals; to new ways of involving the reader—including feedback cards in the magazine, for example. The title of the issue was "California: A New Game with New Rules," but strangely enough, we kept circling back to the most basic themes: home, family, God. . . .

In mid-afternoon, just as our session was about to break up, Jim's wife, Dorothy, came in. She was a lovely woman with particularly striking eyes. When she first looked at Jim, Paul saw something in her expression, a sort of ecstatic intimacy, which, as far as he was concerned, completely solved the problem of the picture portfolio. He spent the next day shooting pictures of Dorothy alone, and then with Jim. Two days later, Paul came to the office with a selection of slides. Everyone there, including the ad people, gathered in a darkened room to view them. There were close-ups of Dorothy looking at golden acacia blossoms, eyes wide with wonder, and Dorothy in a field of golden mustard flowers embracing Jim. The pictures were stunning. The blossoms burned like molten gold on the screen. The expression on Dorothy's face entirely justified my reckless line "The joy of now."

I sent out for champagne, and we toasted Paul, the California issue, and the future. Our session on psychedelics and our six-hour creative problem-solving session hadn't really been necessary for Paul to get those pictures of Dorothy Fadiman. Or had they? In any case, things had worked out perfectly. It seemed we were operating in a state of grace and nothing, absolutely nothing, could go wrong.

[Several days later], on Monday morning, Mike and I walked into the *Look* offices [in New York City] to join up with Paul and T. George Harris [Leonard's immediate superior] in putting the final touches on the issue.

Actually, things were in great shape. If we were a bit on the far side of euphoria, we were also very well organized; all the stories were in the house and laid out ahead of schedule—a rare situation for any magazine. In effect, this gave the members of the editorial board two easy weeks, and everyone on the eleventh floor was in a holiday mood. As for our little group, it seemed that we were under a charm, that we could walk through fire, and that all of life was a wonderful game.

Back in the San Francisco office, I had three weeks to write two essays as well as the captions for two photo portfolios. The photographs and layouts had already been shipped to the printer. The words, as usual, had to fit exactly into the space allotted to them.

I was writing for *Look* magazine, for more than thirty million readers. What I was writing was true. The trends were there no doubt, but I was also writing about a personal dream. As I neared the end of the closing essay, I was flying high again, and ideas I'd thought about for years were pouring out. . . . As I typed out the closing paragraphs, I had a totally unexpected vision of a checkered flag waving in front of me, signaling a victorious finish.

Up to this point, the ferment of ideas and activities centered on Esalen [the first and most important "growth center" in Big Sur] and other similar California institutions had achieved no significant degree of public knowledge. Millions of people would first learn of them through the June 28, 1966, issue of *Look* magazine. If that issue was reportage, it was also manifesto, and I might have guessed that it would occasion a certain amount of controversy. But I had no idea of the storm it would whip up on June 14, 1966, the day the issue went on the newsstands.

As the summer of 1966 deepened, I realized with increasing certainty that June 14 had been a pivotal day in my life. In producing an issue of *Look* on a new game with new rules, I had uncovered some of the unwritten rules of the old game. And I had created a new game with new rules for myself. I didn't know then that before the decade was over, I would attract disapproval from the national administration and that *Look*'s editor in chief would be offered a million dollars to fire me, but I did know that nothing would ever be quite the same.

14

CLOSING THE DOORS
OF PERCEPTION
The Day the Research Ended

In 1966, there were about sixty projects around the country actively inves-tigating LSD. Some were therapeutic studies: one at the University of California, Los Angeles, showed remarkable success in getting autistic chil-dren to communicate; others were working with animals from monkeys to rats to fish, even with insects. Spiders, it turned out, make radically differ-ent web designs when given different psychedelics. A year earlier, the psy-chiatrist Jolly West gave an elephant enough LSD, it is fair to say, to kill an elephant. It did, the dose being several hundred thousand times what any human being had taken or would ever take.

Even that well-reported disaster did not stop research from continuing worldwide. Sandoz Pharmaceuticals in Basel, Switzerland, the developer of LSD, had recently made available summaries of the first one thousand human studies. LSD was the most studied psychoactive drug in the world. This chapter is edited from "Opening the Doors of Perception," in the book Time It Was: American Stories from the Sixties,[1] *edited by Karen Manners Smith and Tim Koster.*

The date is early in 1966. Four of us are seated around a table, called out from the session room for a moment to respond to the contents of a special delivery letter. Back in the room, four men are lying on couches and cushions, eyeshades blocking out the daylight, hearing a Beethoven string quartet on stereo headphones. Each man, a senior scientist, had taken 100 micrograms of LSD—a low dose—about two hours earlier. Two of these men are working on different projects for Stanford Research Institute, another works for Hewlett-Packard, the last is an architect. They are highly qualified, highly respected, and fiercely motivated to solve technical problems. Each one brought to this session problems that he had worked on for at least the past three months and had been unable to solve. None had any prior experience with psychedelics. In another two hours, we plan to lift their eyeshades, take off their headphones, turn off the music, and offer them finger food, which they will probably not touch. We will then help them focus on the problems they came in to solve. They are the fifth or sixth group we have run. The federal government has approved of this study as an experimental use of a "new drug," a drug still under review and not available commercially.

LSD was remarkable in two ways. One, it was effective in micrograms (one-millionth of a gram doses). This made it one of the most potent substances ever discovered. Two, it seemed to have the effect of radically changing perception, awareness, and cognition but not in any predictable way. These results seemed to be dependent not only on the drug effects, but equally so on the situation of the subjects—what they'd been told about what they were going to experience under the drug and, even more interesting to science, the mind-set of the researcher, whether or not he or she had communicated a point of view to the subjects in any given study.

In short, here was a substance whose effects depended in part on the mental expectations of both subject and researcher. Often people in the studies had experiences that appeared to be deeply therapeutic, blissful, and life changing, religious in content or mystical, but they also might have experiences that were profoundly disturbing, confusing, or terrifying. The aftereffects of the experience looked more like learning than simply the passage of a chemical through the brain and body. LSD was the genie in the bottle, and there were bottles of it all over the country and at a growing number of outside laboratories and research institutions as well.

When that special delivery letter came from the U.S. Food and Drug Administration, none of us yet knew that many of the early conferences of LSD researchers had been sponsored by foundations that were covertly funded by the CIA or that the U.S. Army had been giving psychoactive substances to unsuspecting members of the military, prisoners, even some of their own staff. Nor did we know that every project in the country, except those run by the military or intelligence agencies, had received a similar letter on the same day.

Sitting in Menlo Park, California, in the offices of the International Foundation for Advanced Study, we four plus a small support staff were running the only study designed to test the hypothesis that this material could improve the functioning of the rational and the analytical parts of the mind. We were trying to find out if, instead of diverting people into amazing inner landscapes of colors and forms or into adventures of mystical exploration or psychopathological terror, LSD might be used to enhance personal creativity in ways that could be measured.

There had been a string of very successful studies in Canada showing that LSD administered in a safe and supportive setting led to a high rate of curbing long-term alcoholics' drinking. Other studies conducted in Southern California by Dr. Oscar Janiger showed that artists' work changed radically during an LSD session and often was changed thereafter. However, there was an argument in the art world, and in the science world, as to whether or not that art was "better." Our team wanted to see if another aspect of the creative process—technical problem solving—could be helped by the use of these agents.

The answer thus far in our study was a resounding "yes." We were amazed, as were our participants, at how many novel and effective solutions came out of our sessions. Client companies and research institutions were satisfied with the results (if not fully informed of how they occurred). Other members of research groups, including one whose members had worked with us, were asking to be included in the study. It was a deeply satisfying time.

The letter from the U.S. Food and Drug Administration was brief.

It advised us that upon receipt of the letter, our permission to use these materials, our research protocol, and our capacity to work with these materials—in any way, shape, or form—was terminated.

I was by far the youngest member of the research team, a graduate student at Stanford in a psychology department that I'd not informed about this research. Two of the others were full professors of engineering at Stanford in two different departments, and the fourth was the founder and director of the foundation, a scientist in his own right who had retired early and set up a nonprofit institute to better understand the interplay between consciousness, deep personal and spiritual experiences, and these substances.

Very soon, we would need to go back into that room where the four men lay, their minds literally expanding. I say, "I think we need to agree that we got this letter tomorrow." And then we attended to our subjects—now the last group of people who would be allowed the privilege of working with these materials on problems of their choosing with legal government support and supervision for at least the next forty years.

How did I come to be in that room at the International Foundation for Advanced Study? Only a few years before, I'd been a writer in Paris residing in a sixth-floor walk-up, living on as little as possible, sleeping in train stations and hostels when I traveled and staying with whoever would put me up and feed me. As was said of many of our lives then, it was a long strange trip.

What sent me from Paris to Stanford and headlong into psychedelic research was not only a visit from my favorite college professor, Richard Alpert (later known as Ram Dass), and his friend Timothy Leary, but also a cordial note from my draft board asking about my whereabouts and future plans. I realized that there was an M-1 rifle waiting for me to cradle it across my elbows as I crawled through mud and dense vegetation in Vietnam while overhead shots were being fired in both directions, giving me the opportunity of dying by enemy or friendly fire. In my mind, being in a war made no sense, so I returned to the United States to the draft-deferment haven of graduate school.

For the good of the military and for the nation, I was sure then and remain just as convinced today that keeping me out of the war was the better alternative. When you have a long history in junior high and high school of being picked last for team sports, you don't assume that you will thrive in the infantry, let alone rise to the higher level of competence needed in actual combat. I saw my government fellowship to study psychology as the government saying that it was better to keep me out than to deal with any potential hazards to others and myself that it risked by inducting me.

My reasons for plunging into psychedelic research, however, did begin with that visit from Alpert and the first night we spent together.

Paris, 1961. I'm sitting at night in a café on the boulevard Saint-Michel, watching all the people who in turn are watching me. I'm twenty-one and have just taken psilocybin for the first time, and I've no idea what it is or does. I know that the man sitting next to me is Richard Alpert, who has given it to me as a gift. The colors are getting brighter, people's eyes are flashing light when they look at me, and street noise is playing inside me like a multichannel broadcast. I say, as evenly as my quavering voice allows, "It's a little too much for me." Alpert grins at me across the tiny, round glass table. "Me too, and I've not taken anything."

We return to my walk-up a few blocks away. The hotel has a plaque on the side of the front door that says that Freud stayed there. I am writing a novel and sometimes imagine that in the future, they will add a second plaque. But not tonight.

I lie down on my bed. Alpert takes the chair. That about uses up the space in the room. I watch my mind discovering new aspects of itself. Alpert keeps letting me know that whatever my mind is doing is safe and all right. Part of me is not sure what he is talking about, another part knows how deeply right he is, another part of me hopes he is.

One week later, I left Paris and followed Alpert and Leary to Copenhagen, where they joined Aldous Huxley to jointly present a paper to an international congress. Leary and Alpert were teaching psychology at Harvard and were already in the midst of controversy over giving psychedelics to graduate students and other members of the academic community. Six weeks after their conference, I flew to California to begin graduate work in psychology.

While at Stanford, I led three lives. In life one, I wore a sport coat and tie and made sure I showed up every day in the psychology department, visibly a student doing what he could to learn from the lips of the masters. In my second life, two days a week, I was a research assistant at the off-campus International Foundation for Advanced Study. There, I sat in on daylong, high-dose (and legal) LSD therapy sessions.

Each client had at least two people supporting the experience. A man and a woman stayed with every client, plus there was a physician who checked into the session now and then, if needed. I can't recall when we ever had any medical needs, but she added to the feeling of total support and reassurance that made the LSD sessions more beneficial. In addition, a Freudian psychoanalyst had met with each client when he or she first volunteered for our program to determine that each person was likely to benefit and unlikely to run into problems beyond his or her ability to cope. Given the government's skittish stance at the time, the analyst told us we needed to have close to a 100 percent success rate, something not demanded or achieved by any other therapy.

My third life was spent with people who revolved around Ken Kesey. They used psychedelics of all sorts, as well as uppers, downers, and marijuana, even alcohol and cigarettes. One member worked for a pharmaceutical chain and arrived at any event with his pockets stuffed with samples.

It was a group of outlaws, but not lawbreakers—more like paradigm breakers. LSD and many of the other drugs were not illegal in the early 1960s, but their use, especially outside of any research or medical setting, was not socially acceptable. These explorers of inner space were doing field research, exploring what it was like to have free access to these drugs outside of any control or restraint except self-preservation. During these times, when these drugs were opening doors throughout one's mind, the Kesey group used psychedelics while playing, singing, drawing, watching TV, cooking, eating, making love, watching the stars spin and dance, and asking aloud the sorts of questions that their experiences brought up:

- Who are we, really?
- Is the soul mortal or immortal?
- What did Blake or Van Gogh or Plato really experience?
- Is my identity inside my body or does it interpenetrate my body and yours?
- What is common between my mind and the nearest redwood tree?
- Are time and space subjective?
- What is fixed? What moves?
- What stays constant from session to session (that is, what is remembered)?
- What happens in a group where all the minds are opened, loosely linked, and apparently in telepathic communication with one another?
- When someone in such a group becomes terrified, do the rest get sucked into the downdraft? Or can the combined weight of the other minds right the one who has fallen away?

These questions and more were at the heart of the Kesey group experiences: not outlaws in the usual sense but outliers. Better to think of them not as the cultural icons they eventually became but as people who had outgrown the limitations of the laws and who were furiously developing a bigger set of laws to bring order to their own larger sphere of behavior and experience. What the Kesey group was doing sounds philosophical, and it was, but it also had all the raw immediacy of putting your arm across the throat of a drowning swimmer so he or she wouldn't panic, drag you under, and kill you both.

For me, a critical moment happened one morning at the edge of the Pescadero town dump. Pescadero is a tiny town two miles from the California coast and about fifteen miles from Stanford. The dump was a hillside; the bottom was littered, but the top and sides were covered with vines sporting small patches of flowers. One dawn I went there with Kesey and Dorothy, his girlfriend at the time, a woman who would later become my wife (after forty-five years of marriage, we think it will probably last). The night before, she'd taken some LSD ("dropped acid," to say it the way it was) and was in a state of delighted wonder at the personal discoveries she'd made about her own consciousness and how it shaped and reshaped her world. Kesey had taken us to Pescadero because it was a wonderful place to meet the dawn. It is correct to say he took Dorothy there, but because I had been guiding her through parts of the night, she wanted me along.

I was not in the inner circle of the Kesey world. I was too straight and too unwilling to take drugs with everyone. None of the women in the group was interested in me, and I didn't have much in common with any of the men. However, because I worked with LSD legally by day, I was welcome as an odd ornament, as one might want to have someone around who trained tigers or who could chew broken glass.

Dorothy recalled that the defining moment of that dawn came when she was about to step on a small flower. Instead, she lay down on the path and stared at it. I suggested she let the flower do the communicating. What she saw—not thought or contemplated but saw, such is LSD's curious power—was the flower fully open up, go through its cycle, and wither, but she also watched the flower reverse this same flow: recovering from its dried state, re-flowering, and returning to being a bud. She could see it go in both directions, forward and backward in time, dancing its own birth and its own death. When she told me what she was seeing, I confirmed that her experience was one that others had shared. Relieved, she returned to her plant contemplation.

She looked up at Kesey—handsome, rugged, talented, a natural leader, possessed of enormous energy and power. Also married. Kesey had two kids; he was fully committed to the marriage and also to having it open to other partners as well. Dorothy looked at me. I was engaged, but my fiancée was six thousand miles away in Scotland. What she saw was that I seemed very knowledgeable, even comfortable, about her newly discovered inner world. From the moment of the encounter with the flower, her gyroscope began to spin away from Kesey and toward me. Our courtship and marriage are outside this moment in time, but as one can trace a river back to a small spring emerging from a cleft in a rock on a mountainside, our three lives shifted that day from Dorothy's encounter with a single flower.

What about my legal research? What was it like to do legal drug research? Because of the sixties, on most college campuses today it is no trick to find a psychedelic drug, take it, have a wild ride, and wonder about it all. To give it to people in a setting so supportive that 80 percent of our subjects reported that it was the single most important event of their lives—ah, that was a different time! For more than two years while the experiments were going on, I'd slip away from Stanford classes when I could and sit with people who were having their introduction to psychedelics and, through psychedelics, to other levels of consciousness, and perhaps to other levels of reality.

Since I was usually introduced as "a graduate student who will be with us today," I was not primarily responsible for conducting a session. I was truly a sitter and could watch, sometimes help, and sometimes record what people reported as they went through the events of the day. Sometimes I would only appear in the late afternoon and take a person home for the evening. We found that while the effects of the LSD would have worn off after eight hours, a person's newly found capacity to move in and out of different realities diminished but did not stop until he or she was too tired to stay awake. I often had the treat of being with people as they puzzled out the major events or insights of the day. I also helped them deal with their families, who were usually baffled by the combination of tales of bizarre inner experiences and the sense of being with someone, a husband or wife, who was so much more totally open and loving and caring than he or she had been the day before that it often brought the spouse to joyful tears.

By day, in my graduate studies, I was being taught a psychology that seemed to me to cover only a small fragment of the mind. As I've noted earlier in this book, I felt as if I were studying physics with teachers who had no idea that electricity, atomic power, and television existed. I would listen, take notes, ask appropriate questions, and try to appear as if I were not dumbfounded by the tiny little nibbles my instructors seemed to assume were the whole of the apple of knowledge.

By night, having completed my school assignments, I would read books that helped me to piece together the larger world I'd been opened to: *The Book of the Dead,* the *I Ching,* the works of William

Blake, Christian mystics, and Buddhist teachings, especially those of the Zen masters, whose cutting-through-it-all clarity was wonderfully refreshing. I also struggled with Tibetan texts that were hard to comprehend but clearly had been written by people who knew about what I was discovering. I would sit and read those books, wrapped in plain covers the way one had wrapped dirty comics with a magazine in high school to hide pictures of women with disturbingly large breasts from one's teachers.

When I could no longer follow the texts, I would sit cross-legged on the bare linoleum floor of my graduate student "office," a slot in a trailer turned temporary classroom, a space smaller than my bedroom in Paris. I'd look through the sliding glass door at a small pine tree planted to deny the fact that we were in a temporary trailer in a large parking lot. I would breathe and stare, breathe and stare, until the tree began to breathe with me. It would not move or sway but would begin to shine with an invisible illumination, the fact of it extremely alive. It would grow and shrink before my eyes, a very tiny movement, but reminiscent of the flower at the Pescadero dump. I'd attune to that tree until I felt balanced again and then go home to bed.

A Moment of Reflection

A few months after we ended our research program, California passed a law declaring the possession or distribution of LSD to be a crime. Federal policy concerning LSD was later consolidated with the enactment of the Comprehensive Drug Abuse Prevention and Control Act of 1970.

Why did our drug research frighten the establishment so profoundly? Why does it still frighten them? Perhaps because we were able to step off (or were tossed off) the treadmill of daily stuff and saw the whole system of life-death-life. We had discovered that love is the fundamental energy of the universe, and we wouldn't shut up about it.

What we found out was that the love is there, the forgiveness is there, and the understanding and compassion are there. But like water to a fish or air to a bird, it is there, all around us, and exists without any effort on our part. There is no need for the Father, the Son, the Buddha, the

Saints, the Torah, the books, the bells, the candles, the priests, the rituals, or even the wisdom. It is just there—so pervasive and so unending that it is impossible to see as long as you are in the smaller world of people separated from one another.

No wonder enlightenment is always a crime.

PART FOUR

▼

NEW HORIZONS

Introduction to Part Four

After a long quiet period, psychedelics are back in scientific journals, the mainstream press, television, YouTube, and social media. There are clinical studies, spiritual studies, and reports of using psychedelics for problem solving and artistic production.

Some LSD uses are still well below the radar. The most intriguing of these uses are sub-perceptual doses of about 10 micrograms. In that tiny amount, LSD acts like a cognitive enhancer, but without the side effects of larger doses.

Also, curiously, there has been almost no research on current users. The annual large-scale government surveys ask little more than if the respondent has ever taken various substances. My current graduate student research team found that the present college-age generation is not only experienced but knowledgeable about the effects of many different psychedelics and well versed in the range of positive and negative experiences. Older groups are even more so. Chapter 16 describes the initial findings of a study that asked several groups with an interest in psychedelics about the variety of their drug experiences, the reasons for their own use, and the results.

The first-person accounts presented in chapter 3 were brief excerpts of first and early experiences. Chapter 17 offers an in-depth interview in which I talk about the effect that the psychedelic experience has had on my career choices and worldview. The final chapter in this part examines current trends. Public research is emerging from a decades-long underground of whispered events, secretive connections, and closet chemists. Current work is showing substantial spiritual, personal, and scientific benefits.

The surge in research, the large and growing numbers of people attending scientific conferences to discuss psychedelics, and the serious interest in many synthetic and plant-based psychedelics suggest cultural shifts are in the offing. Shamanism in general and ayahuasca in particular are growing in importance, partly because lawsuits for ayahuasca's religious use are being settled in its favor and partly because of its reported healing properties for cancer and other serious conditions.

There is a pressing need to restore what we can of the harmony between humanity and the natural world that existed for millennia. Effective and informed use of psychedelics appears to be one way to help that restorative process.

15

CAN SUB-PERCEPTUAL DOSES OF PSYCHEDELICS IMPROVE NORMAL FUNCTIONING?

Although no formal research exists on sub-perceptual doses, a growing number of people have been using psychedelics this way. When people take a sub-perceptual amount—for LSD, about 10 micrograms (also known as a micro-dose, sub-dose, or "tener")—the common sensory effects associated with higher doses of LSD or psilocybin—a glow or a sparkle around the edges of living things, sensory interweaving such as hearing in color or tasting music, and a loosening of ego boundaries—do not appear. What follow are reports from people who have used these small doses of LSD and psilocybin. Some are from longtime users and others are from people trying them for the first time.*

Indigenous cultures have known about and used sub-perceptual doses of different psychedelics for centuries. Until recently, this knowledge has been overlooked. After being involved in research on sub-perceptual dosages for over a year, I found myself embarrassed at my own cultural bias as I came to realize I had ignored the obvious, and that indigenous heal-

---

*There is some talk of doing a small book on these uses. Such a book would include some of the early work reporting on the uses of "morning glory seeds, peyotl, homgos [mushrooms], and more, prescribed for various maladies." A prominent anthropologist (who forgave my lack of awareness of early extensive and sophisticated low-dose use) sent the aforementioned list to me.

ers or shamans, working with their own psychedelic plants, have systematically and fully explored every dose level.

As these reports are the first to appear in the literature, I've avoided coming to any general conclusions about these low doses beyond noting that all the reports in my files indicate, as these individuals have, that low-dose use has been positive.

Reports: LSD

Charles

"Charles," an environmental expert and a ghostwriter of nonfiction books, took sub-perceptual doses of LSD once every three days. His report is part user's guide and part personal response. He lives in Madison, Wisconsin, with his wife, two children, and three cats.

When the idea of micro-dosing was suggested, it was made even more intriguing by the notion that this was something I could do during my regular workday and that nobody else even had to know what I was up to.

Some Recommendations

There are also some cautions, some hard-learned do's and don'ts, and I just wanted to quickly run through them here before describing what you might expect (or at least what I experienced).

- Be conservative in following the protocol, including the amount and the days between doses.
- Stick with your normal patterns, especially eating, working, and sleeping.
- Be very discreet as to whom you let know.

So first, be conservative in how much you take and how often you take it. It's best to start small. The goal isn't the McKenna-size heroic dose or even the standard 80- to 120-microgram "effective" dose, but something one-tenth the size of that, that is, 10 micrograms, or somewhere between 6 and 12 micrograms. So be conservative, especially if you aren't exactly sure of how much you're giving yourself. If you take more, if you really start "getting off," then if you're like me, you'll have a hard time proceeding with your "normal" day. So start small, and if it's too small, you can always add more the next time.

Also, go slow. The protocol I followed had me take a micro-dose one day, then carefully observe any ongoing or lingering effects the second day, and then give myself the third day completely off. By going slow, you give yourself a chance to *really know,* to really observe what is different, why it's different, and how you can best take advantage of it. The day you're completely off is great as a reset day, kind of like clearing the mind/body palate. Then you're fresh and ready to undertake the experiment again.

Second, *do what you normally do.* Make sure you eat your regular meals, stay hydrated, do your regular exercise, meditations, and practices, and so on. The idea here is to stay grounded while you are being stimulated, ever so slightly, beyond your normal parameters.

Third, *be discreet.* You may want to, or need to, tell your mate, your housemate, or your best friend, but generally speaking, the fewer who know, the better. Note that by going small, your behavior, your demeanor, and your external appearance will be pretty much like normal.

Effects: Making Infinity More Transparent

I've regularly felt four kinds of effects from micro-doses: physical, emotional, creative, and spiritual.

Physical: Within an hour after I swallow my little glass of water or sugar cube, I start feeling more energy. It's a kind of bubbling burning on a very low level; my cells and systems are pumped up with a noticeable kind of buzz that is very different from caffeine (which I often use), speed (which I never use), or pot (which I'm very familiar with). What's lovely is that it's a kind of *good* secondary energy, that is, I can use it to work out with weights, do Pilates, ride my bike, or really just enjoy being with my body. And if, like me, you're a regular caffeine user, you might ingest a little less caffeine than usual, but it's also fine to continue with your regular amounts. That is to say, I haven't found any negative combinatory effects with caffeine (or pot for that matter). And yes, you will need to have a good night's sleep afterward; buzzing with extra energy eventually tires you out.

Emotional: My micro-dose mentor once told me that at the very lowest micro-doses you see how much God loves you, if you take a bit more, you also see how much you love God, and if you take quite a bit more, then of course it gets pretty hard to disentangle exactly who you are and who God is. What I find is that it's easy for me to appreciate everyone and everything in my life, to very easily and naturally step into a space of gratitude and sustain it.

Creative: I've found that I've had some brilliant outbursts (at least they seemed brilliant to me) with respect to both work product and personal creative projects. What seems to happen is that the "flow" state described by Mihaly Csikszentmihalyi and noted frequently in the sports arena is a lot easier to access and stay in. Also, it's relatively easy to access and stay in the state that the consciousness explorer John Lilly once called your "professional satori," that is, you are doing what you do professionally, you are doing it well, time passes quickly, and you are pleased with your output. If you have a serious work project, if a lot is due all at once and you feel under the gun, you will want to think twice about micro-dosing but it may just pay off.

Spiritual: What I feel that micro-dosing does is to slightly rearrange my neural furniture so that glimmers of full-on psychedelic states are constantly pouring into my awareness. I can see how the spider, her web, the wall the web is on, the house the wall is part of, the town the house is part of, and so on, are all connected. It becomes *easy* to see those connections, in fact, practically self-evident. And from there, it's just a short step to radically affirming the rightness of the spider's web, just the way it is in this moment.

And this occurs not in a distracted way, but in a marvelous, enlightening, synchronistic, divine way. The Truth of What Is is simply easier to spot, and that makes everything else easier. Even the next day—the day after—the hint of universal connectedness is still quite apparent.

It's unclear to me whether I'm just becoming sensitized to LSD or whether something else is going on, perhaps an ongoing yearning and learning to make just a little bit more out of the reality that I'm perceiving. That is, over my months of micro-dosing, my expectations as to what is easily possible to see have grown. My Amazing Meter seems to be permanently set to a slightly lower threshold, in a way that I feel has made my life more pleasurable, more powerful, and more effective in terms of my being able to take care of myself and contribute back to others.

It's almost like I was born to be like this, and now I *get* to be like this, on an increasingly regular basis, all thanks to an astonishingly small amount of the substance LSD-25. I don't know if this will help me to reach beyond the one-hundred-year mark like Albert Hofmann did, but I'm pretty certain I'll have a more interesting, effective, and joyous ride regardless.

Madeline

Madeline, a tall, almost willowy, woman in her early thirties, lives in Manhattan. Her report fills in some of her different occupations. She is married and has a four-year-old child.

As the subway rumbles along toward downtown, my observation of the passengers around me is that they put utter poison into their bodies! A woman in a camel-colored suit and white gym shoes uses a plastic knife to spread cream cheese on a giant bagel, washing it all down with gulps of soda. A few others enjoy fast-food breakfasts; enough sandwiches and hash browns are withdrawn from steamy paper sacks to scent the entire car with fryer oil. I wonder for a moment about what these people would think about my peculiar breakfast ritual—20 micrograms of LSD chased a bit later by green juice made from juiced cucumbers, sunflower sprouts, and pea greens.

I arrive at my temporary office where I'm on a seven-week contract editing film. The documentary I'm working on has a budget of nearly nine hundred thousand dollars and will air on the second best network. My job is to screen nearly fifty hours of historical footage and knit it together into a story arc. I snip the footage down to its most essential bits, add narration notes, and harvest sound bites. I feel deeply connected to my work, focused and in the flow. I barely come up for air for the next five hours because I am so sincerely enjoying what I'm doing. I laugh aloud and occasionally cry at poignant moments. I love my work. Although I'm not hungry and don't feel in need of a break, I know that it is healthy to take one. Once outside, the world is too bright, even with my sunglasses on. I have very large blue eyes and naturally large pupils, and anything above 10 micrograms of LSD makes them as big as saucers.

After a six-block walk, I feel hungry, and I sit my lunchbox and thermos on a ledge at my favorite park. I begin Chinese exercises and deep breathing. The movement feels wonderful, and I feel so healthy and connected to my body that I begin to tear up for a second and enjoy a little laugh that can only be described as a release of joy and gratitude. I plan a longer than average workday today and will skip the gym, so this stolen moment of movement and sunshine is essential. My lunch is a thermos of mild green tea and four small salads that I made a day earlier. One is seaweed with sesame seeds, another chickpeas, another quinoa, and the last is fruit with coconut and pecans. Exquisitely nourished, I head back to my office for another four-hour stretch.

Sub-doses of 10 to 20 micrograms allow me to increase my focus, open my heart, and achieve breakthrough results while remaining integrated within my routine. While a full dose requires that I carefully plan my surroundings, on a sub-dose I am fully able to navigate all manner of logistics and social interactions. I would venture to say that my wit, response time, and visual and mental acuity seem greater than normal on it. I utilize a sub-dose about six days each month and sometimes more often if I am engrossed in a project requiring extraordinary focus. This has been my practice for more than ten years, and it has facilitated my success working in mainstream and independent media, staff-level positions in government, and publishing dozens of pieces of journalistic work.

I am not saying that I wouldn't have done *any* of this without LSD, but I am saying that I wouldn't have done *all* of this without it. The practice of sub-dosing transforms my work from being work to being creative play.

I'm a naturally persuasive person, able to enlist others in my vision, but never more so than when I am enhanced by a sub-dose. Therefore, I find it essential to my work as a grant writer and coalition builder to open myself in this way. One of my standard responses to the question "How are you doing?" from a colleague is to reply that I am doing "soaringly well." It really sums up what it feels like to perform my work while sub-dosing: it's somewhat like flying.

I had never heard of sub-dosing when I began doing it. After a couple years of wonderful success with the practice, I met a friend of Terence McKenna's who, upon hearing about my practice, explained that he uses sub-doses too—something he learned from McKenna. He explained that Albert Hofmann did the same thing, and that McKenna told him that Hofmann believed that LSD sub-doses would have gone on to be widely prescribed in much the same way as Ritalin, had it not been so harshly scheduled.

I played with big doses before I played with small ones. I experimented with 250- to 800-microgram doses and learned to surrender to their intensity. My experiences at these doses were profound, amazing, and fun, but ultimately, I couldn't bring too much back with me. I left super-high doses in the late nineties.

Then I began to experiment with sub-doses. I don't drink alcohol because I find it a bit harsh and numbing, so I was looking for something to make me feel sparkly and *up* at cocktail parties and networking events. I tried a few cups of coffee, but I wasn't quite loose enough and I'd still get tired, so I began trying small doses instead. I found that on sub-doses, I made more meaningful and lasting connections, and my own evolution seemed to accelerate, as if I were able to accomplish more living within the same span of time.

I wondered how sub-doses could be employed within my career, and I began using them for bigger assignments and events. I also expanded my role within my own family during this time, and became the one most often consulted. Following conversations with relatives and friends, they would report feeling truly seen. Within only a few months of discovering sub-doses, my skills as a listener and communicator had blossomed. Interestingly, a number of family members appointed me executor to their estates almost immediately after I began using sub-doses.

I find that 10 to 20 micrograms of LSD is both a stimulant and a calming agent at the same time. For me, the only challenge that remains with sub-doses is increased light sensitivity, which I mitigate by wearing sunglasses or dialing down the brightness of my computer screen. This minor inconvenience is certainly worth it to me, because when I'm enhanced, I feel more passionate. I feel more energized. I feel more focused and enlisted. I feel *more.*

I'm not completely comfortable with how little is known about the long-term effects of LSD and other drugs. I'm a healthy young woman, and I want to do only what is safe and smart for myself and my family, so I wish to know what the long-term effects of LSD use are. Albert Hofmann seemed perfectly sharp at 101 years old, and the friends I know who are twice my age and use LSD frequently are some of the most brilliant people I know. And I want the fear of criminalization removed from this field of research so that people like me will be willing to share their experiences openly and have their data quantified.

James

"James" is a warehouse manager in Waco, Texas, for a large home improvement company. He is active in his church and is also writing a family history of what he describes as "my more colorful relatives."

I hadn't used psychedelics for some years, but when a still-tripping friend offered me a few hits divided into teners and told me I could drop one and still go to work, I gave it a try. From the first time out, I liked how I felt. Got my work done easier, rarely lost my temper, my paperwork got done on time, and when I got home at night, I was a lot more fun to be with. What was cool is I found out that I was as good the second day after I'd dosed as the first, maybe better. I didn't say when I was using and when I wasn't, but after a while, my wife would say, "Hey, did you do it today?" Usually, she was right on.

Clifford

"Clifford" is an important psychedelic researcher, group leader, and writer. He is currently writing a book of personal essays.

Student days at the University of California at San Diego were a whirlwind blending of 1960s' issues with the academic pressure necessary to enter postgraduate training of some sort. My personal choices were between psychology and medicine. My introduction to psychedelics had convinced me of their value. I was taking a biology course to prepare for medical school, and we were studying the development of the chick embryo. After the first meeting of the one-quarter-long course, I realized that in order to stay alert, a tiny dose of LSD could be useful. With that in mind, I licked a small, but very potent, tablet emblazoned with the peace sign before every class. This produced a barely noticeable brightening of colors and created a generalized fascination with the course and my professor, who was otherwise uninteresting to me.

Unfortunately, when finals came around, my health disintegrated and I missed the final exam. The next day I called my professor and begged for mercy. She said, "No problem, come to my lab."

"When shall we schedule this?"

She suggested immediately. With some dismay, I agreed that I would meet her within an hour. I reached into the freezer and licked the almost exhausted fragment of the tablet I had used for class. I decided that there was so little left I might as well swallow it all.

At the lab my professor suggested that, since it was such an amazing day, perhaps I could take the exam outside in the wetland wilderness reserve that surrounded the lab. The view of the swamp was stunning! Somehow it had never seemed beautiful to me before. She asked that I take my notebook and pencil out. "Please draw for me the complete development of the chick from fertilization to hatching. That is the only question."

I gasped, "But that is the entire course!"

"Yes, I suppose it is, but make-up exams are supposed to be harder than the original, aren't they?"

I couldn't imagine being able to regurgitate the entire course. As I sat there despondently, I closed my eyes and was flooded with grief. Then I noticed that my inner visual field was undulating like a blanket that was being shaken at one end. I began to see a movie of fertilization! When I opened my eyes a few minutes later, I realized that the movie could be run forward and back and was clear as a bell in my mind's eye, even with my physical eyes open.

Hesitantly, I drew the formation of the blastula, a hollow ball of cells that develops out of the zygote (fertilized egg). As I carefully drew frame after frame of my inner movie, it was her turn to gape! The tiny heart blossomed. The formation of the notochord, the neural groove, and the beginnings of the nervous system were flowing out of my enhanced imagery and onto the pages. A stupendous event—the animated wonder of embryonic growth and the differentiation of cells—continued at a rapid pace. I drew as quickly as I could. To my utter amazement, I was able to carefully and completely replicate the content of the entire course, drawing after drawing, like the frames of animation that I was seeing as a completed film!

It took me about an hour and a quarter drawing as fast as I could to reproduce the twenty-one-day miracle of chick formation. Clearly impressed, my now suddenly lovely professor smiled and said, "Well, I suppose you deserve an A!" The sunlight twinkled on the water, the cattails waved in the gentle breeze, and the gentle wonder of life was everywhere.

Reports: Psilocybin Mushrooms

Stephen Gray

Stephen Gray describes himself as "a lifelong student, teacher, and researcher of spiritual paths, in particular Tibetan Buddhism and the peyote ceremonies of the Native American Church. I've studied and practiced several other modalities in the healing and awakening fields. I've also devoted much time and love to music as a teacher, singer-songwriter, and composer of music for healing and spiritual work under the artist name Keary." The following excerpt is a portion of an essay, "The Benefits of Low-Dose Psilocybin Mushrooms." The full essay can be found at www.stephengrayvision.com by searching for "benefits of low-dose psilocybin mushrooms."

It's well known to the experienced that medium to high doses of psilocybin mushrooms, given advantageous internal and external conditions—often called set and setting—can provoke experiences of stunning insight, visions of great beauty, an abundance of love, contact with spirit entities, and authentic mystical experiences completely beyond the boundaries of the separate ego. Much less frequently discussed are the benefits of very low-dose experiences with these mushrooms.

I often get together with friends on weekends to play music. On one of these evenings, I went to the home of some friends who have a collection of dried and frozen *Psilocybe cyanascens*. We decided to try an experiment. We wanted to see how a very low dose would affect the emotions and the mechanics of playing and singing.

We each ate two medium-size dried mushrooms, the stems perhaps an inch and one-half long and the caps one-half to three-quarters of an inch across. Although we didn't weigh them, previous experience suggests we're talking about less than a gram of dried weight. We didn't engage in any special preparation such as fasting for several hours beforehand, although I always attempt to make a connection with such medicine plants before consuming them by offering a short prayer, a dedication, and/or an expression of gratitude to the spirit of the plant.

This was in no way a reliable scientific experiment. We included a little cannabis smoking with the mushrooms, knowing that the two often complement each other quite nicely. The result was that you might say the mushrooms overrode the somewhat more fuzzy effects of cannabis with a subtle but noticeable sharpness of mind and emotion.

One of the results of this sharpness was that my guitar playing became more focused and agile. I don't play guitar enough anymore to get through most songs flawlessly, but on those nights, my playing was definitely more on the mark. I also noticed that my ability to recollect lyrics was noticeably superior to my norm.

In conjunction with the sharpness has been a softening of the heart, which helped me connect to the emotion of the songs. A lot of the songs I like to play have poetic lyrics that don't necessarily reveal clear and simple meanings. The songs of Bob Dylan and Leonard Cohen can be like that. . . . During these low-dose mushroom sessions, I've noticed that my mind instantaneously grokked meanings that had previously eluded me.

I've noted before with *Psilocybe*s and had confirmed again in these experiences that the mushroom appears to temporarily dismantle inhibition and hesitation to seeing things clearly and talking about personal topics straightforwardly. And it appears to be just as easy to hear these truths spoken about oneself as it is to say them. I've had some very intimate conversations with friends where we revealed ourselves without embarrassment and spoke about sensitive issues without raising defensive reactions.

Ingesting such small doses is something most people can do safely on their own. No particular ritual is necessary to elicit beneficial effects, although in my experience the spirit of the plant is always potentially present and is much more likely to bless and empower even these mild experiences if petitioned and treated with respect.

I'll mention a couple of cautions. Although the *Psilocybe*s are all around us in certain areas of North America, they are not easy to identify at first and can easily be mistaken for similar-looking but poisonous mushrooms. I had an experienced mycophile point out the local *Psilocybe cyanascens,* and since then I've shown another friend how to identify them.

Not all mushrooms have the same potency, of course, and not all people respond the same. One time I ate two small ones and the effects were too subtle to have much impact. Another time I experimented with a slightly higher dose, somewhere between one gram and a gram and a half. For playing music that quantity proved to be a bit much. The effects interfered with my functionality.

If we're able to shift our cultural understanding of these plants and begin to see them as medicine, I would say that, used with respect and good intentions, low-dose psilocybin is good medicine. . . . The important thing is to provide the right kind of space for the medicine's effects to manifest. There has to be enough space in the mind's "busy-ness" to notice the subtleties, to feel the softening of the heart, and to catch the insights as they arise.

.

Anita

"Anita" is a professional artist's model.

Once, while being very professionally overextended in New York, I got hold of a good-sized dose of mushrooms. But instead of taking it all at once, I took a pinch of it each day. I found that I was much more emotionally even and more able to see the world as interrelated rather than disjointed. It was a fully pleasurable experience.

Nathan

"Nathan" is a professional bass and guitar player and a dedicated surfer living in a beach town in Southern California.

I took a small hit of mushroom the other day . . . went out surfing. It was a life-changing event. I was so much more in my body and could feel deeper into it. I sensed the wave had come thousands of miles and that we were coming together for its last few seconds before it hit the beach. But what was best was feeling like I connected back into the greater world. What was so special is that for the past few weeks, I've been really down. A great long-term love relationship broke up, and I've been devastated. I'm still sad about it, but I know it's only a part of me. I got attuned that day, and I haven't lost it. Oh, yeah, my surfing was definitely awesome.

The Question of Tolerance

I asked a once prominent LSD chemist if the "every three days" regimen like the one "Charles" used was necessary, since it is well known that one cannot take repeated doses of most psychedelics and have them continue to be effective.

His initial reply was, "As far as I can determine, less-than-obvious doses do not cause tolerance, which could argue in favor of benefits from ten a day. I'd have to test further, but so far I suspect that sub-detectable doses several days in a row cause no tolerance for a similar barely detectable dose the day following. At this sub-detectable level, there is really at most only the tiniest of intimations you took something."

Preliminary Conclusions

These reports are representative of those I have received in 2010. The reports have several things in common. Everyone said their experiences were positive and valuable. "Charles" suggested that there was a gradual buildup of openness and awareness, eventually spilling over into non-sub-perceptual days. Madeline and Stephen both indicated they did better at what they do well—not excessively, but enough to notice.

As several reports stated, someone taking a dose this low functions, as far as the world is concerned, a little better than normal. To date, I received no reports that sub-perceptual doses have caused any social disruption, personal upset, or any form of work-related difficulty. However, this is a very preliminary look at an area that may become of considerable interest as more opportunities for research open up. We may yet get to know more about what Albert Hofmann called "an under-researched area."

16
SURVEYS OF CURRENT USERS
This Is Your Brain on Drugs

Several years ago, the Open Center in New York City invited me to talk about the current psychedelic situation. My talk included a brief rant about the dearth of research during the forty years of what psychedelic researcher Dr. Charles Grob calls "a protracted lull." During this lull, neither the government nor any individual researcher had bothered to research what millions of us were up to.

A year later, having recovered from my bout of righteousness over "what all those other people were not doing," a student group at San Francisco State University asked me to talk about psychedelics. I decided to ask them about their own drug use and designed a one-page questionnaire to that end.

That questionnaire took about five minutes to complete. It asked what psychedelics people had taken and their reasons for doing so. It asked about best and worst experiences, if they had ever been guides or been guided, what their future intentions were, and asked some questions about demographics. That night, seventy-eight people filled out the forms.

Soon afterward, a few students at two midwestern universities taking courses about psychedelics filled it out, as did some Stanford students, self-designated "psychonauts." Because there were no significant differences between the student groups, these students were added to the first group to make up the complete student sample.

While starting to analyze the data, I turned to psychological, medical, and psychometric research databases to review the many studies that I assumed had preceded this one. It was a surprise to find out that little data existed beyond an annual survey by the U.S. government asking high school students if they had ever used various substances.

Nothing in the literature for the past thirty-five-plus years had asked users anything like the questions I'd asked. There were only two studies that were even close. The first one, published in 1983, interviewed seventy-one people. Without presenting numerical data, it concluded:

- "Moderate polydrug use was the norm."
- "Most people had a 'drug of choice.'"
- "Few people appeared to continue to use psychedelic drugs for a long time."[1]

The second study, done in the nineties, asked different questions than ours of nine psychedelic users in Sweden. That was it. Two studies.* In light of this dearth of information, my low-cost research project seemed worth extending.

I was able to add 163 individuals as a second sample in April 2010 during my presentation at a conference on psychedelic research. (Two other samples—one of some attendees at the Non-Dual Consciousness Conference and one from an interest group in Chicago—are being analyzed.)

What follows are some preliminary findings from the student and the conference samples. These are field notes, not finished formal research; therefore, I am presenting the data with very little interpretation or analysis. For updates about the research, please check www.jamesfadiman .com and www.psychedelicexplorersguide.com.

---

*However, as this book was going to press, news of a dissertation, "Psilocybin and Spiritual Experience" by Kevin Bunch, Psy.D., was just released. He surveyed 504 individuals about their use of this one psychedelic. Conclusions included that 58 percent found their experiences to be "among the five most significantly spiritual experiences of their lives" and 90 percent "claimed that it had positively affected the way they live their lives."

The Student Sample

There were 108 respondents in the total student sample.* Of that total, forty-eight men and forty-three women listed their gender. Except for two older people, the age range of this sample was from 17 to 28 years, with an average age of 22.7 years.†

Substances Taken

Students were asked what they had taken and were presented with eight possibilities: six psychedelics, MDMA, and "other." The percentages of students who used each of the eight are presented in figure 16.1.

Over 50 percent of the group had taken mushrooms/psilocybin, LSD, MDMA, and *Salvia divinorum*.‡ By contrast, only two people had tried ayahuasca. Substances not on the list included: (their terms) Nitrous, DXM, 2-CB, ketamine, LAS, morning glory seeds, and laughing gas. The number of psychedelics taken (excluding "other") ranged from eight (one person) to zero (five people). However, some of those counted as zero had used "other" substances. The average number of different substances a student had taken was 4.3. Students were not asked how many times they had used each substance.

Reasons for Taking

Students chose from a list of ten reasons why they'd taken these substances. The results are presented in figure 16.2.

The reasons picked most often were, in order: fun, self-healing, and problem solving; all were above 50 percent. The least-picked reasons were sexual enhancement and social pressure. There is no way in this sample to

---

*Sophia Korb created all the analysis and all the tables about the student sample. The research was originally presented and developed into poster form by Alicia Danforth. She presented it at the Science of Consciousness Conference in Santa Rosa, California, in October 2009.

†The sample of 108 students comprised:
    seventy-eight at San Francisco State University
    twenty-one at Stanford University
    six at the University of Northern Illinois (class taught by Tom Roberts)
    three at the College of DuPage, Glen Ellyn, Illinois (class taught by Bruce Sewick)

‡Those wishing to know more about *Salvia divinorum,* go to www.sagewisdom.org.

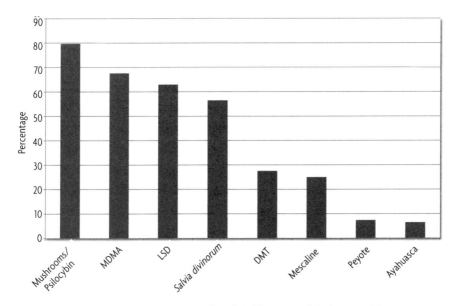

Fig. 16.1. University Students' Self-Reported Substance Use

determine how many of the "fun" choices were related to using MDMA, as it is more often used for social and recreational purposes than any of the other psychedelics.

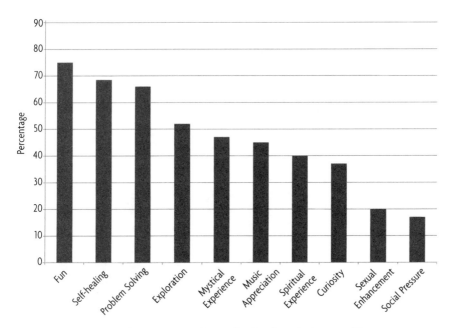

Fig. 16.2. Reasons Given for Student Substance Use

Reasons for Taking: Male/Female Differences

The reasons for drug use differed between men and women as shown in figure 16.3.

As can be seen, women were more likely to take a substance for self-healing. Men take a substance significantly more often out of curiosity, to undergo a spiritual experience or a mystical experience, and to better appreciate music. In fact, men were more likely to have taken psychedelics for all the reasons except self-healing.

Positive and Negative Effects

The students were asked to describe the greatest benefit and the highest cost from all of their experiences. Representative statements for benefits and highest costs are listed below.

Benefits

- I encountered this amazing presence—God?—and felt a complete sense of the perfection in everything.
- I had self-healing, understanding experiences that opened my

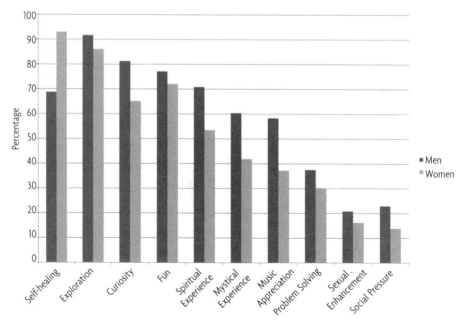

Fig. 16.3. Reasons Given for Drug Use

mind, and lots of visions of creativity and my potential.

- I was the happiest me that I can be and realized the magic of life for the first time.
- I underwent a total change in personality for the better.
- I've been able to express my love for people and nature with MDMA. With LSD, I found my spirituality for the first time and had the best night of my life.
- Communication with the more-than-human world (LSD).

Highest Cost

- Saw ancient patterns all over body, which broke me down to nothing. But relationships came back with the morning sun and life was joyous.
- First time I did LSD, I got left alone in my trip and cried about pain I felt from life experiences. It was scary and I felt unloved and alone. I also had disturbing visuals due to my sadness.
- Oil dripping all over, technology taking over the planet.
- I had been pulling up pickle weed at the beach; when I took the salvia I felt the plants were angry at me and it was not enjoyable.
- I felt sure that I was going to die and could feel what it is like to be killed in a car crash.
- Two hours of misery, but still learned a needed lesson about who to trust.

Those Who Had Been a Guide or Were Guided

The value of guides for these experiences has been a central theme of this book, so the questionnaire also asked if experiences had involved guides. Thirty-seven percent of the sample had either guided or been guided. Their reasons given for substance use, ranked according to whether they had been guided or had been guides, are presented in figure 16.4, on page 218.

Students on either side of the guiding relationship used psychedelics more often for exploration, self-healing, spiritual and mystical experiences, and curiosity than did the complete sample. No one who was guided or was a guide said that the reason was for "fun."

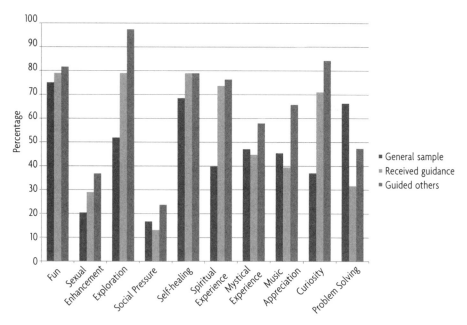

Fig. 16.4. Reasons by Those Who Had Guidance or Guided Others

Future Intentions

The final question asked was whether or not they intended to take psychedelics in the future. Eighty-two percent said yes, seven percent said no, and seven percent didn't answer or were unsure.

Initial Observations

While the results of this questionnaire were what one might expect from a group interested in psychedelic research, keep in mind that data like these had not been collected before. This sample is unique in the drug literature. Reviewing the results presented, it became evident that

- Students have wide access to psychedelic drugs
- They have taken them in a wide variety of situations
- They had bad experiences but rarely blamed the drug itself
- They intend to keep taking them

One item asking about "highest cost" was dropped because some of the students thought it was asking about the dollar cost of the drugs used. Subsequent survey samples asked instead about "worst aftereffects," a better way of framing the same question.

We did find out that the price students paid for enough of a substance for a single "trip" rarely rose above eight dollars. None of the students seemed the slightest bit concerned that these substances were illegal. For about the price of a first-run movie ticket, they could have a powerful, meaningful, transformative, or fun time.

When I questioned the first group, I was not sure if I'd be able to get another student sample, so I requested their cell phone numbers as a way to follow up. ("If you wish, please give me your cell phone number; no names please.")

Several of my professional colleagues insisted that no one would be so foolish or trusting as to give a stranger a list of illegal behaviors and his or her phone number. Perhaps in the spirit of the evening or the casual way students considered their own drug use, not only did thirty-seven students write in their cell numbers, but several added their e-mail addresses as well.

The ease of data collection and the richness of the responses led to the collection of data from other groups, most especially a sample from a professional conference.

The Conference Sample

The Psychedelic Science in the 21st Century conference, held in San Jose, California, in April 2010 and hosted by the MAPS foundation, brought together almost every legal psychedelic researcher in the world. Over 1,200 people attended. At my presentation on entheogenic experience, I asked those present to fill out a questionnaire; 161 people filled it out. Of the 117 people who listed their age, the range was from 16 to 74 years, and the average age was 42. Of those listing their gender, there were 88 men, 51 women, and 1 transgender person.*

---

*All the data about the conference sample were analyzed and all presentations created by Sophia Korb.

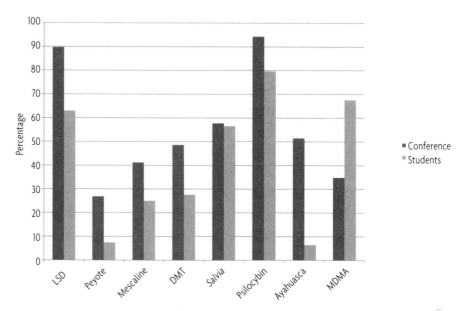

Fig. 16.5. Substances Used by Students and by Conference Attendees

Substance Use

Over 50 percent of the group had experience with mushrooms/psilocybin and LSD (both over 88 percent), *Salvia divinorum,* and ayahausca. The percentages using ayahausca and MDMA differ significantly from those of the student sample, with many more having used ayahausca and far fewer having used MDMA.

As might be expected, given how much older these conference attendees were, their overall use was greater than that of the students for every drug except MDMA. In the student sample, there were only six substances added as "other." In this conference sample, there were far more. Drugs listed included (list is incomplete) nitrous oxide, 2-CB, ketamine, ibogaine, San Pedro, 2-CT7, 2CI, 5-MBO, MDA, @-CE, 2CX, TCB, LAS, DOB, DOI, DOC, seratonin, TCT9, Rue, 4Aco-DIPT, methylone, bufo, GHB, baby rosewood, morning glory seeds, and DXM. A few younger members of the sample also listed cocaine. It is highly unlikely that they considered cocaine to be a psychedelic but they probably just listed every drug they'd tried.

The average number of different substances a conference member had taken was 5.4, significantly more than the student sample of 4.2. The difference might be explained by the fact that this group was older and therefore had had more years of opportunity. Other possibilities abound but those will wait to be explored after further analysis.

The maximum number of drugs listed by a single individual was twenty-four and the lowest was zero (he wrote that he had a heart condition).

Education: 142 Responses

Individuals in the student sample were asked their age, their year in school (e.g., junior, senior), and their major area of study; the individuals in the conference sample were simply asked their level of education.

The five largest groups were:

Level of Education	Number of Responses
B.A./B.S.	53
M.A./M.S.	25
Ph.D.	22
M.D.	14
Some college	10

The people in this sample were generally well educated. It was not a random sample of the entire group, but a subsample of the less science-minded participants. The meeting where this information was collected was in the "cultural" track of the conference, which ran at the same time as the "scientific" main track.

Occupation or Profession: 141 Responses

There were forty-two different occupations listed by the respondents. The five most common occupations only represented 50 percent of the sample. They were, in order:

Occupation	Number of Responses
Student (almost all graduate students)	32
Psychologist	22
M.D./psychiatrist	13
Information technology	9
Business owner	6

No one listed himself or herself as unemployed. Everyone in the sample population listed him- or herself as educated and employed. While this may seem to be a trivial finding, it contradicts the long history of speculation that the use of psychedelics makes one less functional, less productive, and less likely to succeed in a highly competitive society. Put simply, this sample of multi-drug users does not support the stereotypes.

Best Experiences: 120 Responses

We asked which substance had been used for a "best trip." Of the twenty different substances or combinations cited, the five most common were:

Substance	Number of Responses
LSD	42
Mushrooms/psilocybin	24
Ayahuasca	16
MDMA	9
DMT	6

Worst Experiences: 126 Responses

While many respondents indicated that their most difficult or disturbing experiences had been also the most beneficial, we did ask what substance had been taken for their worst trip, however they defined the term *worst*. Of the twenty-one substances or combinations cited, the five most often mentioned were:

Substance	Number of Responses
LSD	47
Mushrooms/psilocybin	32
Ayahuasca	11
Salvia divinorum	9
DMT	6

These two lists are almost identical, but *Salvia divinorum* almost did not appear under "best trips" (one person listed it), and MDMA does not appear at all in the "worst trips" list. In general, the variables of set, setting, sitter, and so forth are what determine a good or bad experience, and that seems true here with the most-cited substances (LSD, mushrooms/psilocybin, and ayahausca), but not with *Salvia divinorum* and MDMA, which were more likely to be either best or worst, but not both.

Worst Aftereffects: 152 Responses

Most of the research and the popular literature about any of these substances focuses on the experience itself or feelings shortly after the experience is over. In our survey, respondents were asked to look back over their long years of experiences and mention the worst aftereffect they'd noticed. Of the forty-nine different effects cited, the eight most commonly mentioned were:

Aftereffect	Number of Responses
Tired	28
Depressed	26
Headache	9
Anxiety	7
Physical aches and insomnia	6 each
Vomiting and paranoia	5 each

Reviewing this list, it is fair to conclude that, at least in this population, the substances used do not appear to be too dangerous. There were, however, individual reports of more-serious aftereffects, including "complete breakdown," "almost died of hypothermia," and "mild PTSD" as well as the more serious "I fell down some stairs and needed physical therapy for three months," and my personal favorite, "lost interest in math class."

Even the most pro-psychedelic advocate needs to keep in mind that these substances, when misused and even used with care, have caused serious and lasting mental damage.

At the same conference, I spent time with an open and personally magnetic young man who was looking for a psychedelically aware therapist. Some nine months earlier, he'd had a bad trip that so disturbed him that he had lost his job and had spent several months homeless and sleeping in his car before he began to recover. While much better, he felt he still needed help.

This being noted, this sample described the relatively minor aftereffects of using many different drugs multiple times over many years.

Substances Used for Specific Effects

The questionnaire given to the conference sample, unlike the student sample, asked respondents their reasons for taking each substance. A few specific pairings suggest the span of questions that can be considered.

Question: What Substances Have You Taken for Exploration?

Substance	Number of Responses
LSD	128
Mushrooms/psilocybin	125
Salvia divinorum	62
DMT	60
Ayahuasca	57
Mescaline	46
Peyote	24

Compare the listing above with the following responses to a question about which drugs were taken for a different reason.

Question: What Substances Have You Taken for Spiritual/Mystical Experiences?

Substance	Number of Responses
Mushrooms/psilocybin	105
LSD	99
DMT	51
Ayahuasca	48
Mescaline	37
Salvia divinorum	35
Peyote	27

LSD and mushrooms/psilocybin are the preferred psychedelics for both exploration and spiritual/mystical experiences. However, far fewer people took psychedelics for spiritual and mystical experiences.

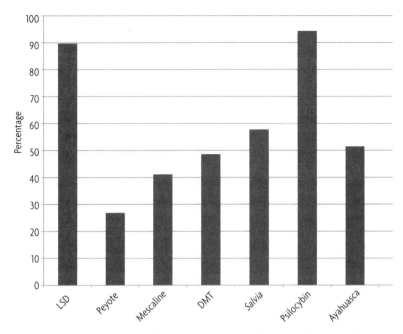

Fig. 16.6. Psychedelics Chosen for Exploration and Spiritual/Mystical Experience

MDMA does not appear on either list because so few respondents listed taking it either for exploration or for spiritual/mystical experiences.

These results may be easier to see as a histogram (figure 16.6).

Sexual Enhancement as a Reason for Taking a Substance: 141 Responses

This was another question asked about the relationship of substance use and sexual behavior. It is well established in clinical and entheogenic literature that these substances do not improve sexual experience, especially in dose levels where there is a feeling of decoupling from the body entirely. However, when we asked the sample if one of their reasons for using substances was for sexual enhancement, the finding was unanticipated.

Substance	Number of Responses
Mushrooms/psilocybin	46
LSD	40
MDMA	28
2-CB	5

There are numerous ways to interpret this finding. One is to assume that the literature is wrong or at least that studies done in settings with guides or observers will underreport sexual behavior because their presence inhibits it. An alternative explanation might be that this question only asked for a *reason* that substances were taken, not whether sexual pleasure or performance actually was enhanced. A third possibility might be that this is a question of dosage and that a "disco hit" (e.g., 50 micrograms of LSD) that enhances sensory awareness enhances sexual awareness as well.

As scientific papers almost always say at the end of whatever they have been reporting on, "Further research is indicated."

Reasons for Taking a Given Psychedelic

We also asked about reasons for taking a given psychedelic. For example, "Why did you choose to take ayahausca?" (Often multiple reasons were given; thus the total number of reasons can exceed the number of individuals in the sample.) The five most chosen reasons were:

Reason	Number of Responses (92 Respondents)
Spiritual/mystical experience	55
Self-healing or understanding	54
Exploration	52
Curiosity	37
Problem solving	19

One can see that ayahausca is taken for a variety of reasons and that no single reason predominates.

Conclusions

As with the student sample, we can make a few general conclusions about the conference population.

- They have had access to many different psychedelic drugs
- They have taken them for a variety of reasons

- They have had few serious, lasting, or bad aftereffects from their use
- Their use pattern differs only slightly from that of the much younger student sample

As can be seen from these last few tables, we have the opportunity to mine this data to answer many more questions such as those given above. There are a great many questions not yet answered that these surveys will allow us to explore. As was noted earlier, these results are early findings from just two of four group surveys. The rest of the data is being entered and analyzed, and the results will be made available in due course. Several other researchers have indicated an interest in the data as it accumulates. These researchers have different interests than the core research team, so there will be other kinds of research being published. In the future, the entire database will be published online for later researchers.

These two samples are not representative of the twenty-three million people in the United States alone who have taken LSD, but they raise provocative questions about the extent of use in larger populations, which hopefully will be of sufficient interest to the regulating and policy-making agencies to fund and expand this kind of research.

THE INADVERTENT PIONEER

My Personal Account

In 1995, two far-sighted foundations, the Fetzer Foundation and the Institute for Noetic Sciences, realized that much of the knowledge and experience of the early psychedelic researchers would soon be lost. Aldous Huxley, Timothy Leary, and Alan Watts, whose books and lectures opened the eyes of a generation to the possibilities inherent in these substances, were gone, as was Richard Evans Schultes, discoverer of dozens of plants used by indigenous healers, and Gordon Wasson, who had rediscovered psilocybin mushrooms in Mexico. Even the CIA operatives who had done sloppy and often terrible research trying to use psychedelics as instruments of torture or interrogation were no longer alive.

The Fetzer Foundation offered to host as many original researchers as could come for a weekend of sharing and reflection. Before the meeting, however, the conveners interviewed each of the potential participants at length, on video, asking them to discuss their roles in the research, to ensure that even those who could not attend could still contribute.

This chapter is composed of portions of my interview. It is a series of answers to questions intended to elicit recollections of my part of psychedelic history. A longer version can be found in Higher Wisdom: Eminent Elders Explore the Continuing Impact of Psychedelics, *edited by Roger Walsh and Charles Grob (both major researchers in their own right) and published by SUNY Press in 2005.*

I'd have to say that I'm an inadvertent psychedelic pioneer.[1] As mentioned elsewhere in this book, I was an undergraduate at Harvard, and in a small tutorial with a young, dynamic professor named Richard Alpert. We became friends and ended up renting a house together for the summer at Stanford, where I worked for him on a large research project.

After my senior year at Harvard, in 1960, I went off to live in Europe. The following spring, Alpert showed up in Paris with Timothy Leary, on their way to Copenhagen to deliver the first paper on their work with psilocybin. He was in great condition and said to me, "The most wonderful thing in the world has happened, and I want to share it with you." I replied, as anyone would, "Of course." Then he reached in his jacket pocket and took out a little bottle of pills.

My reaction was, "Pills? Drugs? What kind of weirdness is this?" However, that evening, I took some psilocybin from that little bottle, sitting in a café on a main street in Paris. After a while we withdrew to my hotel room, where he was basically a sitter for my session.

Out of that night's experiences came my first realizations that the universe was larger than I thought, my identity was smaller than I thought, and there was something about human interaction that I had been missing. It was definitely a powerful bonding experience between us. However, this session did not involve any stripping away of levels of reality. That came later.

Several psilocybin experiences later, one more with Alpert and one with my brother, I returned to the United States. I had received a letter from my draft board basically saying, "Would you like to join us in Vietnam? Or might you consider the alternatives open to you by law?" At the time, graduate school did not attract me but seemed very much the lesser of two evils.

I started my graduate work at Stanford that fall, feeling disappointed with psychology because now I'd used psychedelics and I knew there was a lot more. I didn't know what "more" was, but I sure knew that the psychology department was not teaching it. However, hidden in the back of the course catalog, I found a "graduate special" called The Human Potential, taught by Willis Harman, who was, of all things, a professor of electrical engineering. The little write-up said, "What is the highest and best that human beings can aspire to?" and suggested various readings. As I read it, I thought, "There is something about psychedelics in here. This man knows something of what I know." At that point, I was dividing the world into people who knew what I knew—which wasn't very much, but more than I'd known two months earlier—and those who didn't. (Whether I knew *correctly* was totally beside the point to me at that time.)

Anyway, I found my way to Willis Harman's office, a typical associate professor of electrical engineering's office in a building as drab as a hospital, and said, "I'd like to take your graduate special." He replied gently, "It's full this quarter, but I'll give it again. Perhaps you would be interested at a later date." I looked at him and said, "I've had psilocybin three times." He got up, walked across his office, and closed the door. Then we got down to business.

As it turned out, I had guessed correctly. This course was his way of dealing with the question, How do you teach about psychedelics in a way that doesn't get you either discovered or fired? After talking for a while, we decided that not only would I take the class, but also I would kind of co-teach it, because unlike Harman, I was willing to be open with what was happening for me and thought I had much less to lose.

The class opened with the question "What is the best and highest a human being can be?" Gradually, we moved from psychology to philosophy, then to the mystics, and eventually to personal experience.

Around the same time, I started to work with the International Foundation for Advanced Study in Menlo Park. Funded by Myron Stolaroff, an electronics executive who left that field to devote himself to psychedelic research, this foundation had been set up to work with psychedelics. Harman was involved, as were a few other people. As they had no psychologist on their team, I offered to step into the role. This was a little ludicrous since I was about two months into my first year of graduate work at the time and hadn't studied psychology as an undergraduate, but I was game. We began by working on a paper, "The Psychedelic

Experience," which described the results of the foundation's LSD therapy sessions.

After working together in class and at the foundation for a few weeks, Harman asked if I'd like to have a session with them. Filled with my Dick Alpert/Tim Leary/human closeness/low-dose psilocybin experiences, I said, "That would be great!" I showed up on October 19, 1961, at the foundation: two living room–like suites and some small offices above a beauty shop looking out over a parking lot with one giant oak in it. I was offered the opportunity to take some LSD. Harman was one sitter, and a lovely female engineering professor was the other.

Dr. Charles Savage, medical adviser to the research, did his physician thing of giving me the material and then went down the hall to resume his psychoanalytic practice. I took the material, looked around, and asked my sitters, "Well, aren't you folks taking something?" because that had been the model with Alpert and Leary in my prior sessions. (I think Harman took a little amphetamine, just to keep me cool.) I put on eyeshades, lay down on a couch, and listened to music, the format that they had developed through the work of Al Hubbard, now standard for almost all the ongoing studies worldwide.

Over the next few hours, in that room, much to my surprise, my little mind washed away. My session was a classic psychedelic high-dose entheogenic journey. I discovered that my disinterest in spiritual things was as valid as a ten-year-old's disinterest in sex, arising from a complete lack of awareness of what the universe was made of.

I went to a place of total aloneness—the you've-got-to-walk-this-valley-by-yourself deep awareness of separation from the universe, and the realization that there really was nothing at all you could hold on to. Fortunately, this state is a hair's-breadth away from the place next to it, in which there was only one thing, and I was part of it. At that point, there was what might be described as songs of jubilation throughout the heavens: "Another jerk wakes up!" Not jubilation at the realization of who I, Jim Fadiman, was, but who I was *part* of. What a relief! I moved into a space of feeling that I was not part of everything—but that *everything* was part of everything, and I was clearly part of that. Suddenly, it was obvious that there is no death and that the fundamental waveform of the universe is best described in human terms as love. This was all incredibly obvious. And for some peculiar reason, I, Jim Fadiman, was being given this awakening to my true self.

From that place, I looked at various structures in my life. They were all, at best, amusing. It struck me that being a graduate student to avoid serving in a war seemed to be a perfectly plausible thing to do since one had to do something in this incarnation. It was unclear to me whether I, Jim Fadiman, as a personality, had lived before. But it was also not very important, because the Jim Fadiman that was in that room on October 19 wasn't very important, serving only as the container in which "I" found myself.

That evening, before going home with Harman, we went up to the top of Skyline, a mountain ridge above Stanford. I looked out and had an amazing feeling of identification with Creation. I walked around saying things like, "I've really done a splendid job at all of this." The "I" here was clearly not me, not Jim Fadiman, but the "I" was pleased with Creation and pleased that part of me was observing other parts of me. Now, singing songs of praise to the Lord is an Old Testament notion, and you might wonder why the Lord is at all interested in that, since He wrote the songs, and everything else for that matter. But when you're in the praising mode, it feels nice to congratulate yourself for jobs well done.

I continued as part of a team with Harman, Stolaroff, Savage, and others, but now I was looking at the work from a very different level than before, because *now*, finally, I understood what on Earth we were doing. We were trying to discover whether—if you used psychedelics in a totally supportive, nonmedical setting, with a high enough dose—you could facilitate entheogenic experience. And if so, would that be beneficial?

There was also "advanced training," as it came to be called, with Hubbard, usually in Death Valley. This was the most intense outdoors set and setting one could imagine and allowed openings not easily achieved in any other situation.

A typical session would involve driving in from Lone Pine and stopping at some point to take the psychedelic. Then we would go to several locations and spend time there, usually "eyes open," dealing with what was visible—or visible on the invisible planes there. You were faced with your own life much more directly because of the harshness, enormous beauty, and enormous barrenness of the landscape. The advanced training was a major way of making sure you didn't get caught in your personal belief systems.

While part of the time I was doing government-sanctioned research, I was also, as mentioned in chapter 14, involved with novelist Ken Kesey's world, because Dorothy, my wife, had been involved with Kesey. This made me one of the few people who was fully involved in totally legal psychedelic research and also hanging out with the primo group of psychedelic outlaws, explorers operating without restrictions.

How long were you able to work with psychedelics at Stanford, and how did it end?

It took me two years to get a committee that was willing to have their names on my dissertation, "Behavior Change Following (LSD) Psychedelic Therapy," a title I came up with so Stanford wouldn't throw me out.

The federal government by then had allowed us to do a study on the question of creativity, looking at whether psychedelics could facilitate problem solving of a technical nature. Dr. Oscar Janiger in Los Angeles and others had done work with artists—but we took on a different challenge. Could we use these materials and get people to work on highly technical problems? One difficulty, we knew, was that if we upped the dose enough, our volunteers would all be much more interested in seeing God and in letting go of their personal identities, time, and space than in focusing in on work-related problems.

In 1965, we began to run this really gorgeous study with senior research scientists from a number of companies. We told them that we'd assist them in their most pressing technological problems, particularly if they were really stuck. Our criterion for admission to the study was that they had to bring at least three problems that they had worked on for at least three months. A number of patents emerged out of that study.

But all good things come to an end. One morning, we were running our seventh group. Four people were in the first, relaxing part of the experiment when we got a letter saying, in effect, "Hello, this is your federal government. We are now concerned that psychedelics are available, that people are misusing them, and that there are bad things happening in the youth culture. As far as we can tell, we can't do a thing about the problem that is bothering us. But we can stop somebody somewhere, which will make us feel better. So, we've decided this morning to stop all research in the United States. Yours included." The wording, of course, said it differently, but the message was clear: your work is over.

That effectively ended our research.

We did, however, publish those results, and there are a number of rather distinguished, very happy scientists who were involved in those studies. One became a vice president of Hewlett-Packard; another has won every major scientific award that the computer world offers. The irony was that our studies were a totally acceptable way to bring psychedelics into the culture. Yet we were asked not only to stop the research, but also to deny whatever we had already learned and to keep society ignorant of the work. We were asked to do this while millions of people in the culture at large were running around experimenting without knowledge, help, or support.

Given that you'd had such profound experiences yourself, what did you do next?

I really stepped back at that point. I felt more aware of the absurdity of this moment than I felt personally affected because I was at a place where things didn't affect me much personally; they just happened, and I did whatever I needed to do. So I stepped back and thought, "Well, what else is available?" At that time, because of the millions of people using psychedelics, enormous other spiritual pathways were starting to open up. Most came from existing traditions and various practices including meditation, fasting, vision quests, shamanistic rituals, and the Peyote Way, developed and used primarily by Native Americans. As I could no longer use what seemed to be the cleanest, best, easiest way to work with myself and other people, I looked at what else was out there.

I was almost offered a position as a counselor at San Francisco State

University because they were desperate for someone who had experience with psychedelics and who could work with students with related issues. When they thought about it, however, they realized that if they hired me, or anybody like me, it would imply that there was some truth or legitimacy to what was going on. So, rather than have someone who really *knew* what was going on, they withdrew their offer and decided not to hire me.

This made me realize that my career was on shaky ground since my dissertation exposed me as one of "them," whoever "them" were. I had made it through Stanford. But by the time I was done, Stanford's great terror was that they would actually be, by supporting psychedelic research, what they liked to call themselves, the "Harvard of the West," since Leary and Alpert had been fired from Harvard by that time while doing research less controversial than mine.

One of the things I did work on became the *Journal of Transpersonal Psychology*. I also worked to establish the Transpersonal Psychology Association. This was to become a forum in which different religious and intellectual traditions could come together to talk, not about doctrine, but about experience. It allowed them to cooperate with each other in a way that hadn't previously been possible in either religious or psychological circles.

One model that existed, run by the same core group, was the *Journal of Humanistic Psychology* and its association. We began to form something similar. We wrote to the editorial board members of the *Journal of Humanistic Psychology* and said, "We're moving on. There is more to the human condition than we have experienced with our humanistic orientation. We don't quite know where we're going, but here are some of the things that we're going to look at. . . . Would you like to join us?"

The editors split down the middle. Half of them said, "I have some vague idea of where you're going, and I'll go with you," and the other half said, "Absolutely not." The major negative responses that I recall were from Victor Frankl, who wrote, "This is total nonsense," and Rollo May, who, for various reasons, became a serious enemy of the spiritual implications of the work and worked actively against it.

In many respects, the humanistic movement was very progressive for its time. Why do you think the psychedelic issue and the transpersonal movement were so antithetical to its belief system?

Having been on both sides, my guess is that if you have been brought up with a worldview in which there is only *this* world, you've been brought up intellectually provincial. The only experiences you've had with religion have been with people who also have never had any *true* spiritual experience. What you have, perhaps, is formal religion, which gives you a community of nice people who speak in the metaphors of religion because that's the best language they have. All this adds up to, however, is a rather impoverished vision of spirituality.

You then project onto others, onto people like me at the time. If I'm speaking about being a divine agent of God, then I'm *clearly,* for example, a paranoid schizophrenic because paranoid schizophrenics also talk about being the divine agents or angels of God. What you find is a group of people who are dealing with the profound fear that their entire worldview is small. And when your worldview is small and you're in a position of power, it seems neither unrealistic nor difficult to say that the people who seem to be attacking it must be wrong.

Psychology has a wonderful knack of turning disagreement into derangement, disability, or pathology. In the scientific world, "fear" is usually called "skepticism." Think about it this way: if you knew only a little bit of biology, it would seem highly unlikely that a duckbilled platypus exists. If you've never seen a giraffe or an elephant, it's easy to believe that they don't exist. So, if someone comes to you and says, "I would like you to meet my friend the elephant, who will carry us into the jungle where the giraffes are," it is not surprising if you say, "I'd rather you go away, and I certainly don't want to hire you. And I most certainly don't want to publish your articles."

Would you say that this is also reflective of why the culture at large became so hostile to psychedelics and why, after the initial enthusiasm, there was a wave of repression that included shutting down your program at Stanford?

Psychedelics were a waveform growing in magnitude, and Vietnam was a stone wall. When psychedelics met Vietnam and the country split apart, the old guard who had created and maintained Vietnam and were into war and so forth were terrified and correctly threatened. Why? Because the psychedelic people were saying, "We are not really interested in any of your institutions. We're willing to do whatever's necessary to tear them down. We're willing to eliminate your university, not to add some courses. We're willing to eliminate your military, not improve training. We're willing to empty your churches, because true religious experience does not happen inside walls."

So the old guard said, "I don't know what you guys are up to, but I'm feeling so deeply threatened that I will stop you to whatever extent I can." As a result, you had an amazing unity of the major institutions pushing back against the psychedelic wave. What they said was, "We control the guns; we control the universities; we control medicine. And, by God, we are at war with these people who are not content to let us live our lives but are determined through the most vulnerable part of us, our children, to take away the love and respect and support of our institutions and ourselves." From that point of view, it's hard to know what else they could have done.

In the past few years, there seems to be a resurgence of interest in psychedelics. What's going on?

The culture is gently beginning to admit that—while the federal government has long since stopped research, the journals have stopped accepting articles, and funding for research has dried up—young people are still taking psychedelics. And these young people, who are mostly well educated, are beginning to admit to each other that the decades of misinformation haven't worked as well as the makers of that misinformation would like. It's another generation, some of whom are saying, "I've honestly looked at my own experience versus the platters of misinformation I've been fed, and my own experience seems to be more valid."

So now psychedelics are coming out of the closet again. In what contexts might they become more accepted by society at large in the future?

You need to look at the use of psychedelic material in two contexts. One is entheogenic, and the other is psychotherapeutic. The entheogenic context says that religion is a private act and that government suppression of private, internal events is fundamentally against humanity. That's the entheogenic path, the path that I am committed to. I now realize that the government did not just stop my research by halting the creativity study. What it really did was to tell me, "You may not practice your religion or we will physically imprison you."

The other context is the use of psychedelics to help people live better lives by having less neurosis, less psychosis, fewer fixations, fewer perversions, and so forth. This is a very different realm, which should be in the hands of the people who historically administer therapeutic interventions.

Personally, I've become more radical. In the United States around 1830, the laws were that anyone could practice any kind of healing or medicine he or she wished. If you hurt people you could be sued, but if you didn't hurt people, then you wouldn't be sued. I'd like to be free to help people.

What would you say to young people about psychedelics?

I would basically give them my lecture on set, setting, substance, sitter, session, and situation, which is summed up by: If you're going to use psychedelics, do it with someone you love, and hopefully someone who has been there before you, and be aware that you may find out that the world is better than you ever thought. Beyond that, what I generally say is that it would be an awful lot better if you knew what the truth was before you worked with psychedelics. Many people beginning to use psychedelics today may be a little too young. What I learned from my own research is that psychedelics take your life experience and compost it, so that something new can grow. If you don't have much to compost, you may not get much out of it. I always looked at psychedelics as learning tools. Even in the middle of a psychedelic experience, I would begin to think, "I wonder what I'm going to do with this?" In a sense, I wanted it to be over so I could start to get to the digestion and assimilation phase, because the psychedelic experience itself wasn't my major interest.

What do you think you would have been like without psychedelics?

Without psychedelics, I would have been more neurotic and more boring. I have a decent idea of who I was as a Harvard undergraduate: silly, smart, clever, sarcastic, childish, and arrogant. Yech! I mean, I'm amused by who I was, but I certainly wouldn't have him for dinner. My world was very tiny, grounded on having a large vocabulary, a moderately high IQ, and so little soul that if you measured it in teaspoons, you probably wouldn't have been able to taste me. Psychedelics are the fundamental resource upon which I have drawn to become a human being.

Shifting gears a bit, who do you think should take psychedelics? Say, if it was in your power to design policy?

I feel strongly that we should return entheogen use to the context of a guided relationship, which has been the model in every traditional culture that I have studied. The idea that people should go off and trip with others their own age who don't know any more than they do, be they fifty or twenty or twelve, has never worked well in any culture, and it certainly doesn't work well in ours. So if I were the spiritual experience czar and decreed that people would be allowed to have freedom of religion in the United States of America, I would start by saying that freedom of religion of an entheogenic sort will be done similarly to the way one has the freedom to fly a private plane. You don't start by going up alone. You first go up with someone who knows more than you do. The trained pilot is in charge and tells you when you're ready to fly it yourself.

From the long view, are you optimistic?

If you look through history with entheogenic eyes, you realize that since the truth is always available, some people are going to discover it one way or another in every generation. In these last few generations, a lot of people had a chance to discover it and did.

Every spiritual tradition that is worth its salt has, at its origin, somebody who had a breakthrough into the *true* reality. When they came back into being in their bodies they wondered, "How am I going to share this with anybody?" Somehow, they found a way to do it, and eventually they had a lot of people who hung out around them, some of whom said, "I'll do the shit work. I'll arrange the meeting, I'll bring in the food, I'll handle things."

The handlers gradually—as they always do—got control of the situation. The original founder passed away, and the handlers started to make it easier for themselves. It's easier to bring in the food if it's every Sunday; it's easier if everyone has a certain place to sit; it's easier if the people pay the handlers; and so on. So the bureaucrats always end up eating away at the spiritual food of the founder. Without a continual infusion of spiritual food, you end up with what we would call an "organized" religion. The spiritual urge—the need to be part of your whole self—cannot be repressed any more than the sexual urge. But the expression of it always, inevitably—and I say that without any ill will—gets ossified. Inflexibility leads to further inflexibility.

I have been looking toward the next psychedelic generation to say to us, "What a bunch of tired old farts you are with this or that journal, this association, and your so-called research when God is all around you!" And I want to say to them, "Carry me out of the palace. You win! Tear down the walls. Get back to basics. I mean, I'd appreciate it if you wouldn't *shoot* me. But please take my job!"

It's starting to happen, and I love it.

18

POSITIVE POSSIBILITIES FOR PSYCHEDELICS

A Time of Tentative Celebration

The chemicals of transformation of revelation that open the circuits of light, vision, and communication, called by us mind-manifesting, were known to the American Indians as medicines: the means given to men to know and to heal, to see and to say the truth.

HENRY MUNN, *HALLUCINOGENS AND SHAMANISM*

For those of us involved with psychedelics, this is a time of unexpected changes, a time of tentative celebration. After decades of winter, the ice is thinning. The warming trends toward legalization; increased religious, medical, and psychotherapeutic use; scientific exploration; and cultural acceptance are encouraging.

After so many years, why now? Perhaps because the generation that suppressed research, criminalized personal use, and jailed users is passing from power. This next generation is better able to admit to the ineffectiveness of the legal clampdown and to temper it. It is much easier for those who never voted for the current laws to recognize that some, passed in haste and ignorance, are unworkable and counterproductive.

While the agenda of the research community has focused on a restoration of therapeutic use,[1] the most striking changes have been in the legal status of private personal use. The community of nations seems to be shaking off the fear induced by the excesses of the sixties, the phobic response of the American government, and the pressure from the United States on other nations to follow its lead. Like wildflowers coming up through cracks in concrete, other countries are starting to set their own policies.

For example, Gilberto Gil, the culture minister of Brazil, spoke of the importance of Brazil's efforts to recognize its culture through the national heritage program and characterized the ayahuasca churches as part of the "religious diversity that Brazilian democracy must respect." This characterization of the sacramental use of ayahuasca as "religious" allowed Brazil to deftly sidestep its international treaty obligations to restrict drug use.

The Netherlands has long allowed some psychedelics to be quite easily available but has stopped short of formal legalization. Portugal decriminalized all drugs in 2001 and made it explicit that treatment would be available for any drug user needing it. The naysayers fretted that this would have terrible consequences, but results have been entirely beneficial: less addiction, less social disruption, less overall crime, less actual use, more treatment facilities, and huge savings in law enforcement.[2] Mexico legalized small amounts of all previously illegal drugs in 2009. This was done, in part, to free up resources to try to eliminate criminal drug cartels. Since illegal addictive drugs, including cocaine, heroin, and their derivatives, are produced primarily for the U.S. market, the focus is on cross-border activities. The Czech Republic relaxed its laws to the point that many psychedelic plants may be owned or grown legally. It has also relaxed its penalties for possession of small amounts of manufactured substances like MDMA.[3]

The basis for these reforms is the recognition of the following realities:

1. Psychedelics are not addictive. They never were.
2. Marijuana, unlike tobacco and alcohol, does not cause systemic medical syndromes. In the United States alone, tobacco—legal, addictive, and regulated—directly contributes to the deaths of four hundred thousand people a year, while marijuana—illegal, nonaddictive, and unregulated (and perhaps used by more

Americans than still smoke cigarettes*)—does not kill anyone.

3. Illegal drugs are crime and violence magnets. It was true when the United States prohibited alcohol in the 1920s; it is equally true of any other desired and prohibited substance. We forget the huge increase in drinking and crime that Prohibition brought on. Author Simon Louvish wrote, "Times Square— between 34th and 52nd streets—boasted 2,500 speakeasies, where before Prohibition there had been only 300 saloons. In the entire country, in 1925, there were estimated to be three million 'booze joints,' where 'pre-Prohibition cafes numbered 177,000.' In other words, a nation of moderate drinkers was turned into a nation of obsessive alcoholics, paying for criminals to build up an immense black market that would affect the nation's economy for decades."[4]

If one removes criminal penalties for benign or at least nonaddictive drugs, personal use actually declines—at least in Holland and Portugal, the only two countries for which we have data. The other equivalent statistics that we have indicate that those states with medical marijuana laws have not seen a rise in total marijuana smoked, as had been forecast by those trying to stop those laws from going into effect.

A second group of countries have not changed their laws, but their courts have ruled that their constitutions affirm the right to private consciousness-changing activities. Brazil and Argentina's highest courts have concluded that the state cannot deny people the right to personal use of any substances as long as such use does not lead to socially unacceptable or criminal behavior.

The third group of countries, still uncertain of what direction to take, includes the United States. In the United States, policies that lumped marijuana, psychedelics, and addictive drugs together led to a bulging jail population, the proliferation of highly profitable international criminal

---

*The National Institute of Drug Abuse 2009 Survey results of high school students indicate that for twelfth-grade students, marijuana use in the past month was 38.2 percent and tobacco use in the past month was 20.1 percent.

activities, the distortion of the national economy in countries producing illegal drugs for American consumption, and a growing disdain for the U.S. government's failure to cope with the situation. These policies also cost billions of dollars annually. In spite of Washington's reluctance to change, state after state has used its prerogative to allow people to use marijuana as a medication.

Until the Obama administration, the federal government did its best to subvert these laws and keep all marijuana users criminalized. An indication of the pent-up demand for legal medical use is that within a few weeks of the administration's decision to stop federal blocking of medical marijuana use that had been approved under state laws, eight hundred marijuana dispensaries opened up in Los Angeles alone, outnumbering banks and public schools in the city. The trend toward legalization is accelerating as it becomes more and more self-evident that marijuana use does not lead to violence or to criminal behavior. That the last three presidents have smoked marijuana at one point in their lives has not been lost on reformers or the general public. Marijuana is not a psychedelic, but it is a consciousness-altering substance used traditionally for spiritual and therapeutic purposes. As its status changes, other consciousness-altering plants and substances are less likely to remain demonized.

In 2010, several states, notably California but Nevada and Florida as well, had drives to allow the right to vote on initiatives to decriminalize or legalize marijuana. The California drive succeeded and put "Proposition 19" on its ballot. In California, the primary argument is that marijuana production, although one of the state's largest industries, is totally untaxed and that its interdiction is expensive and unsuccessful.[5] The idea is to turn a sinkhole of wasted money into a source of revenue. The California ballot proposition makes possession of up to one ounce legal; it allows individual cultivation in a garden of no more than twenty-five square feet, forbids sales to minors, and forbids smoking in public. The specifics of regulation and taxation are left to local jurisdictions.

The proposition was defeated 54 percent to 46 percent. Medical marijuana initiatives in Oregon and South Dakota also lost. The loss, at least in California, was due solely to the demographics of the turnout. As was true nationally, a far smaller number of younger voters participated than in 2008. The older the voter, the less likely he or she was to vote for the proposition.

More directly pertaining to psychedelics and religious freedom, several court cases in other states have established that religious groups using ayahuasca as their central sacrament can practice their faith without fear of imprisonment. These cases are a major step toward the restoration of religious liberty regarding other psychedelics in other settings.

Even the nonsense of forbidding the cultivation of hemp as though it were marijuana (comparable to putting root beer in the same class as Coors) has been getting a fresh look. Imported hemp products, including those for human consumption, are again available. One state, Washington, following the example of Canada and a dozen other countries, allows hemp to be grown, harvested, and sold. There seems to be, if not an end to the lack of common sense in the regulatory establishment, at least some cracks in it.

Making marijuana legal and taxable would have greatly reduced the budgets and staff needs of the drug-enforcement establishment—and its clout. The push-back came from law-enforcement agencies, private prisons, and prison guard groups, whose profits or very existence depend on strict enforcement and long sentences (in addition, from alcohol and tobacco interests). Many police departments, for example, depend on the seizure of property and money from drug arrests as a major revenue source and will fight a loss to their incomes. For example, authorities in Los Angeles in 2008 seized assets valued at $7,709,355; in San Francisco, $938,012; and in Sacramento, $1,633,282.[6]

Only now, in the preliminary phase of liberalization, are we starting to have available evidence-based science about psychedelics. It would be unduly optimistic to expect evidence-based legislation to become widespread anytime soon, but more countries can be expected to relax some of their restrictions as the benefits of doing so become more widely apparent.

Entheogenic Use

Although legal restrictions put an end to conventional research, they did little to prevent the continued proliferation of psychedelics throughout the culture. It is difficult to say which of many cultural areas have been most affected by psychedelics. For example, Jack Kornfield, a noted Buddhist teacher, says, "It is true for the majority of American Buddhist teachers that they have had experience with psychedelics either right after they started their spiritual practice or prior to it."[7] This use, in fact, is not contrary to Buddhist vows.[8] My own experience is that teachers in many other spiritual disciplines also began their spiritual journeys after important psychedelic experiences.

Since 2006 a team at Johns Hopkins University has been engaged in a series of studies to determine if psychedelics taken in a safe and sacred situation lead subjects to spiritual experiences.[9] Hardly surprising, the answer has been yes. More important than the research itself was that it crossed a major barrier: the government allowed, for the first time, a research study that asked spiritual questions, not medical ones. Most telling was the amount of media attention given to the findings. More than three hundred publications took note of the results after their publication in a peer-reviewed academic journal. Surprisingly, a positive account even appeared in the *Wall Street Journal.* More instructive, in looking at trends, was a short article in the *Scottish Sporting News.* The headline read, "Shrooms Get You High." The editors assumed that their subscribers knew the slang term for psychedelic mushrooms and that it would not require a lengthy article to say that science had discovered what their readers already knew.

Equally important, a host of websites now meet the need to have easy access to basic information for safe, sane psychedelic use. The foremost site is Erowid (www.erowid.org), which has reports and information, technical articles, interactive molecular dictionaries, visionary art, descriptions of dangers and contraindications, as well as thousands of personal reports on dozens of substances. The site averages sixty thousand visits a day, a figure that has grown every year since its inception. Browsing through the site makes it clear that while forty years of inadequate information may have worked against wise use, a widespread underground is thriving unimpeded.*

Another recent phenomenon is the growing popularity of ayahuasca. While other psychedelics are often used recreationally, ayahuasca is almost always taken under the direction of experienced guides or shamans. In the sixties, a prototypical rite of passage was to visit India, study with a guru, and practice austerities in an ashram. Today's psycho-explorers head for the South American rain forest to work with traditional healers and traditional plant medicines, of which ayahuasca is the best known. While the trips to India were mostly about personal self-realization, the intentions of those seeking today's South American immersions almost always include healing (physical and mental), but the seekers are equally concerned with repairing the rift between humanity and the other biological kingdoms.

Two debates continue, holdovers from the wide-eyed sixties. One is about the validity of experiences induced by plants or chemicals versus experiences achieved by meditation, prayer, movement, or fasting. The argument smolders and flares up now and then but will never be settled. The other debate—between those who scorn synthetic psychedelics and those who don't—goes on as well, with no hope of either side convincing the other. Gordon Wasson, who discovered psychedelic-mushroom use in the New World, was asked about the difference between the mushrooms and psilocybin, manufactured by Sandoz. He said, "I did not discover any difference. I think the people who discover a difference are looking for a difference and imagine they see a difference."[10] What is important is the effect that taking the substance has on one's life and well-being, not the subtleties of this or that product.

Medical and Psychotherapeutic Uses

Medical and psychotherapeutic psychedelic research is back! Though one researcher calls this time a golden age in psychedelic research, it

---

*See also www.quantcast.com/erowid.org, an analytic site that describes the demographics of Erowid users.

would be more realistic to say that a tiny tip of the camel's nose has been allowed into the tent. Outside the tent, a large community of researchers is eager to begin work delayed for decades. In 2006 and 2008, scientific conferences honoring the work of Albert Hofmann in synthesizing LSD and other psychedelics brought more than two thousand people from thirty-seven countries to Basel, Switzerland. Two hundred journalists from all over the world covered those presentations. More recently, the Psychedelic Science in the 21st Century conference, held in San Jose, California, in April 2010, sold out at twelve hundred participants and was widely and favorably reported in the media. These are remarkable turnouts for gatherings about substances that have been illegal for so long.

While some current research is a repeat of work done before everything closed down, new areas of research reveal how psychedelics help alleviate medical conditions that have not been amenable to conventional treatment. It is important to note that there has been no outcry to stop the work. By taking on more difficult syndromes, the researchers have skirted such opposition, and, in fact, have been well supported by their medical colleagues.

One example is work being done with cluster headaches.[11] The healing effects of LSD for this condition were first claimed by illegal users, whose communications with one another became public,[12] and they are now being evaluated in a study conducted at Harvard. It remains to be seen if what is already fairly well proved can make it through the double-blind pharmaceutical hurdle to peer-reviewed publication and, more important, can become available, not only for research but also for use in normal clinical practice.

Another successful study used psilocybin with late-stage cancer patients who had high levels of anxiety. Results show that a single session in a safe and supportive setting, allowing the sacred to be experienced should it occur, benefits the patient and the patient's family.[13] Within two days of the release of the results, which were published in a major journal, there were over four hundred media mentions. What was striking about the coverage was that, as in the earlier Johns Hopkins study, the stories reported not only the findings but also that the study affirmed what was already known. It is not unreasonable to assume that the extensive press coverage was due in part to the fact that many journalists and media editors these days have tried psychedelics while in college and thus are more open to positive reporting of even the smallest new study.

A more controversial treatment, once allowed inside the United States but now pushed out to other countries, uses iboga, an African psychedelic plant, to break the cycle of heroin addiction. Given the poor track record of conventional treatments and the high cost of addiction, untreated as well as treated, this area should be getting more attention and support in the future. In fact, several recovered addicts found it to be so valuable that they now treat their brethren illegally in inner-city environments without medical support.

What is yet to resume is research on psychedelic therapy to overcome alcohol addiction, which was far and away the most fully researched, tested, and proven therapy from before the psychedelic prohibition era. Nothing has been written about it since then, not even in underground circles. It is, for now, a large missing piece of the current medical research renaissance.[14]

A number of other countries, including Germany, Switzerland, Jordan, and Israel, are allowing or supporting psychedelic projects, primarily with MDMA, to help people overcome chronically debilitating effects of post-traumatic stress disorder (PTSD). With hundreds of thousands of veterans returning home from the wars in Iraq and Afghanistan with PTSD, demand for a treatment with a higher improvement rate than the present therapy is intensifying. That Vietnam veterans, decades after that conflict, are still in treatment makes it all the more likely that eventually MDMA-based therapy programs will be offered to veterans.

The first research study of veterans with PTSD to be given MDMA-based therapy was approved in 2010. Perhaps, as with cluster headaches, the first reports will be from veterans who are self-medicating and helping one another, as is already happening with marijuana. However, as long as the U.S. Department of Veterans Affairs' hospital system remains underfunded, understaffed, and overcrowded, it will be unlikely to institute new treatment protocols soon.

Extensive illegal use of psychedelics for self-exploration, with and without trained guides, will continue. A survey of college students found that the most cited reason for taking psychedelics was self-exploration, not spiritual or recreational use.[15] Just as the acceptance of medical marijuana has spawned the "dispensary," where patients can buy their medications, so can we expect the emergence of clinics and institutions specializing in psychotherapeutic treatment with different kinds of psychedelics.*

Creativity and Problem Solving

The term *psychedelic* is already in popular use to describe a certain kind of music and visual art. It carries no stigma for an artist to avow that psychedelics influenced the creation of a song, a painting, or a dramatic production. Their use is widely accepted in the technical world as well, even though there is, as yet, hardly any discussion about it.

During the "dot-com" revolution, companies were formed by people young enough to have grown up with psychedelics readily available. Drug use for them was casual and frequent. That two Nobel Prize laureates acknowledged the impact of psychedelics on their scientific breakthroughs suggests that there has been far more use of these substances in the scientific community than is reported.[16]

Paralleling the thousands of people who attended the scientific conferences in Basel and San Jose are the much larger groups that flock to the yearly Boom Festival in Portugal and the Burning Man Festival held in the Black Rock Desert in Nevada. While not all of the fifty thousand people who attend Burning Man each year have taken psychedelics, the vast majority of attendees have.

On YouTube, over one million people have viewed individual factual and conceptual videos on psychedelics. In 2009, National Geographic Television was able to sell advertising space for a full evening of programming about "drugs." The evening began with an hour about methamphet-

---

*In 2009, the federal government allowed therapists who use MDMA with patients to take MDMA themselves for training purposes. This breached another invisible wall, treating MDMA not as a substance like a medication, but as a substance whose effects must be experienced to effectively offer it as part of a treatment.

amine. A second hour toured the world of marijuana planting, growing, selling, and use. The final hour was on contemporary psychedelic use, primarily biomedical and therapeutic studies, but it included urban drug dealing and the use of psychedelics by artists to improve and expand their skills.* Such programs indicate how far we have come since nonsense like *Reefer Madness* was touted as "informational."

Conclusions

The overall trend is toward greater openness and greater availability of information. Trained guides for spiritual and scientific sessions are still hard to come by, but cultural and market forces are favorable for institutions to be created for such instruction. In fact, over one hundred not-yet-legal guides and those working in approved research studies met together—unofficially—at the San Jose conference. They agreed to pool information and approved the establishment of a wiki site, www.entheoguide.net/wiki, to be administered by the Guild of Guides. The first two chapters of this book and the checklist (chapter 19) are already part of that website. The guild is planning to have its first national conference in 2011.

Both the overview in this chapter and this whole book support the optimistic hope that the proper uses of these remarkable substances will not be overwhelmed by trivial popularization, as was the case when psychedelics were made illegal. The counterforces to wider acceptance include the usual suspects: stupidity, fear, greed, self-interest, and inertia. The law enforcement–prison establishment employed to enforce drug laws are already becoming active. In California, the prison guard unions donate heavily to political campaigns and will undoubtedly spend a great deal of money, time, and energy fighting any marijuana initiative. Some members of organized religions will also be among the opposition. In almost every religious institution, there are those who act as intermediaries between the faithful and the Divine. Psychedelic experiences that

---

*While I was on segments of this television program, I had no control over the content or the narration. (To be honest, I really tried to influence both.)

offer the possibility of direct contact, bypassing this establishment, have been seen as a threat in the past and may be so today.[17] Other money to oppose the initiative has come from liquor and tobacco interests, perhaps concerned with a potential competitor for recreational use.

Additional opposition may come from the international banking system. If this sounds unlikely, it is only because most of us are unaware of the value of illegal drug sales. A United Nations study of the world financial meltdown of 2008 and 2009 concluded that one of the few continuing sources of liquidity was the $232 billion (that's the real number) of estimated drug profits during that period.[18] The majority of these profits were from drugs such as heroin and cocaine, but keeping the laws muddy and confusing serves these interests better than laws focused solely on addictive drugs.

As favorable as these trends may be (and whatever else you read in this book that you feel good about or are surprised by or want to share with someone), what matters most is how your understanding of yourself and your place in the natural order has been made clearer or richer or of more value because of your actual or anticipated psychedelic-supported experiences. If the resultant insights are not integrated into your life, they can be trivialized, ignored, or even "pathologized." Huston Smith, probably the world's foremost scholar of religion, says the question is not "Do these substances support religious experience?" but "Does their use lead to a religious life?" Psychedelic researcher and Buddhist practitioner Rick Strassman says, "'Spiritual experience' alone, even repeated, is not the basis for becoming a better person. Rather, psychedelic insights tempered and put into practice, using ethical and moral considerations, appear to be the best way to harness the power of psychedelic drugs."[19]

This round of prohibition of highly desired substances is starting to wind down. Like the first attempt with alcohol, it has been a failure along every dimension that can be measured. These words by Albert Einstein, speaking of the first prohibition, sadly are just as valid today: "The prestige of government has undoubtedly been lowered considerably by the Prohibition law. For nothing is more destructive of respect for the government and the law of the land than passing laws which cannot be enforced. It is an open secret that the dangerous increase of crime in this country is closely connected with this." In many cultures, psychedelic explorers are called upon to find something of use to their society, such as learning about the healing properties of a plant, bringing back a healing song, or recovering a nugget of wisdom to help people live in greater harmony with themselves and with the natural world. That psychedelics make such experiences more easily available does not lessen this responsibility.

The question posed by the poet Mary Oliver, "What is it you plan to do with your one wild and precious life?"[20] is one that psychedelics impel you to take seriously.

THE NECESSARY,
THE EXTRAORDINARY,

and Some Hard-Core Data

Introduction to Part Five

When you write fiction, you soon learn that readers don't need to know much about the characters at the beginning of a story. So fiction writers wait. They fill in the backstories about their characters later. Another truth that fiction writers know is that all books are mysteries; but unless the "mystery" keeps the reader curious enough to turn the next page, the book isn't working.

For nonfiction writers, the tasks of holding the readers' attention and bringing in back stories are much the same. This final section is back story. It contains important information for your own personal exploration.

Chapter 19 is a checklist of the information contained in the first two chapters about giving or taking a high-dose entheogenic session, restating the basic elements to take into account. (There is growing evidence, especially with complex medical procedures, that the mandatory use of checklists reduces mistakes and vastly improves success rates. For that reason, a checklist is included here.)

Chapter 20 contains examples of personal journeys taken without using the psychedelics LSD, mescaline, and psilocybin. The first four sessions are reports from two people taking ayahuasca with indigenous guides. These sessions are samples of the experiences Westerners have with this plant mixture. The last report describes what took place during the last part of a fourteen-day darkness retreat; it reads like a classic mystical experience. All these reports are reminders included to remind us that that there are many methods and practices that can open awareness and that different methods open different doors.

Chapter 21 explores actual behaviors (described more generally in chapter 8) that are changed and remain changed as the result of therapeutic sessions with psychedelics.

The final chapter presents the results of a very early study that asked individuals who had had a single high-dose psychedelic journey with LSD or mescaline what they felt was important about their experience. Perhaps because of the long research lull, this simple self-report study is still the best available today.

In a good novel, we look forward to loose ends being tidied up, mysteries solved, and characters' behavior explained as events complete their cycle. The real world is not like that at all. Nothing ever ends; it just blends into the next thing. Every nonfiction book is only a snapshot of what is currently known and what remains unknown. Some of what we know now as being ever so true will turn out to be wrong, and whole areas will be revealed as the new unknown.

This tour of psychedelic studies is no different. Some will not hold up, and some will turn out to be critically important. Each of us must evaluate public information and scientific research reports and, above all, test everything against our own personal experience.

19
ENTHEOGENIC JOURNEYS
A Checklist for Voyagers and Guides

This checklist is designed to help the voyager and guide create the best possible opportunity for a voyager having an intentional entheogenic session. The checklist is meant to supplement the guidelines fully described in chapters 1 and 2, not to serve as a substitute for it. It's best to work through the checklist a few weeks ahead of time, but it can also prove useful just before and even during a session. See www.entheoguide.net for possible updates and expansions.

General Preparation

Voyager and Guide
- Read through chapter 1, "Meeting the Divine Within," and chapter 2, "The Entheogenic Voyage."
- Feel good about each other. Feel that you can trust one another.

Voyager
- Clarify your personal preconceptions about psychedelics and entheogenic experiences in general.
- Consider and reflect on your personal understanding of mystical experiences, cosmic consciousness, and God, Goddess, or the Divine in general.

- Find an appropriate and qualified guide for the session.
- Set your intention clearly enough to be able to say it to your guide.
- Ideally, have three full days set aside for the experience: a day to prepare, a day to have the session, and a day to integrate the session.

Guide

- Determine whether you are qualified and experienced enough to serve as a guide. If you are feeling uncertain, determine whether you can be supervised (with the voyager's acknowledgment) by a qualified mentor.
- Agree to serve as voyager's guide.

One Week Before the Journey

Voyager and Guide

- Make sure in advance that you have your voyage day off for all commitments from work, family, and friends. For people with whom you keep in regular contact or people who might call you spontaneously and worry when they can't find you, let them know that you will be unavailable all day and evening. If you use an Iphone, BlackBerry, or tweet or use another instant service to communicate with others, make sure that those people know there will be times when you will be offline and that you are fine.

Set

Voyager and Guide

- Feel reasonably well prepared for the coming session.
- Have a good understanding of the general flow of time and the likely types of internal visions and external changes anticipated during a session.
- Have a positive overall mind-set with respect to the coming session.
- Feel good about and trusting of each other.

Voyager

- Make sure to spend part of the day before the session quietly, in preparation.
- Be in touch with thoughts and feelings and have positive expectations.
- Be comfortable with the guide, physically and emotionally.
- Have no unusual or intense, suicidal, dark, or otherwise troubling thoughts and don't intend to delve deeply into suffering or the nature of evil.
- Be prepared to have *highly unusual experiences,* including: experiencing different realities or historical periods; being in a different body of either sex; becoming an animal, plant, or microorganism; experiencing your own birth; meeting the Divine within in a wide variety of possible forms, including gods and goddesses, divine beings, or transcendent light.

Guide

- Have the intention to wholeheartedly and effectively be present for the voyager.
- Be emotionally and spiritually ready for the upcoming session.
- Be prepared to handle whatever arises during the session, internally or externally.
- Be prepared to deal with any fear that arises in the voyager (or yourself) with gentleness and presence.
- Remain neutral and nonjudgmental about the voyager's issues, relationships, and personal history.
- Understand that there are an infinite number of ways for the voyager to meet the Divine.
- Verify that the voyager has no suicidal, dark, or otherwise troubling thoughts and is not intending to delve deeply into suffering or the nature of evil.
- Be willing to cancel or postpone the session for a specific reason or based on an intuitive gut feeling.
- Check the existing level of trust between yourself and the voyager.

Setting

Voyager and Guide

- Ensure that you have a private, safe, comfortable indoor space to use for the session's duration.
- Ensure that there are comfortable spots—couches, beds, rugs—where the voyager can lie down, sit down, and hang out.
- Have soft pillows and blankets available.
- Music capability: have headphones, ear buds, or speakers available in accordance with voyager's preference.
- Have eyeshades, eye pillows, and a folded washcloth or scarf available for eyes-closed music listening.
- Have flowers and candles available, if desired.
- Have water available for the voyager and the guide.
- Have access to adequate restroom facilities.
- Silence or turn off electronic devices (including phones).
- Minimize the likelihood of other external interruptions.
- Have art materials, journals, and other creative tools available for the voyager's use, if desired. Also have family photographs, a mirror, artistic objects, flowers, and other beautiful natural or man-made objects available.
- Agree on whether the outdoors will be safely accessible for the latter part of session.

Voyager

- Be adequately and comfortably dressed and have warm layers available.
- Consult with the guide on music and, if desired, provide the guide with specific musical requests and selections.

Guide

- Feel good about the space and overall setting.
- Provide for personal food, drink and other needs for the duration of the session.
- Consult with the voyager on music.

- Have appropriate music available for different phases of the session.

Substance

Voyager and Guide
- Agree on the desired entheogen and dose.
- Have obtained the entheogen from a trusted source.

Voyager
- Understand the likely overall effects from the entheogen at the chosen dose.
- Be prepared to be quiet and lie down as the entheogen takes effect over the first twenty minutes to one hour.

Guide
- Have an adequate way to measure out and administer the correct dosage.
- If the voyager is moving around or otherwise seems substantially under-dosed after the first hour or so, possibly administer a booster dose.
- If, after two hours, with or without a booster dose, the voyager is not deeply inside, DO NOT continue to press for an entheogenic-level session.

Session

Voyager and Guide
- Be prepared, positive, and overall ready for the duration of coming session.
- If either the voyager or the guide has sudden, intense forebodings or misgivings about going forward with the imminent session, cancel or postpone it.
- Create an intentional, sacred space as the entheogen is administered.
- Agree to keep unnecessary conversation to a minimum.

- Have an appropriate sitter available to care for the voyager at the end of the session and after the session.

Voyager

- Eat lightly or not at all before the session.
- Feel physically well (or well enough) to go forward with session.
- Be prepared to take guidance and receive assistance from the guide during the session.
- Be prepared to lie down, listen to music, observe your breathing, and pay attention to any sensations in the body.
- Be prepared to let go of expectations about session, and let go of personal concerns about relationships, personal issues, and habits.
- Be prepared to let go of each experience, feeling, or visual event as it occurs.
- Be prepared to let go of your personal identity and allow physical boundaries to dissolve.
- Be prepared to experience and deepen your awareness of other dimensions of reality.
- Be willing to ask for guide's help, assistance, or feedback whenever desired and trust the guide's directions.
- Be prepared to reintegrate toward the end of the session.

Guide

- Be prepared to give the voyager specific, necessary assistance and guidance, such as a gentle touch and the suggestion to breathe deeply.
- Be prepared to assist the voyager in getting to and going to the bathroom.
- Be prepared to hold the voyager's hand and otherwise maintain supportive, nonverbal contact.
- Remember to let the voyager know when you are leaving and have returned if you need to briefly leave to use the bathroom or do something else.
- Be prepared to go with the overall flow, to trust the voyager's

instincts, and to accommodate the voyager's stated desires when reasonable and possible.

- Agree to take no consciousness-altering drugs before or during the session.
- Be prepared to experience and appropriately deal with any "contact high."
- Refuse to act in a sexual manner, even if asked.
- Validate what the voyager sees and experiences by rephrasing or summarizing it in simple language.
- Be prepared to invite the voyager to go deeper by saying phrases like "Yes! That's good. Would you like to know more?"
- Be prepared to show the voyager personal photographs if requested.
- Be prepared to make electronic recordings or take notes at the voyager's request.

Post-Session Situation and Sitter

Voyager and Guide

- The post-session sitter, ideally a friend or relative with psychedelic experience, should be identified ahead of time and should arrive at the agreed-upon time.
- The sitter understands his or her job is to fully support the voyager during his or her post-session reintegration period.
- In consultation with the sitter, a plan is in place for the initial post-session reintegration period and to assist in getting the voyager back to his or her regular circumstances.
- In consultation with the sitter, a plan should be in place to offer the voyager a light meal after the session.

Voyager

- Be prepared to spend the day after the session integrating insights and experiences.
- Will not make any major life decisions—other than immediately stopping toxic behaviors—for at least the first few weeks.

- Have adequate post-session support available from friends, the sitter, and the guide, if needed.
- Be prepared to wait at least six months before another entheogenic session.

Guide

- Be sure that the voyager is in an appropriate condition to be left with the sitter.
- Be sure that the voyager has an appropriate support system in place in terms of family, friends, people at work, religious group support, therapists, and spiritual teachers.
- Be prepared to meet with the voyager at least once soon after the session to help finish the reintegration process.

Sitter

- Be prepared to listen and do not suggest, interrupt, or interpret.
- Agree to allow long silences, as the voyager may still be doing inner work.
- Agree to help the voyager get ready for bed, to sleep, or to rest.
- Agree to not leave the voyager alone for the night, but that you can leave the voyager with friends or family.

BEYOND LSD— WAY BEYOND
Ayahuasca Sessions and a Darkness Retreat

MICHAEL WIESE, "ANATOLE,"
and LINDSEY VONA

LSD and related psychedelics open up one range of experience. The reports in this chapter show how people have used other ways to explore a significant range of experiences. Each of these reports began as a letter to friends. Each one describes a transformational journey. Each writer had prior experience with other psychedelics. The first two are about ayahuasca taken under shamanistic guidance; the third is about the effect of a prolonged time period spent in total darkness with no substance given at all.

Ayahuasca
Michael Wiese

Michael Wiese is a respected documentary filmmaker, a former television and film executive, and the owner and publisher of Michael Wiese Productions (www.MWP.com), the foremost publisher of books about film and video creation and production. *After his first two experiences with aya-huasca, he wrote a report to a circle of friends. It has been slightly shortened for inclusion here as "part 1."* A year later, Wiese wrote another report about a subsequent session, included here as "part 2."*

Wiese has since made a film, The Shaman and Ayahuasca: Journeys to Sacred Realms, *and is publishing a book of interviews related to this work.[1] He lives with his family in Cornwall, England.*

Part One

The Second Journey

The shaman shakes his rattle. He whistles, breathlessly. His seductive voice weaves through me with beautiful and eerie *icaros* (songs) that create openings in my brain. I remember to focus on my intention. I am here to learn. To go deeper, I breathe slowly in and out. I feel the gritty, molasses-thick medicine of Mother Ayahuasca ripple through my belly, my liver and kidneys, and then jet up my spine to my brain. She is present. It's time to ask. I think, "Show me Divine Love."

Faint at first, with hardly any color saturation, geometric images appear. They brighten and become something. I see a yellow, peach-colored gauze. I feel there is something behind it. Slowly Mother Ayahuasca pulls back the veil to reveal a soft yellow room. I realize it is a nursery. Curiosity draws me near. I try to focus on this amazing vision.

As I look closer, I see a womblike room, secure and comforting. How strange. Why would She show me a nursery? And like any nursery, which may display the first A-B-C letters of the alphabet or a fanciful mobile for the new arrival, this too has pre-school teachings. Everywhere, in this room, is the support and love of all the child's previous ancestors going back to pre-history.

As I move into the room, I begin to see that the designers of *this* nursery have prepared the most fantastic and elaborate carvings—too vast for the eye to take in except in short gasps—for the being who will arrive shortly. Behold the sacred! Complete and total awe! The carvings

---

*For an excellent site on ayahuasca research literature, see www.wasiwaska.org/research .htm.

are perfect and stretch on as far as I can see. It's as if ten thousand crafts-men have been commanded by a king to carve for ten thousand years. It's as if generations of the Universe's most accomplished artisans have been told that a Divine Child is coming and to get the room ready. And they have done so. That's what I see.

These intricate carvings—far more advanced than those of the Taj Mahal or anything in the Forbidden City—are sacred scriptures in Sanskrit, Egyptian, Hebrew, Arabic, and many other texts I don't recog-nize. The walls are filled with knowledge that the child will absorb in its life. I am trying to take it all in and remember it because it's the most extraordinary place I've ever been—a heavenly palace.

I move closer into the room and can feel the breathing presence of two huge black boas that encircle and protect the room. I can't see them, but I can feel their warm, deep electric hum. I think to myself, "Oh great, giant snakes." I am afraid I might see them and be terrified. But as I breathe again, I find out I am not. The Giant Snakes are here to protect the Child. "So who is the Child?" I ask.

"This room is for you. You are the Child."

I am overwhelmed, shocked, stunned. No words can describe the feeling! I am worthy of the love of the Great Mother Ayahuasca! She has poured her most magnificent creativity into preparing and creating this room for me!

I try to take it all in. I notice the room has expanded on the far side. I can see an entire cityscape built with the same exquisite craftsmanship and intent. This is only one room of thousands, millions! Nothing is spared in Her generosity for the Child.

A second, deeper wave of realization comes over me. All humans are Divine Children. She provides for us all. We are already living in a Paradise!

Hours later, when the vision has worn off and I look around at the green field where I've been sitting, the pond with its geese and four goslings and the forest beyond—I see every leaf a masterpiece like the carved detail in the room. Mother Ayahuasca has poured the same love and creativity into providing food and beauty for all human life. We live in an exquisite paradise. We should fall to our knees in appreciation for our sacred Earth and the Universe.

The First Journey

This nursery was one of many visions. I wrote about it first because it was the most exquisite, gentle, and beautiful of the visions. Ayahuasca can also bring very dark and terrifying visions.

The first journey was filled with energy so great I could not stay balanced. It had the force of a tsunami washing over me, and it went on for hours. It started with a beautiful landscape of jewels and a woven electronic blanket of undulating snakes with extremely garish orange and green colors. There is nothing subtle about Ayahuasca's taste in art! The detail was incredible, and there was too much to watch.

When I first saw the landscape, I thought to myself how beautiful it was to look at. Just then, the relationship between the vision and me shifted. Subject and object merged. Duality was gone. I *was* the vision. I *was* the mesh of energy and jewels and snakes that I was seeing.

That's when the scanning began. It was like the medicine plant had a lot of entities working for it, and although I couldn't see them, my body was being scanned and sliced and diced in every direction as if through a giant cheese grater. Later, I realized what I was describing could have been interpreted as an alien abduction.

It was not frightening, but it was overwhelming. I certainly hoped they knew what they were doing. My DNA, my entire operating system, was being reprogrammed—and fast. Billions of terabytes of information were shuttling through every cell.

I breathed through it, trying to stay centered. I found I could ask the plant questions and get immediate answers, either verbally or visually or telepathically. But there was so much energy that for much of the time it was all I could do to surf the wave, let alone try to carry on a master-student conversation. There is a vast amount I don't remember.

Sometime later, I saw other images of organic green-and-flesh-colored entities. At first, the light was beautiful, but when I looked deeper into the shadows, there was real evil, and it was terrifying, and I tried not to look. Wrong. The lesson being taught was that good and evil are part of the same thing, and like it or not, they come into the world of duality as a package deal. I tried to accept this and breathe through the realization, and even though I didn't like what I was learning, I saw it was true.

Sometime later, I entered a black, murky, smoky hell—worlds of scraping electronic sounds and metals. A smoky substance rose like one of those black snakes that kids light on Halloween. I may have been seeing my toxins being released at a cellular level.

All around me throughout the night were the sounds of the other thirty participants puking their guts out. People were growling and bellowing like beasts as they heaved into their buckets. I tried to give them love and compassion and, as we were instructed to do, not get caught up in their dramas because I had my own to attend to—that was my responsibility. Without staying focused on one's breathing and intent (what one wants to learn), it's very easy to get disoriented.

All the time, the energy poured into me and through me like a fire hose pummeling me, so much so that I felt that my energy would be depleted and I would truly be annihilated. I tried to sit up straight in half-lotus and breathe in and out. I was nauseous and vomited several times over the next four or five hours. But little came up because I had eaten very little beforehand so what was purged was probably toxins from my organs.

Once as I leaned into the bucket bright colored pearls—like pop beads—came out of my mouth. The torrent of energy continued to hammer me. Occasionally there would be a one-breath break and then back into it. There is no resisting this force, which is the same as the force of Creativity and Destruction combined. Everything is constantly being born and dying. This force brings everything into being and recycles it in death. I was tapped in directly to the main power current of the Universe. All Powerful does not describe it. It is Beyond Massive! And it is surging through me constantly. I am a part of it; everything is a part of it. Our existence depends on it.

I was on a Mobius strip dying and being reborn again and again and again and again and again and again. . . . It was painful and frightening and dizzying and, like some out-of-control carnival ride, as much as I begged, the operator would not let me off. Nightmarish.

I was sure I wouldn't make it. I had nothing left. Still, I fought to hang on to my last drop of energy, but in the face of ayahuasca—the most powerful—*resistance is futile.*

When the ceremony ended, I stumbled back to my room, heavily intoxicated, shaking and weaving, and dizzily dropped into bed. But the visions continued, and I was hammered for another seven hours. I realized that it was foolish to have eaten so little before the session because I had no fuel and no reserves. I was feeling dehydrated but was too weak and sick to reach the few inches to the bottle at the bedside. It took enormous strength to reach it and suck a few drops. I felt if I didn't nurse myself back to life, I'd be dead by dawn. I wanted to get someone to get the shaman and have him end the journey, and even though I could hear others nearby, I was too weak, too near death, to call out to them. At 7:00 a.m., the visions stopped. The journey had lasted twelve brutal hours, short in Earth time—an eternity in experiential time.

Throughout the day, I was weak, and I swore to everyone, over and over, "I will never, ever, ever do this again."

At one point, I was very paranoid as I realized my entire DNA had been reprogrammed. I felt my hard drive was erased and I had a whole new operating system that had been installed by aliens. I felt that the whole thing was a vast conspiracy—my friends introducing me to the shaman, the literature was all propaganda—and now my previous life was annihilated, and I was one of *them.*

On Sunday was another session. I told my friends and the shaman what had happened and that I wasn't going to do it again, that I didn't have the strength. I was in a mind-space of weakness, of feeling myself small and incapable. It was pointed out to me that in fact I did survive, that the warrior in me did return home. I was indeed changed. I had numerous insights, which busted me out of old beliefs and habits and negative thinking. The treasures were indeed worth the horrific struggles. It was going to the Underworld, Experiencing the Supreme Ordeal, Resurrection, and Returning with the Elixir. The Joseph Campbell/Christopher Vogler mythic paradigm is so powerful because it expresses the real deal.

But I did survive, so I must have had the strength. And yet it was a terrifying journey and the most difficult thing I'd ever done in my life. Only a fool would sign up again. My theory is because I had stayed on a raw vegetable diet for two or three weeks before ingesting the plant medicine, the ayahuasca worked intensively and quickly through an empty stomach. (Hence little came up during the purging.) Even though I was one of the last people during the ceremony to ingest the medicine, I was one of the first to start to journey.

The shaman suggested I take a lesser dose if I wanted to do it again. But I didn't want to do it again! Never! I already had enough content to process for a lifetime.

But as I regained my strength and ate a real meal for the first time in weeks, my confidence was restored. It is a great privilege to be allowed even a glimpse of this multidimensional Universe peopled with gods, demons, fairies, spirits, ancestors, and mythological beasts. Everything described in myth and legend is real, and these creatures are only a sliver of the inhabitants who share the Universe in a parallel dimension. I realized that my ordinary consciousness is asleep, unaware, caught in addictive and habitual patterns. Ayahuasca blows the top off that and with a cosmic tough love takes you on an express train to the true nature of reality. She demands that you "up your game," inherit your birthright, and become all that you are in your own sacred and divine nature. Isn't that what we're all looking to do?

I knew I had to meet the challenge and ingest the healing medicine again. So—since it is all about "set and setting" and preparing your own mental state before journeying, I did my best to drop my self-generated image of weakness and simply go for it.

I realize that at least—as a filmmaker—I've picked the right medium. Words cannot describe what happened. You cannot "language" this experience. I know I sound certifiable, but I am not. I've never used language like Divine Child or Great Mother Ayahuasca before, but it seems appropriate to frame this experience.

For the four days I spent around the shaman and the other participants, there was an incredible feeling of love and acceptance. My mind is usually filled with judgments—judging everything in some way, separating myself from others. The main teaching is we are all part of the same thing. Our bodies do not end at our skin; they extend throughout the cosmos. We do not live on the Earth; we are the Earth. We are not separate and we will suffer until we realize this, at which time our true healing begins.

Part Two
The Third Journey

As a result of our desire to understand more about the dimensions that ayahuasca opened in us, my wife and I were invited to join my same shaman Don José Campos in Peru.

Shortly after our arrival, the shaman conducted a private ceremony to prepare us for the interview process. Since my body requires very little plant medicine to enter other dimensions, I took a cautionary small dose. My intention was to work on some health issues, so 90 percent of my journey focused on healing.

After about forty minutes, I started to have visions. Vast celestial hallways—what I recognized as the Halls of Healing—appeared in soft blues and violets. Columns rose to the clouded heavens. While I didn't see any "gods" or encounter any entities, this was certainly their domain.

About midway through the ceremony of *icaros* sung by Don José and additional songs by singer-guitarist Artur Mena Salas (a Peruvian recording artist), a tropical lightning and thunderstorm was invoked. A rush of wind blew through the circular space, which felt like a flock of spirits flying through. Then the gods began to play. Lightning struck, followed by crashes of thunder, coming closer and closer after the flash. The energy was phenomenal. A torrential downpour shook the trees that surrounded us.

At the climax of the storm, I had visions of entering a deep cellar. I did some deep breathing work to lift and remove black boxes one at a time. They were very heavy, even though I had discovered that by breathing I could lift them from the basement to the ground floor. I found I could do even more work if I synced the lifting with the thunderclaps and their release of energy. It felt like the storm was helping me cleanse.

After what seemed like hours of lifting boxes, I was pleased I had only one or two left to move. But then I discovered a secret cavern beneath the floor loaded with more black boxes! I understood this was content that I no longer needed and I could finally be free of. I hadn't the slightest desire to open a box to see what was inside. It was no value to me anymore. I only wanted to get rid of it now that I had my chance. So, breath after breath, like the broom scene from *The Sorcerer's Apprentice,* I lifted boxes until I was exhausted and there were no more.

At some point in the ceremony, I asked the plant teacher if I could see Buddhas and bodhisattvas, and for a moment, I felt sure they would appear, but then I got the message that, yes, I would see them, but not now because I wasn't ready. Fair enough.

Everyone else had already returned to normal consciousness an hour or two before me. (I've gotta try even smaller doses!) Several times when I opened my eyes, the shaman was sprinkling perfume water, trying to revive me, asking me "Are you back?" I said no, closed my eyes, and went back to work. At some point, feeling I had had enough, he gave me a lemon with salt to taste. In ten minutes, I came back, and I could walk around naturally.

Toward the end of the journey, I saw electric-green snake-like weavings that were unfolding very seductively to draw me in. Apprehensive at being annihilated by this emerald cosmic Cuisinart, I opened my eyes to stop it, then closed them, at which point the process would begin again. I needed to surrender to the visions and let them take me. The vision was simultaneously my vision, my body, and everything in the Universe and beyond: one energy, space and awareness mixing. Hard as it was, the plant medicine's main message was simply, "Let go," join consciousness. There is no annihilation; there is no beginning; there is no ending.

"Anatole"

"Anatole" is a gifted yoga teacher living in Charleston, South Carolina. He has been involved in a successful high-tech start-up company and has written several books that make technology more accessible to the general public. His report illustrates the way ayahuasca, called "Aya" in his report, "teaches." Like any teacher, Aya sometimes finds it necessary to repeat a lesson until it is understood. This was a first experience.

A very, very brief report. I don't want to write too much.

This was one of the most remarkable experiences in my life. One of the things the shaman seems to do is act as a guide, a very highly trained and experienced guide.

After a brief vision of lights and interconnecting lines, my mind kicked into overdrive, and I became very, very lucid and creative. I immediately solved a couple of long-standing personal problems. I lucidly and clearly saw the solutions to formerly intractable problems. The solutions were easy, simple, and clear. (Implementing them will require a lot of work, but I see the solutions clearly.)

I received many teachings, almost all of them verbal. The more important ones were repeated forcefully, several times, so I wouldn't forget.

At one point I asked Aya how to heal a health problem. I got three answers:

ANSWER 1: "Are you sure you really want to know? Here's what healing means." Followed by an explanation.

"Yes."

ANSWER 2: "Are you really, really sure? Here's what it means." The explanation was repeated.

"Yes."

ANSWER 3: "It [the healing process] would probably kill you [you are not strong enough]. So here's what you can do as an alternative. . . ." A detailed teaching followed.

The shaman impressed me tremendously. He struck me as the equivalent—in our culture—of a world-famous doctor or medical professional, a highly educated and gifted professional in his field. The complexity and subtlety [of the technology, psychology, learning] of this [discipline, field, arena] left me in awe.

The most surprising thing about the entheogen is how "practical" it is. I see why they call it a medicine.

I went in with very strong intent and clearly focused questions. The setting was superb and serious. I was told the dose was small.

I am reviewing the "teachings" and seeing if they hold up to scrutiny by my "daily" consciousness. So far, they seem to be valid and very accurate.

Total Darkness Retreat

Lindsey Vona

Lindsey Vona is a talented musician, graphic artist, and poet living in Northern California. With her permission, I've included a section of her report about experiences that resemble classic mystical descriptions and reports of entheogenic journeys. A major difference seems to be that while peak experiences aided by psychedelics last at best a few hours, Vona seems to have spent days in the unitive state. As with a proper use of psychedelics, set and setting were important variables in letting Vona come, on her own, into this state of consciousness and later to begin to integrate her new view of her identity into her life.

Vona spent two weeks in darkness at the Sierra Obscura Darkness Retreat Center. At its blog (go to www.sierraobscura.wordpress.com and click on "overview"), the center is described as "an optimal environment in which individuals enter into perpetual darkness, with all of their basic needs provided for, in support of self-realization." The stated optimal time period for these retreats is fourteen days, with two days post-retreat at the center for integration.

A Darkness Retreat Report

This is a detailed description of my retreat in total darkness for fourteen days at Sierra Obscura Darkness Retreat Center. Recently, I've been getting quite a few requests from friends in the community to share my experience, so I decided to go all out and offer a candid portrait of my journey through the abyss into self-realization.

During my retreat, I had my own bedroom and access to two full bathrooms and a large, comfortable, common space, all totally "en-darkened." Organic food and liquids were delivered, by way of a corridor and a series of doors to ensure no light leakage, at varying hours of day and night.

Food boxes were left on a table in the common space with a wooden number on it associated with the room.

Vona described the first eight days in detail, which included many other kinds of experiences. Her report of the second part of her retreat and her return to her normal life are included here. For her full report and more about her work, go to www.lindseyvona.com.

Around day nine, I felt like I was being teased right on the edge of ego death; it was very different than ayahuasca. The visuals in my meditations began to lessen, and my mind basically stopped for long stretches of time. I was awash with black nothing and the occasional passage of thoughts as I lay waiting for the next stages of internal changes.

Somewhere between day nine and day eleven is when I had my most profound opening into self-realization. I don't remember how long it lasted, but this is a fair description of what I remember. At one point in my meditation, my head opened and flooded with light. I watched and felt this quiet bliss and gladness take over and noticed that my body became pure vibration. I couldn't feel or relate to myself as physical anymore or as Lindsey in any way, and yet I was still myself, but it felt much more real than what we call waking life.

I was absorbed into this light, and this light became the entirety of space around me until I was only this giant, radiant light-filled void. I was real and home again and bigger than a trillion of our suns. In some way of seeing beyond having physical eyes, I looked down and saw the dots that were the earth and sun and solar system and thought of Lindsey. None of it was real. I was the only thing real. The material thing I once identified as and thought of as myself and my world was realized to be a full and total illusion, not even worth defining.

Words like *spiritual* and *Lindsey* and *Earth* flashed before my awareness of perfect peace and were realized as inconsequential, as though they never existed and were only beautiful idea-pictures already come and gone and dissolved back into my actual self of pure light. I zoomed down to Earth and saw Lindsey. It didn't make sense. I was a gigantic bigger-than-all-concept-of-universe radiant unending shimmering ball of light emanating perfect compassion forever without cause. Even now, as I write this, I am aware that it's total illusion and ultimately inconsequential. I am holding this paradox while sitting in physical space and time, not quite sure how to relate it to you at all, really.

The nature of reality is not what it seems. Even my experiences of perceiving the *maya,* of perceiving emptiness and suchness throughout my whole "life as Lindsey" as a spiritual seeker could not come close to this total absorption into self-remembering perfection of total . . . er . . . uh . . . beyond words and description annihilation into truth-light.

During this absorption into light, I also realized that I was able to sit on the rug of my room as a perfected vibrational entity, not as "Lindsey," but as my true self, a vibration of perfect Buddha nature. My best metaphor for this is that we are like living, vibrating, nonphysical Tanka paintings. We're already perfected and beyond even concepts of enlightenment or self-realization, and perfectly realized. We've just forgotten, and rightly so, because these mind-body-desire mechanisms are not us, even though they are. This life is a shadow in a great memory probably already forgotten by unending intelligent light.

I was able to easily shift between my awareness of self as this great unending light and my awareness as this vibrating, perfectly realized Buddha, nonphysical self for what felt like forever. I think this realization state lasted several days while in the dark. All fear of death was completely annihilated in this realization. All relationship to suffering or suffering over the suffering of others at this time was not even a laughable possibility. Identification was futile. I was happy to die into this light forever. Part of me wanted to die. Part of me very much did not want to come back into this room, this body-thing as Lindsey. It didn't make sense, and yet it happened and here I am. I didn't think about my parents or whether they would miss me if I let myself get completely absorbed in the truth of what I am because I knew that ultimately they are the exact same thing and that eventually, whether in this "lifetime story" or at the time of "death," we pretty much all remember because we already are it. I guess I can't really know what is true for you or "anyone," except that you are me, and this life is not at all what it seems.

This idea of physicality is still just a concept, and we have very sophisticated sciences now that describe this process of liberation through all of these body energy centers, and it's funny that you can get back to yourself through this map called a body, but ultimately it is the false identification. What a joke!

It is very much a dream-thought radiating from the one eternal emanation, which is also you, right now, beyond the husk of your worldly identity. The earth herself is a dream and is dreaming, and we are all asleep in it right now. Even though I've had this realization, right now, for the most part, I am sleeping because the dense physical plane is the world of attachment and desire, and ultimately, I am a vibration shapeshifting back and forth between image-vibration and perfect eternal light and identification with the physical, which isn't really physical, even though it seems so real.

This realization completely annihilated my need to "work on myself" in the way I had been during the previous abyss moments of the retreat. I didn't need to feel blissful anymore or have any particular experience or have an identity that I had sculpted well enough to get what I want out of this "life" from you or anyone or any "world." All that was spoiled, and I was free from all fear or notion of death and still am . . . in this moment. It is funny. Right now I am excited about life as well as death, but that's only partially true because I'm right here and life and death are only concepts. It is a paradox.

Amidst this realization as I came back into this husk of illusion sweet self, it occurred to me that perfecting human love will do nicely for now, that I am happy to break open into the depth of love with you in this lifetime and excited for the challenges to come in the hopes that I can maintain these perceptions enough in my awareness to live more gracefully in the truth of the light that we are sharing here together.

A few abyss moments after this, Danielle came downstairs, and we spoke, and she lit a candle next to my bed.

The first time I saw the physical apparition of light in fourteen days, I saw the true nature of reality, this time with human eyes. I could only look at *her* for a few seconds, and then I started shaking and crying and needed the candle to be put out for a while as I integrated what I saw.

Then I went upstairs to be with Paskal and the Sierra Obscura team near the fireplace, the blank slate of my awareness free of all concepts. I saw light dancing everywhere and the unborn world radiating and perfecting itself in presence. A thought arose in my mind, and I saw how its flash across the screen of awareness literally bent reality around me; a projected thought is a distorted lens that conditions this mind-world. Sitting as source, seeing everyone in their God-self-hood by candlelight, I cried and silently noticed how easily the psychic energies from the minds around me danced and played together, refracting off of the screen. Later that evening, I called Rigzin, who I knew had been sending us prayers for the entire retreat, wanting to share the depth of my gratitude from that pure place with her and with the whole team who served us for those two weeks.

The next morning, with sunglasses on, Danielle took me for a drive along a beautiful tree-lined road on our way into downtown Nevada City. The light was so mesmerizing, and it was hard to really talk; I just wanted to look at everything.

As I saw this "world" again, I could barely contain my laughter at how unreal it seemed but tried to hold it together in the restaurant.

This retreat was by far the most profoundly important investment I have ever made in this sweet dream thing I now humbly, temporarily, call myself. I am slowly coming back into my "life" and integrating. Although I have been mainly silent these last few days, I can feel the conditioned world of concepts and desires dancing again, although without as much power over me as it once had. I am excited that my body/mind is now naturally waking up early and wanting to meditate right away. I understand that many, many beings on this planet, including possibly you, have died into this perfect state of self-realization. After all, it is what we are.

I can't really know for sure how my life will unfold from here. All I know for sure is that I am perfect god light temporarily dreaming Lindsey and World and none of this happened or is real at all. Under this husk of temporarily arising selfish thoughts, preferences, conditions, images, attachments, and desires, I am a vibration of pure compassion, which is being itself, already liberated, never born, never died, traversing the great void that holds each of us, whether as gods or humans, as my teacher Maniko says, more perfectly than any living element. I'm filled with emptiness and quiet gladness and gratitude at having an opportunity to take this on alone in the dark, in comfort, with so many beings, physical and nonphysical, supporting me.

21
BEHAVORIAL CHANGES AFTER PSYCHEDELIC THERAPY
Lasting Results of High-Dose Single Sessions

Sixty-seven participants (forty-four men and twenty-three women) were given LSD, mescaline, or a combination of the two for a guided psychedelic session. Before and after that session, they met with a therapist as part of a course of therapy or personal exploration. (Other aspects of this study have been discussed in more detail in chapter 8.) The sessions were run by the staff (myself included) of the International Foundation for Advanced Study in Menlo Park in 1962 and 1963 along the lines of sessions described in full in chapters 1 and 2.

Six to nine months later, the participants were asked what had changed in their lives. Their answers were recorded as the following.

More: Engaging in this behavior more intensely or more frequently than before the therapy.

Less: Engaging in this behavior less intensely or less frequently than before the therapy.

Same: Engaging in this behavior as often as before or not at all.

More-extensive comments by the participants were written down during the interview. Three hundred and thirty-two questions were grouped in eighteen categories. The level of significance for each item was calculated using a sign test.*

The original study, listing the total scores for each question as well as additional comments by participants and more-extensive predictions and analyses, is available online.†

What follows is a brief discussion of most of the highly significant items in each of the eighteen categories, with some predictions about the likely direction and extent of specific changes and some representative comments to clarify and amplify the answers. One complete table (Table 21.1) on page 288 is included to show how all of the data for each category were displayed.

The findings were grouped into six areas:

- Personal habits
- Work and interpersonal relations
- Cultural and creative activities
- Activities involving family members
- Subjective activities
- Physical functioning and health

Personal Habits

It was predicted that participants would become more inner-directed and spend less time doing things just to please or impress others. It was expected that they would be less anxious about being orderly.

Over 50 percent of the sample reported changes in personal orderliness.

---

*A sign test is simply a way of determining if the difference between those who answer more (+) or less (−) is a real difference and not just chance.

†The study was conducted under the auspices of the International Foundation for Advanced Study in Menlo Park, California, under a New Drug Investigational License from the U.S. Food and Drug Administration. This research was carried out during the tenure of my predoctorial fellowship #5 F1 MH-16,900 from the U.S. National Institute of Mental Health.

Representative of those who had become less orderly were comments such as "Before, I was orderly because I was afraid of what others thought" and "Doesn't seem to be so important anymore." Those who had become more orderly made comments such as "Things seem to fall into place more easily" and "Bought vacuum cleaner."

A significant number of men improved their appearance ($p < .01$),* wore brighter colors ($p < .01$), and became more stylish ($p = .01$). Both men ($p < .01$) and women ($p = .01$) reported more interest in household decoration, making comments such as "Now I buy flowers for the house, haven't for years" and "Having a ball using what I have, silly nightlight for bathroom, split big rug in half . . . do things with more pleasure."

It was predicted that changes in eating habits would include an increased enjoyment of the social side of eating and cooking as well as in the pleasure of eating. It was expected that drinking problems would be ameliorated.

The most widespread changes were increased appreciation for fine cooking ($p < .01$), increased interest in cooking ($p = .05$), and, to a lesser degree, an interest in unusual foods ($p = .10$). Individual reports included less interest in sweets and less compulsive eating. Comments included, "No longer crave potato chips," "Not the need for the candy bar now," and "I was a

---

*A brief explanation for readers who have no idea how statistics are used in psychology: Any measurement is rated against how likely it is that the same result would happen by chance. The p means probability. The number following the p is how far from chance the actual result is. In psychology, if your data would happen by chance one out of ten times (written as $p = .10$), you can call it a trend or a tendency or an inclination. If it would happen by chance five times out of one hundred ($p = .05$), you can call it "significant." That means it probably is really so. If it would happen by chance only one time in one hundred ($p = .01$), you do a little dance and thank the gods because that is *very* significant. There aren't many results in psychology better than that.

In this research, however, the data were often overwhelmingly better than ($p = .01$): sometimes one in one thousand ($p = .001$), one in ten thousand ($p = .0001$), or greater. There is almost no other research on any kind of psychotherapy that makes such a strong showing. To keep the data from being criticized as unlikely or impossible, I recorded all results more likely to be real above the one in one hundred chance level as ($p < .01$). There are many such instances in the following pages because, in almost every category, some findings were that strong.

compulsive eater when I was unhappy. I guess I've stopped now." One participant reported, "Melon allergy over." (As mentioned earlier, in chapter 4, Dr. Andrew Weil has written about overcoming a severe cat allergy during a psychedelic session. His proposal to evaluate psychedelic therapy for allergy relief has not yet been acted on.)

Half the sample (48 percent) reported changes in their drinking pattern. Those drinking less said, "Quit entirely. Before, I would have three drinks or more before dinner," "I used to think that drinking would ease tension; I'm not fooled now," "Drink now because I enjoy it. Before I drank to get drunk," and "I don't care for wine since LSD. On skid row I was a wino. I was drinking up to LSD." (*Note:* Three years later, this last participant still did not drink.)

Those drinking more said, "Didn't drink at all before; I had a fear of losing control," and "Apt to have a sherry before dinner. . . . Mother [still] thinks social drinking leads to alcoholism." Twice as many subjects reported drinking less than those reporting drinking more. Most of those who drank more, mostly men, went from abstention to moderate social drinking.

Work and Interpersonal Relations

Since one aim in undertaking psychedelic therapy is to gain information about one's self and one's relationships, changes were expected in the value placed on work and the degree of cooperation with and interest in other people.

Well over two-thirds of the sample reported major changes in their work pattern. The job itself was easier ($p < .01$), more work was done ($p < .01$), with more energy ($p < .01$) and more initiative ($p < .01$). Interest in the job increased slightly overall ($p = .10$). However, a number of people reported less interest, reflecting changing priorities. Comments included, "Last week I demoted myself. I asked not to be boss," "More inclined to study and read than to get ahead financially," and "Before, there was a compulsion to get somewhere, be a vice president. . . . That feeling is gone."

For most, cooperation increased ($p < .01$), as did decisiveness ($p < .01$), and confidence in one's decisions ($p < .01$). Some subjects found it more difficult to make decisions ($p < .01$), and some procrastinated more ($p < .01$). Respect for coworkers ($p < .01$) and listening to them ($p < .01$) increased. Listening to superiors went up significantly ($p < .01$).

As for interpersonal relations, 87 percent of the sample reported being closer to others ($p < .01$). Subjects reported having more friends at work ($p < .01$) and outside of work ($p < .01$), feeling closer and easier with them ($p < .01$), less anxious ($p < .01$), and less distant ($p < .01$). They spent more time talking with others ($p < .01$), and taking part in activities ($p < .01$). They spoke more frankly ($p < .01$), and more tactfully ($p < .01$), and had a heightened interest in talking with others ($p < .01$), and being with others ($p < .01$). They enjoyed parties more ($p < .01$), liked pets more ($p < .01$), spent more time in nature ($p < .01$), and felt more positively about nature in general ($p < .01$) and flowers in particular ($p < .01$).

Across the entire sample, psychedelic therapy clearly had a pervasive positive effect on work and social intimacy.

Cultural and Creative Activities

As psychedelic experience almost always heightens awareness of music, more interest in music was expected. Any increase in reading would probably be in psychology, consciousness, or spirituality.

These predictions were borne out. More time was spent listening to music ($p < .01$). Subjects bought new, higher-quality audio equipment ($p < .01$), and listened more to classical music ($p < .01$). Over 70 percent of the subjects read more ($p < .01$), especially on religion ($p < .01$), ethics ($p < .01$), mysticism ($p < .01$), philosophy ($p < .01$), and psychology ($p < .01$). They watched television less ($p < .01$). While this may reflect interviewer bias, watching less television was considered healthier.

Since participants were encouraged to explore their spiritual orientation and religious background, considerable changes in related behaviors were expected. Many changes were highly significant, the most frequent—reported by more than two-thirds of the participants—being greater tolerance ($p < .01$) and more belief in a higher power ($p < .01$). There was little change in church attendance. However, more religious books were read ($p < .01$), there was greater interest in religious services ($p < .01$) and talking about religious subjects ($p < .01$). There was more feeling for religious music ($p < .01$). Subjects prayed more often ($p < .01$). Comments included, "I have been brought closer to God and the concept of the supernatural. The teachings of Christ are very definite now," "More belief now than ever, but I'm uncertain as well," "Radical change. Now I feel it," and "I believe in a unitive spirit. God is up there; God is down here."

While psychedelic use still causes ripples throughout the art world, the only significant change in creative activities was greater enjoyment of a musical instrument ($p < .01$). Some people reported less interest in prior creative pursuits. Comments included, "Taking less pictures now. I don't feel it is as important to have things recorded," and "Writing is an escape valve. I guess much of my love was repressed and writing got rid of sadness, frustration, and desires." There were changes in painting ($p = .01$). Participants said, "Completely new. I literally learned to hold the brush," "I become more of a colorist. Less interest in pure drawing. Harmony of color is more important," and "From naturalism to abstraction (mandala) as a device for focusing."

It may be that the shifts reported, duplicated in other studies, are manifestations of increased well-being. A 1964 study by Savage and others[1] reported decreased anxiety for 68 percent of the forty-nine patients at six to twelve months after psychedelic therapy. A 1964 study of psychedelic therapy by Downing and Wygant[2] reported 80 percent of the subjects felt greater personal security.

Activities Involving Family Members

Part of the research explored emotional responsiveness in a range of intimate relationships: first in general, then within the family and in marriage, and finally in sexual behavior. Given prior findings, greater emotional openness and responsiveness were likely.

TABLE 21.1. PERCENTAGE, SIGNIFICANCE LEVEL, AND DIRECTION OF CHANGES IN EMOTIONAL RESPONSES— BEHAVIORAL CHANGE INTERVIEWS

(Total = 67: 44 men, 23 women)[3]

Symbols: + = more or more frequently; − = less or less frequently;
  * = statistically inappropriate to assess; ns = not significant

Title of Item	Percent Changed	Percent Level of Significance			Direction of Change
		Total	Men	Women	
General level of responsiveness	88	< .01	< .01	< .01	+
Aggressive responses:					
Verbal	84	ns	ns	ns	*
Sarcasm	67	< .01	< .01	< .01	−
Physical	31	ns	ns	ns	*
By letter	19	ns	ns	ns	*
Loving behavior:					
Verbal	88	< .01	< .01	< .01	+
Physical	78	< .01	< .01	< .01	+
By letter	31	.01	ns	.10	+
Friendly behavior:					
Verbal	84	< .01	< .01	< .01	+
Physical	69	< .01	< .01	< .01	+
By letter	30	< .01	.05	.10	+
Friendships:					
Renewed	37	< .01	< .01	ns	+
Let lapse	36	.10	ns	ns	+
New	57	< .01	< .01	< .01	+
Letter writing	34	ns	ns	ns	*
Takes orders (submissive)	69	.10	.05	ns	+

Title of Item	Percent Changed	Percent Level of Significance			Direction of Change
		Total	Men	Women	
Leads or controls (dominant):					
At work	57	.05	.10	ns	+
At home	54	.10	ns	.10	+
In social groups	49	ns	ns	.10	+
Self-confidence:					
In beliefs	87	< .01	< .01	< .01	+
In decisions	85	< .01	< .01	< .01	+
In actions	87	< .01	< .01	< .01	+
React differently when in error					
Yes or no	61	.10	ns	ns	+ (Yes)
Advice:					
Give it	58	ns	ns	ns	*
Seek it	54	ns	ns	ns	*
Accept it	49	< .01	.01	ns	+
In argument:					
Dogmatic	66	< .01	< .01	.10	−
Excitable	70	< .01	< .01	ns	−
Flexible	76	< .01	< .01	< .01	+
Stubborn	57	< .01	< .01	.10	−
Other behavior					
Singing	36	< .01	< .01	.01	+
Whistling	25	< .01	< .01	.05	+

Table 21.1 is an illustration of how each group of results was presented in the full report of the study. It was picked because it records significant changes in such a large percentage of the sample. The most pervasive changes were heightened responsiveness ($p < .01$), a more loving expressiveness physically ($p < .01$) and verbally ($p < .01$), and greater friendliness ($p < .01$). Participants had greater confidence in their beliefs

(p < .01), decisions (p < .01), and actions (p < .01). They were both more and less aggressive, but less sarcastic (p < .01). Men were more willing to accept advice (p < .01). In arguments, both men and women were less dogmatic (p < .01), excitable (p < .01), and stubborn (p < .01) as well as more flexible (p < .01). There was more singing (p < .01) and whistling (p < .01), most probably brought on by feeling good more often.

Self-confidence increased for almost everyone (p < .01). Except for four people who reported decreases, it seemed that these subjects were more willing to feel their feelings, better able to be angry, and more likely to love. Freer to be aggressive, they were also more open to affection. In short, they appeared to be more social and more vital.

The emotional expansiveness and the increased openness and friendships seen in Table 21.1 did not carry over as fully to relationships within families. There were fewer changes in those relationships than had been expected. These adults did get along better with their parents (p = .01). There were significant shifts in sharing ideas (p < .01), spending time with family members (p < .01), and getting along with siblings as well (p < .01). More participants shifted their behavior toward their children. More time was spent teaching (p < .01), playing (p < .01), reading (p < .01), talking (p < .01), and caring for them (p < .01). Overall, parents and children got along better (p < .01).

Individual changes with a family member were sometimes sizable. One participant, speaking of his father, said, "First time we've been able to talk to each other." Another said, "Under LSD I understood something about my oldest child and now we get along better."

Marriage (Married Subjects Only)

Marriage, the most long-term and intimate relationship, is also one of the most fragile. Spouses were often worried when told that their partner was undertaking psychedelic therapy. We were unsure if marriages would be strengthened or shattered by insights obtained during the course of therapy.

The question that showed the greatest amount of change of any item in the entire interview (92 percent) was the question of marital satisfaction. Every person but two felt that his or her marriage was more satisfactory. And one of those two felt that his marriage had improved, adding, "But I'm less satisfied because I see more possibilities for improvement." Besides the overwhelming amount of improved satisfaction ($p < .01$), communication improved ($p < .01$), as did wishing to please one's spouse ($p < 01$). Quarrels, as did occur, were shorter ($p < .01$), and problems were discussed sooner ($p < .01$). More activities ($p < .01$) and interests were shared ($p < .01$). Over half the sample with spouses (58 percent) had a partner who also had psychedelic therapy, likely a contributing factor for these pervasive positive changes.

Sexual Patterns

Given the greater degree of martial satisfaction, one might predict an equal rise in sexual satisfaction. Most of the changes reported, while not highly significant, were in the predicted direction. For women, sex was seen as more important ($p = .05$) and more central to the relationship ($p = .05$); for men, less so. Both sexes reported that sexual excitement increased ($p = .01$) and reported significantly more satisfaction with intercourse ($p < .01$), which included more variation ($p < .01$). Men reported improved performance ($p < .01$). For men, masturbation decreased ($p < .01$) and was less satisfying ($p = .05$). Both sexes reported more frequent and satisfying kissing and petting ($p < .01$).

While the absolute numbers of individuals whose sexual behavior shifted were not as high as in some other areas, individual comments are illustrative of the importance of some of the changes. Some who reported sexuality to be more important said, "Is changed greatly, and changed for the better. A happy natural instinct for it now," "For the first time in my life, I'm having sexual feelings," and "I never understood how much pleasure was possible in sex." Some who found sexuality less important said, "Previous to LSD, to my mind, sex was important as a problem. Now it is not," "Before LSD, it was beautiful but all else was a mess. Now I realize that it is not so central," and "Used to feel put upon. Now it's enjoyment."

While interest in sex both increased and diminished, most of the comments were about having less anxiety and more pleasure. While the number of women reporting more orgasms was not statistically significant, of the nine women who did report this, seven of their husbands had done psychedelic therapy. The temptation to speculate on this finding has been resisted.

Two subjects reported they had given up sexual behavior. Both gave as reasons their own accelerated spiritual development. However, to their interviewers, neither appeared to be functioning at the level of those explanations. It appeared, instead, that they used the therapy to reinforce defensive structures rather than coming to terms with real difficulties in their sexual adjustment.

Overall, there is clear evidence that the often-reported emotional openness that occurs during well-managed psychedelic therapy was true for this group and that this openness was retained. It is seen in their relationships from the more formal to the most intimate.

Subjective Activities

The list of subjective activities includes:

Material values
Introspective activities
Fears
Dreams

Material Values

The popular and even the pseudo-professional literature of the sixties abounds with how often psychedelic use saps the ambition and denigrates the work ethic, often quoting Leary's rallying cry of "Turn on, tune in, drop out." However, in the study group, men's earnings actually increased ($p = .05$). There was significantly less concern among men over status ($p < .01$), respect from coworkers ($p < .05$), respect from others in general ($p < .05$), and more interest overall in finding new work ($p < .01$). Women's ambition increased ($p = .05$), showing less interest in income, per se, but more in other job satisfaction.

This population may be less interested in materialism, but more interested in productive and satisfying work.

Introspective Activities

Psychedelic therapy so stresses the value of introspection that it would be surprising if there were not significant shifts toward these activities. The participants spent more time in introspection ($p < .01$), self-analysis ($p < .01$), and meditation ($p < .01$). Of those joining outside groups, men gravitated toward therapy ($p = .01$), while women joined religious groups ($p = .10$).

Fears

Overall, fears decreased more than they increased in every category. There were twenty-three reports of increased fears and 156 reports of decreases ($p < .01$). Because the therapy regimen did not focus on fears or attempt to interpret them when they arose, this result is intriguing. As self-concept and self-awareness showed dramatic increases, one would predict that specific fears, especially phobias, would diminish. In fact, fear of insects ($p < .01$), animals ($p = .01$), being alone in darkness ($p = .05$), and snakes ($p = .10$) diminished. Fears of heights, enclosed places, and falling were unchanged, but may have been rare in the sample. For some people, their reduced fears were important. One participant stated, "Less fear of heights. Feeling is still there, but I can control it now." In psychedelic therapy, individuals often experience their identity to be beyond their physical body. Perhaps this is why the fear of death was the fear most often cited as having decreased ($p < .01$).

Dreams

When people become more introspective and more interested in their own inner processes, their actual dream life may become richer or they may notice and recall their dreams more easily.

For whatever cause, in the study population, every aspect of their dreams showed significant increases except length. Different facets of increased dream activity are illustrated by the following representative comments.

Frequency ($p < .01$): "Much more. No dreams for several years prior to LSD session," "Didn't dream at all before LSD. Now I dream."

Length: "Seems longer now, more happens"; "Quick and to the point. Used to be involved and go on and on."

Amount in color ($p < .01$): "Color now. No color before"; "Hadn't dreamed in color before LSD."

In addition, dreams were more intense ($p < .01$), more meaningful ($p < .01$), remembered more often ($p < .01$), and enjoyed more ($p < .01$). For some, dreams were less disturbing. Comments included, "Not scared anymore," "Dreams instead of nightmares," and "Less pain, fewer nightmares."

In summation, the subjects reported a richer, more meaningful, and less disturbing dream life.

Physical Functioning and Health

The therapy staff predicted that physical health would improve alongside mental health.

Physical Functioning

Only about one-quarter of the sample reported changes in any physical activity. Activities that did change, however, increased, including walking ($p = .01$), hiking ($p = .05$), participating in sports ($p = .01$), dancing ($p = .10$), bike riding ($p = .10$), and gardening ($p < .01$). Psychedelic therapy, when it affected physical activities, did so in a healthy direction. The only activity that decreased was hunting ($p = .01$), a change probably more philosophical than physical.

Health

Most subjects were in moderate to good health prior to entering the program, and most changes reported were improvements. Of the sample, 76 percent felt better after exercise ($p < .01$), and smaller percentages experience less fatigue in general ($p < .01$), fewer headaches ($p < .01$), and less boredom ($p < .01$). Participants reported improved vision ($p < .01$), hearing ($p = 10$), smell ($p = .01$), taste ($p = .01$), and touch ($p = 01$). Some slept less ($p = .10$), used fewer medications, ($p = .05$), and had fewer pains or complaints in general (p < .01). Comments included, "No more tranquilizers," and "I had a pain in my leg. X-ray showed arthritis. When I was upset it became more painful. Since LSD the pain has been eliminated entirely." Some subjects reported new complaints, many of which seem to be psychosomatic in origin.

The increases in physical activities and improved health appeared to be more from an indirect consequence of establishing a more workable psychological equilibrium than from any direct effect from the psychedelic therapy itself.

Conclusions

It can be seen, from this lengthy and somewhat exhaustive presentation of results, that changes in this group of sixty-seven people were numerous, extensive, positive, and lasting. It can be concluded that this therapeutic protocol of short duration, at least with this moderately healthy population, was beneficial. That this therapy is not yet legally available to the general population is unfortunate.

A QUESTIONNAIRE STUDY OF PSYCHEDELIC EXPERIENCES

WILLIS HARMAN, Ph.D., and
JAMES FADIMAN, Ph.D.

From the beginning, reports about the effectiveness or dangers of psychedelic experience relied on individual reports as their primary source of data. This was supplemented with opinions based on varying amounts of knowledge, from none (most common) to considerable knowledge based on experience (rare). What was missing was a straightforward look at the self-reports of a large number of people who had been given a psychedelic under similar conditions and who were long enough away from the experience to realistically evaluate it.

The following questionnaire was given to provide answers to a few basic questions. It does not offer any interpretations of the results. Because almost every item reported would test as statistically significant (a term that means it is unlikely one would get the same results by chance), that statistical measurement was not used here. Because of the protracted lull in legal research, we do not have similar reports from current psychedelic therapists. I spoke with one nonlegal therapist, however, who indicated, considering his own experience with over one thousand clients, that these results were in line with his own perceptions. As the number of legal studies increases, we can hope for a replication of this kind of questionnaire research in the future.

Questionnaire Study of the Psychedelic Experience

The following is a brief summary report* on the results of a questionnaire sent to the first 113 clients of the International Foundation for Advanced Study in Menlo Park, California, and to forty nonpaying, experimental subjects who had single LSD sessions at the same location under similar conditions. Of these, ninety-three patients (82 percent) and twenty-six non-patients (65 percent) returned completed questionnaires.

The treatment of the patients in this report was similar to the treatment described in chapters 1 and 2.[1] Preparation lasting approximately one month preceded the LSD session. Doses were moderately high (200–400 micrograms of LSD with an additional 200–400 milligrams of mescaline when deemed necessary). The groups of volunteer subjects were not strictly comparable, since in addition to the selective factors operating for the two groups, the non-patient group in general received less preparation and lower doses.

The questionnaire was patterned after one used in a similar study.[2] It consisted of seventy-five statements wherein the subject was asked to rate his or her level of agreement with the statements: 0 (not at all), 1 (a little), 2 (quite a bit), 3 (very much). Additional questions requested subjective reports on particular aspects of the experience (e.g., impression of preparation and atmosphere, most meaningful insight).

Summary of Results

In overall summary, the single most significant figure is perhaps the percentage of respondents who claimed "quite a bit" or "very much" for lasting benefits (83 percent). The claimed improvement rate rises from 76 percent at one to three months after the single LSD session to 85 percent

---

*This chapter consists of an edited version of a longer report with the same title that was never published but was referred to by others in the literature.

after twelve months or more have elapsed since the session. The most commonly reported benefits include an increase in the ability to love (78 percent), to handle hostility (69 percent), to communicate (69 percent), and to understand self and others (88 percent); other changes included improved interpersonal relations (72 percent), decreased anxiety (66 percent), increased self-esteem (71 percent), and a new way of looking at the world (83 percent). Of particular interest is a high correlation of 0.91 between "greater awareness of a higher power, or ultimate reality" and "claimed permanent benefit.

As regards negative responses, none of the experimental volunteers and only one patient felt that they had been harmed mentally. (By the time a year had elapsed since his session, that one patient had revised his negative opinion.) Immediately after the LSD session, 24 percent found that daydreaming and introspection "interfere with getting things done"; that fell to 11 percent after one year. Problems within the marital relationship not previously present were reported by 27 percent of non-patients and 16 percent of patients.

In the following tables, items marked with an * are the percentages based on the number of respondents who answered this question, because some items, such as those about marriage or work, were not applicable for everyone.

I. Sex Differences

One question was whether there were significant differences in response to the LSD according to sex. The figures given below are percentages of the total group of clients whose first LSD session had been at least three months prior to the filling out of the questionnaire and who marked each statement either "I agree with the statement very much" or "I agree quite a bit" (3 or 2, according to the questionnaire instructions). Three percentages are given for each item, in columns marked **M** (men), **W** (women), and **T** group (total). There were many differences, some statistically significant, but none that seemed important clinically. There is no later research that has looked at or found major differences between how men and women respond to specific psychedelics.

Table 22.1. Looking back on your LSD experience, how does it look to you now?

	M	W	T
A very pleasant experience	75	85	82
A very unpleasant experience	38	29	34
A very confusing experience	27	41	34
Something I want to try again	82	94	88
An experience of physical discomfort and illness	9	24	15
An experience of great beauty	82	79	81
Greater awareness of reality	88	94	91
Feel it was of lasting benefit to me	85	85	85
Gave me great understanding of myself and others	82	88	85
Greatest thing that ever happened to me	82	74	78
A transcendental experience, beyond my usual comprehension	85	82	84
A religious experience	82	88	85
A pleasant memory, but nothing more	0	0	0
An experience of insanity	24	20	22
Did me harm mentally	3	0	1
A very disappointing experience	3	0	1

Table 22.2. How were you, or what were you left with, after the LSD experience?

	M	W	T
A new way of looking at the world	88	82	85
A sense of futility and emptiness	11	7	9
A greater understanding of the importance and meaning of human relationships	85	85	85
A new understanding of beauty and art	59	68	63
A new understanding of music	68	71	69

(Table 22.2 *continued*)	M	W	T
A greater awareness of God, or a Higher Power, or an Ultimate Reality	91	91	91
A sense of greater regard for the welfare and comfort of others	77	79	78
A frightening feeling that I might go crazy or lose control at any time	9	9	9
A feeling that I "missed the boat" or somehow failed to get out of the experience what was potentially there	35	29	32
Beneficial changes noticed by the person closest to me	62	68	65
Improved ability to communicate with others	71	71	71
Greater tolerance of others whose opinions, preferences, habits, and attitudes differ from mine	71	77	74
Deeper understanding of others	77	85	81
More sensitivity to the feelings of others, even when not expressed	68	71	69
Increased reliance on my own values and judgment, less dependence on others' opinions	65	88	77
Increased interest in universal concepts (e.g., the meaning of life, my place in relation to the rest of life)	85	91	88
More tendency to view such matters as telepathy, reincarnation, spiritualism, foreseeing the future (clairvoyantly or in dreams), as possibilities warranting investigation	74	83	78
Introduced some problems in relationships that were not present before	26	38	32
*Improved relationship with wife or husband	66	70	67
*Problems within the marriage relationship that were not present before	21	18	20

II. Effect of Time

We were interested if the effects of the LSD session tended to "wear off" and whether the answers would differ depending on the length of time since the session. Percentages are presented from participants who fit into four time frames: **A** (less than three months since the LSD session; $n = 21$), **B** (3–6 months; $n = 26$), **C** (6–12 months; $n = 19$), and **D** (over 12 months; $n = 27$).

Table 22.3. How were you, or what were you left with, after the LSD experience?

	A	B	C	D
A new way of looking at the world	75	88	72	92
A greater understanding of the importance and meaning of human relationships	80	81	78	88
A greater awareness of God, or a Higher Power, or an Ultimate Reality	60	92	89	92
More tendency toward feelings of depression	5	8	17	12
More intense swings in feelings from "high" to "low"	20	23	50	29
More frequent and persistent feelings of happiness	55	81	72	83
More ability to handle hostility creatively and get over it	55	73	72	75
More ability to love in general	75	81	83	75
Generally decreased anxiety	55	65	72	71
More ability to relax and be myself	60	77	67	75
Increased self-esteem, higher evaluation of myself	60	69	78	79
Frequent or persistent feelings that might be described as wonderment at the miracle of Being	55	65	72	83

Table 22.4. What changes in attitudes and behavior do you feel have occurred directly as a result of your LSD experience?

	A	B	C	D
*Generally improved relations with persons I work and live with	74	73	95	63
*Improved relations with superiors at work	20	64	67	53
*Improved relations with subordinates at work	40	50	73	47
Seem to have more energy	40	38	61	54
Find decision-making easier	50	62	72	71
Find I do more daydreaming and introspection, which interferes with getting things done	20	15	17	4
*Increased effectiveness in my work	35	48	50	64
*More dissatisfaction with my present work	15	21	24	23
*Feel I am of more value to my employer	37	62	58	71
New freedom from old habit patterns	40	58	50	58

III. Outstanding Event or Insight

The answers to the question "What single event or insight, if any, during the LSD experience do you consider to have been of greatest meaning to you?" are of sufficient interest to be worth summarizing briefly. (The actual number of people responding is used here, not a percentage.)

Table 22.5. Outstanding Events or Insights

Answers	Number of Respondents
Experiencing an underlying reality, a sense of oneness with all of life, of unity and purpose, of love, of the presence of a Higher Power	53
Discovering that I have the necessary resources to solve my problems, that answers can come from within; coming to a deeper understanding of my own personal dynamics	20
Coming to understand the meaning of forgiveness and acceptance	9
Insight into my relationships with other people	7
Seeing the essential simplicity of life, the miracle of just Being, that there is nothing to fear	6
Realization of how much my own outlook has been restricted	2
Experiencing music in a new way	2
Realization of the vastness of inner space, that there is much yet to explore	5
Miscellaneous	5
No particular insight	10

LAST WORDS

When you publish a book, your editor becomes your most knowledgeable supporter and critic. My editor, Anne Dillon, said that the readers of this book needed a few final words to pull it all together.

I agreed with her, in part because this book includes so many different uses of psychedelics and also because I had some loose ends left to discuss. I've described the positive trends in research, personal use, and lowered legal restrictions. Those trends continue: more countries are establishing clean-needle clinics for heroin users, more states are voting on compassionate medical use of marijuana, and more research is being published on marijuana's varied healing properties. Also, marijuana growers in Oakland, California, organized a union and joined the Teamsters, which is about as mainstream as you can get.

Some of what you've read in this book has been presented by me at conferences, heard on podcasts, and distributed via a few websites, to which I've gotten a variety of responses, some of which have been gratifying, others emotionally disturbing. Most upsetting for me are stories of people damaged by psychedelics misused, like this one: "When I was seventeen, I was at a keg party with my best friend. He set his drink down and went to the bathroom. During that time, someone dropped a massive dose of LSD in his drink. To cut to the chase, he is in a state mental hospital to this day. I am now forty-eight. He was a 4.0 student, very popular, and one of the nicest people that God put on this planet."

In a more perfect world, that tragic outcome could have been avoided had there been experienced people available to intercede. Now, at least, at concerts, at festivals, and as best exemplified at Burning Man, there are well-trained individuals, with and without the right degrees, to assist people who have taken psychedelics and become disoriented as a result. Most of these disoriented individuals emerge from the experience, not only undamaged, but also healthier and more prudent than before their crisis.

The fact that we, as a nation, have made it highly unlikely that people can get this kind of training as part of a psychology, medical, or nursing degree has served no one. I've become part of a movement to alert teenagers and younger people that "dosing" someone—giving them a dose of a psychedelic (or any drug) without their knowledge—is as morally repugnant as rape or physical assault.

People often ask me to give them a psychedelic or entheogenic session or connect them with a guide. As an author and a researcher, I need to be—and I am—totally law abiding; thus I am not able to provide that service. I hope that will change and that soon I will be able to fulfill these requests, but that day has not yet come. There is, however, and has been for some time, a quiet underground of guides, each of them actively working with clients. If and when the barriers come down, this Guild of Guides is ready to move aboveground and continue their work. Clandestine out of necessity, recently they have started to form networks; this is a good sign.

I also get asked about psychedelic research that someone should be doing related to, for example, lupus, multiple sclerosis, stuttering, or allergies. I hope that such studies will be part of the second wave of research because there are individual reports that each of these conditions has been vastly improved after a psychedelic experience.

The survey studies that we are currently conducting have taken a new turn in that we have established baselines about use, such as bringing to light the fact that people who are interested in psychedelics have used many different substances in a great variety of settings. That's now known.

The second level of questions we are asking includes the following.

- **Health:** Are there long-term stable changes in prior physical conditions? If, in taking a high dose in a safely managed experience, you realize that your identity is not limited to your personality, not even to your body, does that affect overall health and, if so, in what ways?

- **Sexual identity/orientation:** Have psychedelic experiences changed either your sexual orientation or your point of view about your orientation?

- **Bad trips:** Most of the use reports indicate that bad trips are not usual but not uncommon. We are asking people to describe the anatomy of such trips: their cause, content, impact, insights, and aftereffects. We know already that a bad trip rarely stops a person from having additional psychedelic experiences, although typically they don't have many more.

A different team is gathering reports on the use of teners (subperceptual doses). Communities of users are reporting on their experiences, adding to the reports in chapter 15. Why this interest? This community leader's (a member of the Guild of Guides) opinion seems spot on: "If the modern world is ever going to accept these medicines, in our experience, maybe it would be a good idea to start at a more manageable dose versus the blow your mind Death/Rebirth (full dose or more) experience that has been the norm for the last forty years."

My task is to collect, compile, analyze, and publish these reports.

A new project for me is team-teaching a class titled Psychedelics: Theory, Research, and Clinical Applications with David Lukoff and Alicia Danforth at the Institute for Transpersonal Psychology, in Palo Alto, California. It is the first graduate-level clinical class like it in the country. We already have requests from other U.S. schools and for people in Canada and England to teach it online. This interest argues that the period of institutionally induced ignorance is giving ground to commonsense education. If millions of people have taken psychedelics, it is sensible for psychotherapists and spiritual guides to know enough about these substances and their vicissitudes to be helpful to clients coming to work with them.

Whether these projects will be encouraged or suppressed again is unclear given that some institutions remain phobic about psychedelics. Consider the following research-supported observation by Stanislav Grof: "One of the most remarkable consequences of various forms of transpersonal experiences is spontaneous emergence and development of genuine humanitarian and ecological interests and need to take part in activities aimed at peaceful coexistence and well-being of humanity. . . . As a result of these experiences, individuals tend to develop feelings that they are planetary citizens and members of the human family before belonging to a particular country or a specific racial, social, ideological, political, or religious group."

The question that has bedeviled those of us who have been involved in this work since when LSD was the most widely researched psychiatric drug in the world has been to understand what deep fears drove those who outlawed more research. Ironically, it may be what Grof describes.

Many people in the sixties who became involved in self-discovery through psychedelics and other methods went through, to some degree, what the expert in understanding world mythologies Joseph Campbell calls "detribalization." This is a loosening of the ties that individuals had to groups they identified with, be it a union, a school, a sports team, a profession, a nation, or a religion. To the extent one detribalizes from dogmas and codes of conduct, that assertive behavior threatens the group itself. Lay Catholics who practice birth control or Jews who marry outside their faith have both partly detribalized, as have individuals who drop out of professional careers to live in rural communes or join ashrams.

People who have used psychedelics are more likely to detribalize and, after so doing, to create new institutions. The antiwar movement, the civil rights movement, women's liberation, the ecology movement, communes, the sexual revolution, and even organic farming were all fueled and strengthened by those who had taken psychedelics. The backlash against all these movements was inevitable. What was not predicted was that the backlash would extend not only to what people did, but also to their personal, private psychedelic use, eventually suppressing work by scholars and researchers in the field who were not making any counter-cultural waves themselves.*

Perhaps this is why the current researchers have been tiptoeing so cautiously, publishing in only the respectable journals and, as much as possible, not rocking any cultural boats.

An author usually ends personal remarks like these with "Buy my book." But if you're reading this, you or your library or your friend already has done that. My request, then, is that you share what you've learned with those around you. Let's support legal research in every way we can and support one another as well. Keep in mind that even those most disturbed by and opposed to psychedelics want, as much as we do, a better world for us all.

JAMES FADIMAN, PH.D.
JFADIMAN@GMAIL.COM

---

*While Timothy Leary was still at Harvard, he met with the staff of the West Coast research foundation I worked with. We said we were concerned that his insistence on liberalizing the use of these substances would harm us all. His answer was, "If I win, and psychedelics are widely available, you win as well. If I lose and use is restricted, you researchers will still be left standing." It didn't work out that way.

NOTES

To readers looking at these endnotes ~

Every quote or citation in this book is as accurate as I could make it but, this being the age of fluid and flexible information, some of these notes may lack a portion of what an old-fashioned citation would have. Every URL worked the day I included it in the manuscript. That said, some of those references to sources no longer are live, books may be out of print, and the online presence of some journals may be obsolete. In those cases, for anything you are looking for and can't find, please write to me at jfadiman@gmail.com.

Overview—Why This Book?

1. From the National Drug Intelligence Center, 2001, "Data reported in the National Household Survey on Drug Abuse indicate that an estimated 20.2 million U.S. residents aged 12 and older used LSD at least once in their lifetime." From the National Survey on Drug Use and Health, 2008, "In 2006, approximately 23.3 million persons aged 12 and over used LSD in their lifetime, 666 thousand used it in the past year."

2. See Tom Roberts's suggested plan in Michael J. Winkelman and Thomas B. Roberts, eds., *Psychedelic Medicine: New Evidence for Hallucinogenic Substances as Treatments,* vol. 1 (Westport, Conn.: Praeger Publishers, 2007), 288–95.

3. Terence McKenna, *The Archaic Revival* (San Francisco: HarperSanFrancisco, 1991). For example, chapter 10, page 142, begins, "I propose to show that the human/mushroom interaction is not a static symbolic relationship, but rather a dynamic one through which at least one of the parties has been bootstrapped to higher and higher cultural levels."

4. Stephen Harold Buhner, *The Lost Languages of Plants* (White River

Junction, Vt.: Chelsea Green Publishing, 2002), 229. Buhner writes, "We have facilitated the loss of plant species, the loss of health in ecosystems and our bodies, and the loss of the sense of who we are." See also J. P. Harpignies, ed., *Visionary Plant Consciousness: The Shamanistic Teachings of the Plant World* (Rochester, Vt.: Park Street Press, 2007).

5. Michael J. Winkelman and Thomas B. Roberts, eds., *Psychedelic Medicine: New Evidence for Hallucinogenic Substances as Treatments*, 2 vols. (Westport, Conn.: Praeger Publishers, 2007).

6. Jeremy Narby, "Shamans and Scientists," in *Hallucinogens,* ed. Charles Grob (New York: Tarcher/Putnam, 2002), 159–63. A study with scientists working directly with ayahuasca is a rare exception. Three scientists, each from a different scientific discipline, took part in an ayahuasca session with a shaman as their guide. They had been instructed to "ask ayahuasca" for suggestions and information and did so. Each received what he felt to be useful and not at all predictable advice or information directly related to his research.

Chapter 1. Meeting the Divine Within

1. J. Norman Sherwood, Myron J. Stolaroff, and Willis W. Harman, "The Psychedelic Experience—A New Concept in Psychotherapy," *Journal of Neuropsychiatry* 3 (1962): 370–75.

2. William James, *The Varieties of Religious Experience,* 1902. Many other editions.

3. Albert Hofmann. *LSD: My Problem Child* (Sarasota, Fla.: MAPS, 2005).

4. Rick Strassman, "Preparation for the Journey," in *Inner Paths to Outer Space,* Rick Strassman, Slawek Wojtowicz, Luis Eduardo Luis, and Ede Frecska (Rochester, Vt.: Park Street Press, 2008), 268–98. The first section of this chapter is a more extensive discussion of the need for substantial preparation for any psychedelic voyage. Strassman reviews what a voyager can do long term, what one's intent is, and what is the short-term work that will make a voyage safer and more meaningful. This book is highly recommended reading for voyagers and almost always required for guides.

5. Frederick R. Dannaway, "Strange Fires, Weird Smokes and Psychoactive Combustibles: Entheogens and Incense in Ancient Traditions," *Journal of Psychoactive Drugs,* vol. 42 (4) (December 2010): 485–97.

6. Every guide has his or her own favorites as well, as the following comment makes clear. "So much more [than was in the section of the guidelines]— among the best seem to be the Brahms *Requiem,* Barber's *Adagio for Strings,* Gorecki's *Third Symphony,* the slow movement of the Brahms *Violin*

Concerto, etc. The challenge for every guide is to differentiate between the 'very good' and the 'excellent.'" (personal correspondence)

7. Torsten Passie, John H. Halpern, Dirk O. Strichtenoth, Hinderk M. Emrich, and Annelie Hintzen, "The Pharmacology of Lysergic Acid Diethylamide: A Review," *CNS Neurosciences & Therapeutics* 14 (2008): 295–314. Their conclusion, after reviewing nearly ten thousand scientific papers and citing 199 references, was, "The pharmacology of LSD is complex and its mechanisms of action are still not completely understood" (p. 295).

8. Roland R. Griffiths, William A. Richards, Una D. McCann, and Robert Jesse. "Psilocybin Can Occasion Mystical-Type Experiences Having Substantial and Sustained Personal Meaning and Spiritual Significance," *Psychopharmacology* 187, 3 (2006): 268–83. Also in *Psychedelic Medicine: New Evidence for Hallucinogenic Substances as Treatments,* vol. 2, eds. Michael J. Winkelman and Thomas B. Roberts (Westport, Conn.: Praeger Publishers, 2007), 230. For a longer and more complete discussion, see Peter Stafford, *Psychedelics Encyclopedia,* rev. ed. (Los Angeles: Tarcher Inc., 1983), 271–73.

Chapter 3. Qualities of Transcendent Experience

1. Excerpt from Alan Watts, "Psychedelics and the Religious Experience," *California Law Review* 56, no. 1 (January 1968): 74–85.

2. Hinduism regards the universe not as an artifact, but as an immense drama in which the One Actor (the *paramatman* or *brakman*) plays all the parts, which are his (or "its") masks or personae. The sensation of being only this one particular self, John Doe, is the result of the Actor's total absorption in playing this and every other part. For fuller expositions, see S. Radhakrishnan, *The Hindu View of Life* (1927); and H. Zimmer, *Philosophies of India* (1951), 355–463. A popular version of this concept is in Alan Watts, *The Book—On the Taboo Against Knowing Who You Are* (1966).

3. *Isaiah* 45:6–7.

4. *Chandogya Upanishad* 6.15.3.

Chapter 4. Experiences of Psychedelic Pioneers

1. Albert Hofmann, interview in *High Times;* and *LSD: My Problem Child* (Santa Cruz, Calif.: MAPS, 2005), 48–51.

2. Aldous Huxley, *Moksha: Aldous Huxley's Classic Writings on Psychedelics and the Visionary Experience,* eds. Michael Horowitz and Cynthia Palmer (Rochester, Vt.: Park Street Press, 1999).

3. Keith Thompson, "Stormy Search for the Self," *Yoga Journal* (July/August 1990): 54–61, 94.

4. Alexander Shulgin and Ann Shulgin, *PiHKAL: A Chemical Love Story* (Berkeley: Transform Press, 1995), 16–17.

5. Timothy Leary, *High Priest* (New York: New American Library, 1968), 283, 255–56.

6. Ram Dass and Ralph Metzner, *Birth of a Psychedelic Culture,* with Gary Bravo (Santa Fe, N. Mex.: Synergetic Press, 2010), 25.

7. Ram Dass, "Walking the Path: Psychedelics and Beyond," in *Higher Wisdom: Eminent Elders Explore the Continuing Impact of Psychedelics,* eds. Roger Walsh and Charles Grob (Albany: State University of New York Press, 2005), 209–11.

8. Ram Dass and Ralph Metzner, *Birth of a Psychedelic Culture,* with Gary Bravo (Santa Fe, N. Mex.: Synergetic Press, 2010), 25.

9. "Empirical Metaphysics," by Huston Smith, in *Cleaning the Doors of Perception* (New York: Tarcher, 2000), 10–13.

10. Rabbi Zalman Schachter-Shalomi, "Transcending Religious Boundaries," in *Higher Wisdom: Eminent Elders Explore the Continuing Impact of Psychedelics,* eds. Roger Walsh and Charles Grob (Albany: State University of New York Press, 2005), 195–206.

11. Charles Tart, "Initial Integrations of Some Psychedelic Understandings into Every Day Life," in *Psychedelic Reflections,* eds. Lester Grinspoon and James B. Bakalar (New York: Human Sciences Press, 1983), 223–33.

12. Frances Vaughan, "Transpersonal Counseling: Some Observations Regarding Entheogens," in *Psychoactive Sacramentals: Essays on Entheogens and Religion,* ed. Thomas Roberts (San Francisco: Council on Spiritual Practices, 2001), 191.

13. Frances Vaughan, "Perception and Knowledge: Reflections on Psychological and Spiritual Learning in the Psychedelic Experience" in *Psychedelic Reflections,* eds. Lester Grinspoon and James B. Bakalar (New York: Human Sciences Press, 1983), 109.

14. Rich English, "The Dried Piper," *Drunkard Magazine,* www.drunkard .com/issues/01-05/0105-dry-piper.html.

15. Peter Coyote, "Smiling with Dr. Hofmann and the Dead: Reflections on the Counterculture and Wisdom," *The Sixties* 1, no. 2 (2008), 271–78.

Introduction to Part Two

1. Gary Fisher, "Treating the Untreatable," in *Higher Wisdom: Eminent Elders Explore the Continuing Impact of Psychedelics,* eds. Roger Walsh and Charles Grob (Albany: State University of New York Press, 2005), 103–18.

2. John H. Halpern, "Hallucinogens in the Treatment of Alcoholism and Other Addictions," in *Psychedelic Medicine: New Evidence for Hallucinogenic Substances as Treatments*, vol. 2, eds. Michael J. Winkelman and Thomas B. Roberts (Westport, Conn.: Praeger Publishers, 2007), 1–14.

3. From a personal communication with the author.

4. Rick Strassman, "Adverse Reactions to Psychedelic Drugs: A Review of the Literature," *Journal of Nervous and Mental Diseases* 172 (1984): 577–95.

5. Almost all current studies are reviewed in Michael J. Winkelman and Thomas B. Roberts, eds., *Psychedelic Medicine: New Evidence for Hallucinogenic Substances as Treatments*, 2 vols. (Westport, Conn.: Praeger Publishers, 2007). A much more detailed review of these findings can be found in chapter 21 of this volume.

6. Jeremy Narby and Francis Huxley, eds., *Shamans Through Time: 500 Years on the Path to Knowledge* (New York: Jeremy Tarcher/Penguin, 2004).

7. Robert Tindall described several contemporary shamanistic therapeutic settings in *The Jaguar That Roams the Mind* (Rochester, Vt.: Park Street Press, 2008). See also some personal experiences in Daniel Pinchbeck, *Breaking Open the Head: A Psychedelic Journey into the Heart of Contemporary Shamanism* (New York: Broadway Books, 2002). For possible contemporary settings, see Roberts's suggested plan for the creation of psychedelic training and healing centers in Michael J. Winkelman and Thomas B. Roberts, eds., *Psychedelic Medicine: New Evidence for Hallucinogenic Substances as Treatments*, vol. 1 (Westport, Conn.: Praeger Publishers, 2007), 288–95.

Chapter 5. Therapeutic Uses of Psychedelics

1. Willis W. Harman, "The Issue of the Consciousness-Expanding Drugs," *Main Currents in Modern Thought* 20, no. 1 (September–October 1963): 5–14. Harman does not describe the unwholesome beliefs that those with psychedelic experience challenged, but they would have included the smug complacency in the ultimate capacity of material science to overcome all problems, coupled with the rising backlash against the increasingly unpopular Vietnam War. These antiestablishment views were part of the reason for the government's overreaction toward all psychedelic research.

2. Peter T. Furst, "Ancient Altered States," in *Higher Wisdom: Eminent Elders Explore the Continuing Impact of Psychedelics*, eds. Roger Walsh and Charles Grob (Albany: State University of New York Press, 2005), 150–57. "In 5000 BC they were already using peyote that had been traded up to that area from either the lower Rio Grande or from northern Mexico."

3. Paul H. Hoch, "Remarks on LSD and Mescaline," *Journal of Nervous and Mental Diseases* 125 (1957): 442–44. However Hoch gave LSD, his patients did not like it. He is quoted elsewhere saying, "Actually, in my experience, no patient asks for it [LSD] again."

4. Sanford M. Unger, "Mescaline, LSD, Psilocybin, and Personality Change: A Review," *Psychiatry: Journal for the Study of Interpersonal Processes* 26, no. 2 (1963): 111–25. On page 117, Unger describes how different therapists manage to get results in line with their own theories of consciousness. He says, "As a matter of fact, in an amusing and somewhat bemused account, Hartman has described his LSD using group comprised of two Freudians and two Jungians, in which the patients of the former report childhood memories, while those of the latter have 'transcendental' experiences. In addition, for Jungian patients, the transcendental state is associated with 'spectacular' therapeutic results, while for Freudians, should such a state 'accidentally' occur, no such spectacular consequence is observed."

5. One exception is: Mitchael W. Johnson, William A. Richards, and Ronald R. Griffiths, "Human Hallucinogen Research: Guidelines for Safety," *Journal of Psychopharmacology* 22 (2008): 1–18. Exhaustive in detail, it describes how the studies at Johns Hopkins are being conducted. If you already know how to run sessions, you can pull out the helpful parts, but the necessary medical obfuscation and hyper-academic language make using this paper as a training tool a daunting proposition. Also see Myron Stolaroff, *The Secret Chief Revealed* (Santa Cruz, Calif.: MAPS, 2007) for an in-depth look at how one therapist gave hundreds of sessions with all kinds of substances.

6. Alicia Danforth, Sophia Korb, and James Fadiman, "Psychedelics and Students: Motives, Methods, Meltdowns, and Mind-Manifesting Miracles" (presented at the Science of Consciousness Conference, Santa Rosa, Calif., October 21–23, 2009).

7. From a therapy session report that was written seven months after the experience at the International Foundation for Advanced Study in Menlo Park, California.

8. Gary Fisher, "The Psycholytic Treatment of a Childhood Schizophrenic Girl," *International Journal of Social Psychiatry,* 16, 2 (1970): 112–30. "The rationale behind the use of psychedelic agents with psychotic children was that these drugs have the capacity to activate or chemically energize various areas of the brain to an extreme degree resulting in vivid experiencing in the area of perception, emotion, memory and feeling. Experiences and feelings ordinarily denied awareness receive proportionately more energy causing

them to break into a state of consciousness which is less strongly domi-
nated by the usual defenses and values which one has developed. Without
the usual complicated defensive structures and censures, the individual is
able to re-experience himself in a far less distorted way and to reevaluate
the worthiness of his essential self."

9. A complete list, including an excellent video, is kept up-to-date by the
   Multidisciplinary Association for Psychedelic Studies and is available at
   www.maps.org/responding_to_difficult_psychedelic_experiences.html.

10. For example, Peter Webster, philosopher and historian, in a personal com-
    munication with the author, suggested, "The idea that the primary effect
    of the psychedelic drugs themselves (excluding 'noise') may be simply to
    increase the gain or efficiency of the postulated 'significance-detection
    module' of the brain, the key anatomical center for which being the locus
    caeruleus, meshes nicely with personal, rather than pharmacological respon-
    sibility for the 'effects' of psychedelic experience."

11. The website www.clusterbusters.com provides information on entheogenic
    and natural treatments for neuro-vascular headaches, ranging from clusters
    to migraine headaches. "Early research was very successful before it was
    halted when these substances were pulled from the market and removed
    from research labs. This treatment offers hope not only to effectively treat
    ongoing cluster cycles, but to actually break those cycles and to stop future
    cycles from returning. The treatment of cluster headaches with halluci-
    nogens has been kept alive by a few doctors, researchers, and most impor-
    tantly, sufferers searching for a better treatment than exists on the market
    today. Outstanding results have been seen by many cluster headache suf-
    ferers and although clusters have been the major focus, early and current
    'research' shows equally effective results for related vascular headaches."

12. T. J. Haley and S. Ruyschmann, "Brain Concentrations of LSD-25 (Delysid)
    after Intracerebral or Intravenous Administration in Conscious Animals,"
    Experienta 13 (1957): 199–200. Also Max Rinkel, "Pharmodynamics of LSD
    and Mescaline," *Journal of Nervous and Mental Diseases* 125 (1957): 424–26.

13. Michael C. Mithoefer, Mark T. Wagner, Ann T. Mithoefer, Ilsa Jerome, and
    Rick Doblin, "The Safety and Efficacy of ±3,4-methylenedioxymethamphet-
    amine-assisted Psychotherapy in Subjects with Chronic, Treatment-resistant
    Posttraumatic Stress Disorder: the First Randomized Controlled Pilot Study,"
    Journal of Psychopharmacology. Published online July 19, 2010.

14. Edward Tick, *War and the Soul: Healing Our Nation's Veterans from Post-
    traumatic Stress Disorder* (Wheaton, Ill.: Quest Books, 2005).

15. Michael C. Mithoefer, Mark T. Wagner, Ann T. Mithoefer, Ilsa Jerome, and

Rick Doblin, "The Safety and Efficacy of ±3,4-methylenedioxymethamphet-amine-assisted Psychotherapy in Subjects with Chronic, Treatment-resistant Posttraumatic Stress Disorder: the First Randomized Controlled Pilot Study," *Journal of Psychopharmacology*. Published online July 19, 2010.

16. C. S. Grob, et al., "A Pilot Study of Psilocybin Treatment in Advanced-Stage Cancer Patients with Anxiety," *Archives of General Psychiatry* 68 (1) (2011): 71–78.

17. Quoted from P. G. Stafford and B. H. Golightly, *LSD—The Problem Solving Psychedelic* (New York: Award Books, 1967), chap. 4, "Everyday Problems." Out of print but the whole book is available at www.scribd .com/doc/12692270/LSD-The-ProblemSolving-Psychedelic. It is full of specific examples from subjects in many studies.

18. Mike Dinko, the audio recording expert, in a personal communication with me, said that his stuttering had ebbed away after a single session. Also Paul Stemets, the world-famous mycologist, cured himself of severe stuttering in a single self-administered psychedelic session at age fifteen. This is an area easily researched.

19. Sanford Unger, "Apparent Results of Referrals of Alcoholics for LSD Therapy," *Report of the Bureau Saskatchewan Department of Public Health*, Regina, Saskatchewan, Canada, 1962: 5.

20. The director of alcoholism research at the U.S. National Institutes of Health was shown the results from several hospitals in Canada reporting about a 50 percent success rate with chronic alcoholics. He said he did not believe the results. He was asked what research with psychedelics he would believe. "None," was his answer. (Told to author by someone present at the meeting.)

21. A list of LSD studies done with children who have autism is available at www.neurodiversity.com/lsd.html.

22. Robert E. Mogar and Robert W. Aldrich, "The Use of Psychedelics with Autistic Schizophrenic Children," *Behavioral Neuropsychiatry* 1 (1964): 44–51. This article was also in *Psychedelic Review* 10 (1969): 10–15, and can be found at www.erowid.org (search on "Mogar").

23. There may be renewed interest if not renewed research. See Jeff Sigafoos, Vanessa A. Green, Chaturi Edrisinha, and Gulio E. Lancioni, "Flashback to the 1960s: LSD in the Treatment of Autism," *Developmental Neuro-rehabilitation* 10, no. 1 (2007), 75–81. Also at www.scribd.com/doc/37658219/7-75. For a review of truly impressive results, Fisher describes a number of his cases. Gary Fisher, "Treating the Untreatable," in *Higher Wisdom: Eminent Elders Explore the Continuing Impact of Psychedelics*, eds. Roger Walsh and Charles Grob (Albany: State University of New York Press, 2005), 102–17.

24. See Charles Tart, *The End of Materialism* (Oakland, Calif.: Noetic Books and New Harbinger, 2009). The book offers a fine presentation of unassailable data on the reality of the basic "paranormal" phenomena and a well-reasoned analysis of why these areas remain pushed out of the current scientific worldview.

25. John Markoff, *What the Dormouse Said: How the '60s Counterculture Shaped the Personal Computer Industry* (New York: Viking Penguin, 2005).

26. Myron Stolaroff, *The Secret Chief Revealed* (Santa Cruz, Calif.: MAPS, 2007). This book presents a series of interviews with Leo Zeff, who trained several hundred mental health workers and ran sessions for thousands of individuals using a number of settings and a wide range of materials.

Chapter 6. Things Can Go Wrong

1. Neal Goldsmith, portions of appendix 2 in *Psychedelic Healing: The Promise of Entheogens for Psychotherapy and Spiritual Development* (Rochester, Vt.: Healing Arts Press, 2011), 182–204. For more information, see www.neal-goldsmith.com.

Chapter 7. Myths and Misperceptions

1. Originally published as "Strychnine and Other Enduring Myths: Expert and User Folklore Surrounding LSD," by David Presti and Jerome Beck in *Psychoactive Sacramentals,* ed. Thomas Roberts (San Francisco: Council for Spiritual Practices, 2001), 125–37.

2. Albert Hofmann, *LSD: My Problem Child* (Santa Cruz, Calif.: MAPS, 2005).

3. J. G. Hardman, et al., *Goodman & Gilman's The Pharmacological Basis of Therapeutics,* 9th ed. (New York: McGraw-Hill, 1996), 1689–90.

4. P. Weasel, "Trans-high Market Quotations," *High Times* (May 1993): 72.

5. J. E. Beck, "Drug Use Trends and Knowledge among Students Enrolled in a Required Health Course at the University of Oregon, Winter 1980" (unpublished honors thesis, University of Oregon, Eugene: 1980).

6. American Psychiatric Association, *Diagnostic and Statistical Manual of Mental Disorders,* 4th ed. (Washington, D.C.: American Psychiatric Association Press, 1994), 231.

7. A. J. Giannini, "Inward the Mind's I: Description, Diagnosis, and Treatment of Acute and Delayed LSD Hallucinations," *Psychiatric Annals* 24 (1994): 134–36.

8. R. N. Pechnick and J. T. Ungerleider, "Hallucinogens," in *Substance Abuse: A Comprehensive Textbook,* eds. J. H. Lowinson, et al. (Baltimore: Williams and Wilkens, 1997), 230–38.

9. C. R. Carroll, *Drugs in Modern Society* (Dubuque, Iowa: Wm. C. Brown, 1989).

10. G. Hanson and P. J. Venturelli, *Drugs and Society* (Boston: Jones and Bartlett, 1995).

11. C. Kuhn, et al., *Buzzed: The Straight Facts about the Most Used and Abused Drugs* (New York: Norton, 1998).

12. Department of Justice, *Street Terms: Drugs and the Drug Trade* (Rockville, Md.: 1994).

13. "Street Names for Common Drugs," *Journal of Emergency Medicine,* July 1988: 46–47.

14. Albert Hofmann, *LSD: My Problem Child* (Santa Cruz, Calif.: MAPS, 2005), 71–72.

15. J. Ott, *Pharmacotheon: Entheogenic Drugs, Their Plant Sources and History,* foreword by Albert Hofmann (Kennewick, Wash.: Natural Products Company, 1993), 134–35.

16. Lester Grinspoon and James B. Bakalar, eds. *Psychedelic Drugs Reconsidered* (New York: Basic Books, 1979; repr. New York: Lindesmith Center, 1997), 76.

17. J. K. Brown and M. H. Malone, "Status of Drug Quality in the Street-Drug Market," *Pacific Information Service on Street Drugs* 3, no. 1 (1973): 1–8.

18. E. M. Brecher, *Licit and Illicit Drugs* (Boston: Little, Brown and Company, 1972), 376.

19. M. A. Lee and B. Shlain, *Acid Dreams: The CIA, LSD, and the Sixties Rebellion* (New York: Grove Press, 1985), 188.

20. Alexander Shulgin and Ann Shulgin, *TiHKAL: The Continuation* (Berkeley, Calif.: Transform Press, 1997).

21. Jan Harold Brunvand, *The Choking Doberman and Other "New" Urban Legends* (New York: Norton, 1984).

22. Drug Enforcement Administration, "LSD: A Situation Report," Washington, D.C.: 1991.

23. M. M. Cohen, M. J. Marinello, and N. Back, "Chromosomal Damage in Human Leukocytes Induced by Lysergic Acid Diethylamide," *Science* 155 (1967): 1417–19.

24. M. M. Cohen, K. Hirshhorn, and W. A. Frosch, "In Vivo and In Vitro Chromosomal Damage Induced by LSD-25," *The New England Journal of Medicine* 227 (1967): 1043–49.

25. Editorial, "Radiomimetic Properties of LSD," *The New England Journal of Medicine* 227 (1967): 1090–91.

26. N. I. Dishotsky, et al., "LSD and Genetic Damage," *Science* 172 (1971): 431–40.

27. E. Goode, *Drugs in American Society*, 4th ed. (New York: McGraw-Hill, 1993).

28. E. Goode, *Drugs in American Society*, 5th ed. (New York: McGraw-Hill, 1999).

29. S. Grof, *LSD Psychotherapy* (1980; repr. Alameda, Calif.: Hunter House, 1994; repr. Santa Cruz, MAPS, 2009).

30. M. J. Stolaroff, *Thanaros to Eros: 35 Years of Psychedelic Exploration* (Berlin: Verlag fur Wissenschaft und Bildung, 1994).

31. R. J. Strassman, "Adverse Reactions to Psychedelic Drugs: A Review of the Literature," *The Journal of Nervous and Mental Disease* 172 (1984): 577–95.

32. Lester Grinspoon and James B. Bakalar, eds., *Psychedelic Drugs Reconsidered* (New York: Basic Books, 1979; repr. New York: Lindesmith Center, 1997).

33. American Psychiatric Association, *Diagnostic and Statistical Manual of Mental Disorders*, 4th ed. (Washington, D.C.: American Psychiatric Association Press, 1994), 654.

34. Sidney Cohen, "Lysergic Acid Diethylamide: Side Effects and Complications," *The Journal of Nervous and Mental Disease* 130 (1960): 30–40.

35. R. S. Gable, "Toward a Comparative Overview of Dependence Potential and Acute Toxicity of Psychoactive Substances Used Nonmedically," *The American Journal of Drug and Alcohol Abuse* 19 (1993): 263–81.

36. L. J. West, C. M. Pierce, and W. D. Thomas, "Lysergic Acid Diethylamide: Its Effects on a Male Asiatic Elephant," *Science* 138 (1962): 1100–3.

37. Lester Grinspoon and James B. Bakalar, eds., *Psychedelic Drugs Reconsidered* (New York: Basic Books, 1979; repr. New York: Lindesmith Center, 1997), 159.

38. S. Grof, *LSD Psychotherapy* (repr. Alameda, Calif.: Hunter House, 1994; repr. Santa Cruz, Calif.: MAPS, 2009), 134.

39. American Psychiatric Association, *Diagnostic and Statistical Manual of Mental Disorders*, 4th ed. (Washington, D.C.: American Psychiatric Association Press, 1994), 233–34.

40. H. D. Abraham and A. M. Aldridge, "Adverse Consequences of Lysergic Acid Diethylamide," *Addiction* 88 (1993): 1327–34.

41. L. S. Myers, S. S. Watkins, and T. J. Carter, "Flashbacks in Theory and Practice," *The Heffter Review of Psychedelic Research* 1 (1998): 51–55.

42. Drug Enforcement Administration, "LSD: A Situation Report," Washington, D.C.: 1991.

43. L. A. Henderson and W. J. Glass, *LSD: Still With Us After All These Years* (New York: Lexington Books, 1994), 52.

44. Sidney Cohen, "Lysergic Acid Diethylamide: Side Effects and Complications," *The Journal of Nervous and Mental Disease* 130 (1960).

45. E. M. Brecher, *Licit and Illicit Drugs* (Boston: Little, Brown and Company, 1972).

46. R. Bunce, "The Social and Political Sources of Drug Effects: The Case of Bad Trips on Psychedelics," *Journal of Drug Issues* 9 (1979): 213–33.

47. N. E. Zinherg, *Drug, Set, and Setting* (New Haven, Conn.: Yale University Press, 1984).

48. Lester Grinspoon and James B. Bakalar, eds. *Psychedelic Drugs Reconsidered* (Basic Books, New York, 1979; repr. New York: Lindesmith Center, 1997), 159.

49. L. A. Henderson and W. J. Glass, *LSD: Still With Us After All These Years* (New York: Lexington Books, 1994), 55.

Chapter 8. Therapeutic Effectiveness of Single Guided Sessions

1. J. J. Meduna, *Carbon Dioxide Therapy* (Springfield, Ill.: Charles C. Thomas, 1950).

2. Abbreviated from Charles Savage, James Fadiman, Robert Mogar, and Mary H. Allen, "Process and Outcome Variables in Psychedelic (LSD) Therapy," in *The Use of LSD in Psychotherapy and Alcoholism,* ed. Harold Abramson (Indianapolis: Bobbs-Merrill, 1967), 511–32.

3. James Fadiman, "Behavior Change Following (LSD) Psychedelic Therapy." Dissertation, Stanford University, 1965, p. 3. Can be found at www .proquest.com (search for name or title) but you have to be a member to gain access (most academic libraries are members); also available at www .jamesfadiman.com.

4. Norman Sherwood, Myron Stolaroff, and Willis J. Harman, "The Psyche-delic Experience—A New Concept in Psychotherapy," *Journal of Neuropsy-chiatry* 4 (1962): 370–75.

5. Helen D. Sargent, "Intrapsychic Change: Methodological Problems in Psychotherapy Research," *Psychiatry* 24 (1961). Quoted in R. S. Wallerstein, "The Problem of Assessment of Change in Psychotherapy," *International Journal of Psychoanalysis* 44 (1963): 33–41.

6. James Fadiman, "Behavior Change Following Psychedelic (LSD) Therapy,"

Dissertation, Stanford University, 1965. For those who wish to delve even more deeply, the full scoring and discussion of all 332 items across the eighteen categories takes eighty-seven pages of the original dissertation including some correlations with clinical evaluation scales. It may be read or downloaded at www.proquest.com or at www.jamesfadiman.com.

7. Charles Savage, James Fadiman, Robert Mogar, and Mary H. Allen, "Process and Outcome Variables in Psychedelic (LSD) Therapy," in *The Use of LSD in Psychotherapy and Alcoholism,* ed. Harold Abramson (Indianapolis: Bobbs-Merrill, l967), edited from pages 519–21.

8. Charles Savage, Ethel Savage, James Fadiman, and Willis W. Harman, "LSD: Therapeutic Effects of the Psychedelic Experience," *Psychological Reports* 14 (1964): 111–20.

9. Michael J. Winkelman and Thomas B. Roberts, eds. *Psychedelic Medicine: New Evidence for Hallucinogenic Substances as Treatments,* 2 vols. (Westport, Conn.: Praeger Publishers, 2007).

Introduction to Part Three

1. See Margaret Talbot, "Brain Drain: The Underground World of 'Neuro-enhancing' Drugs," *The New Yorker,* April 27, 2009, 32–43. See also Henry Greeley, Phillip Campbell, Barbara Sahakain Harris, John Kessler, Michael Gazzaniga, and Martha J. Farrah, "Towards Responsible Use of Cognitive-Enhancing Drugs by the Healthy," *Nature* 456 (December 11, 2008): 702–705.

2. John Markoff, *What the Dormouse Said: How the 60s Counterculture Shaped the Personal Computer Industry* (New York: Viking Penguin, 2005).

3. Michael Schrage, "A Brave New Prescription for Creative Management," *Fortune,* April 30, 2001. Reprinted in the MAPS bulletin XI, 1 (2001): 31. Michael Schrage was codirector of the Massachusetts Institute of Technology Media Lab's e-markets initiative. Part of his article reads, "Inspiration is elusive. Innovation is hard. Demand for technical and conceptual breakthroughs in global business is intensifying. Organizations are looking everywhere for the transforming insight. Perhaps the best prescription for boosting corporate creativity would be a prescription. . . . Why not the next logical step? Turn these everyday experiments in self-medication into more rigorously designed and disciplined initiatives for innovation. Think of such mediated medicated creativity as a form of creative managerial therapy best done under professional supervision. Picture the Leary-Huxley Institute for Creative Business Visualization on one of the sunnier islands near Crete. Psychopharmacologists and board-certified neuropsy-

chologists dispense small, precise dosages of psychoactive materials to visiting executive teams that want to push themselves beyond the boundaries of conventional business perception. The purpose would not be to get 'high' but to enhance creativity. Skilled facilitators would ensure that the interactions focus on the business tasks at hand. . . . Perhaps a team of hedge fund managers might find investment inspiration in a myco-managed conversation in the hypothetical institute's Coleridge Room. Off in the Lennon Wing, fashion buyers and designers at a global clothing merchant could brainstorm in profoundly different ways. At the newly refurbished De Quincey Pavilion, computational chemistry researchers from—ironically— one of the world's largest pharmaceuticals companies could play with the asymmetrical geometries of a potentially therapeutic protein. . . . To the extent that market imperatives insist that individuals and institutions become ever more creative or fail, there will be growing societal pressure to view psychoactive drugs as a kind of value-added Prozac—a pill to enhance creativity rather than mood. No one is shocked to hear of an 'artist'—a pop musician, a painter, a photographer, a film director, a writer—who credits experimentation with 'consciousness-expanding' drugs as essential to her creative development. Indeed, global media conglomerates knowingly hire such people even as they disapprove of and disavow illegal drug use."

4. Willis W. Harman and James Fadiman, "Selective Enhancement of Specific Capacities through Psychedelic Training," in *Psychedelics: The Uses and Implications of Hallucinogenic Drugs,* eds. Bernard Aaronson and Humphry Osmond (New York: Doubleday and Company, 1970), 240.

Chapter 9. Breakthrough Research

1. Revised and updated by James Fadiman from Willis Harman and James Fadiman, "Selective Enhancement of Specific Capacities through Psychedelic Training," in *Psychedelics: The Uses and Implications of Hallucinogenic Drugs,* eds. Bernard Aaronson and Humphry Osmond (New York: Doubleday and Company, 1970), 239–57. That article was an overview of a longer paper: Willis W. Harman, et al., "Psychedelic Agents in Creative Problem Solving: A Pilot Study," *Psychological Reports* 19 (1966): 211–27.

2. The quote is from James Fadiman, "Behavior Change following Psychedelic (LSD) Therapy," dissertation, Stanford University, 1965. A list of studies from each perspective is on page 3, following the quote.

3. Robert Mogar, "Current Status and Future Trends in Psychedelic (LSD) Research," *Journal of Humanistic Psychology* 4 (1965): 147–66.

4. Robert Mogar and Charles Savage, "Personality Change Associated with

Psychedelic Therapy: A Preliminary Report," *Psychotherapy: Theory, Research, Practice* 1 (1964): 154–62; James Fadiman, "Behavior Change following Psychedelic (LSD) Therapy," dissertation, Stanford University, 1965; Charles Savage, et al., "The Effects of Psychedelic Therapy on Values, Personality, and Behavior," *International Journal of Neuropsychiatry* 2 (1966): 241–54.

5. Those interested in the relationship of these aspects to research and theory on creativity can refer to the detailed technical discussion in Willis W. Harman, et al., "Psychedelic Agents in Creative Problem Solving: A Pilot Study," *Psychological Reports* 19 (1966): 211–27.

6. H. A. Witkin, *Psychological Differentiation* (New York: Wiley, 1962).

7. For a fuller description of these results, see Willis W. Harman, et al., "Psychedelic Agents in Creative Problem Solving: A Pilot Study," *Psychological Reports* 19 (1966): 211–27; Charles Savage, et al., "The Effects of Psychedelic Therapy on Values, Personality, and Behavior," *International Journal of Neuropsychiatry* 2 (1966): 241–54; and A. Hoffer, "LSD: A Review of Its Present Status," *Clinical Pharmacology and Therapeutics* 6 (1965): 183–255.

8. C. Savage, et al., "The Effects of Psychedelic Therapy on Values, Personality, and Behavior," *International Journal of Neuropsychiatry* 2 (1966): 241–54; A. Hoffer, "LSD: A Review of Its Present Status," *Clinical Pharmacology and Therapeutics* 6 (1965): 183–255.

Chapter 11. Case Studies

1. "LSD: A Design Tool?" *Progressive Architecture,* August 1966.

Chapter 13. The *Look* Magazine Experiment

1. Sections from *Walking on the Edge of the World* by George Leonard, (Boston: Houghton Mifflin Company, 1988), chapters 22–24.

Chapter 14. Closing the Doors of Perception

1. "Opening the Doors of Perception," by James Fadiman in *Time It Was: American Stories from the Sixties,* eds. K. M. Smith and T. Koster (Upper Saddle River, N.J.: Pearson Prentice-Hall, 2008), 228–35.

Chapter 16. Surveys of Current Users

1. Norman E. Zinberg, "The Users Speak for Themselves," in *Psychedelic Reflections,* eds. Lester Grinspoon and James B. Bakalar (New York: Human Sciences Press, 1983), 39–60. It is impossible not to notice that, after ten

years of funding, this report offers little more than samples of interviews and generalizations. Given that I collected a larger sample in five minutes and that the total time for sample collections of close to four hundred people took only a few hours, one wonders if this research was a good value for the money. However, given that the first five-year grant was called "Controlled Nonmedical Drug Use" and the second five-year grant was called "Processes of Control in Different Heroin Using Styles," it is likely that this work was slipped in as part of a larger and totally noncontroversial study.

Chapter 17. The Inadvertent Pioneer: My Personal Account

1. Edited from the version published as "James Fadiman, Transpersonal Transitions: The Higher Reaches of Psyche and Psychology," in *Higher Wisdom: Eminent Elders Explore the Continuing Impact of Psychedelics,* eds. Roger Walsh and Charles Grob (Albany: State University of New York Press, 2005), 24–45.

Chapter 18. Positive Possibilities for Psychedelics

1. Rick Strassman, "Biomedical Research with Psychedelics: Current Models and Future Prospects," in *Entheogens and the Future of Religion,* ed. Robert Forte (San Francisco: Council on Spiritual Practices, 1997), 153–62.

2. Maria Szalavitz, "Drugs in Portugal: Did Decriminalization Work?" *Time Magazine,* August 26, 2009, www.time.com (search for article title). "Judging by every metric, decriminalization in Portugal has been a resounding success," says Glenn Greenwald, an attorney, author, and fluent Portuguese speaker, who conducted the research. "It has enabled the Portuguese government to manage and control the drug problem far better than virtually every other Western country does." Compared to the European Union and the United States, Portugal's drug-use numbers are impressive. Following decriminalization, Portugal had the lowest rate of lifetime marijuana use in people over fifteen in the E.U.: 10 percent. The most comparable figure in America is in people over twelve: 39.8 percent. Proportionally, more Americans have used cocaine than Portuguese have used marijuana.

3. Charlotte Bowyer, "Czech Drug Policy," Adam Smith Institute, www .AdamSmith.org. (search on the article title). "As of January 1st, [2010], the Czech Republic's drug policy is changing. While the personal use of illicit drugs was decriminalized a year ago, possession of the vague 'larger than small' amount of a substance still lead to prosecution. The difficulty the public, police and courts faced in judging this amount has led to

government clarifying the levels acceptable for personal consumption, such as 15 grams of marijuana, 4 tablets of ecstasy, a gram of cocaine and 1.5 grams of heroin. Setting out the law in a clear way and using common sense to designate a 'reasonable' level of drug possession makes it easier for all to monitor and respect the law."

4. Simon Louvish, *Mae West* (New York: St. Martin's Press, 2005), 82.

5. John Di Saia, M.D., "Marijuana—California's Salvation," Wellsphere, www .wellsphere.com (search on the article title). Di Saia, a non–pot using plastic surgeon, wrote the following summary of the legalize-and-tax-it argument. "Marijuana is California's largest cash crop. It's valued at $14 billion annually, or nearly twice the value of the state's grape and vegetable crops combined, according to government statistics. But the state doesn't receive any revenue from its cash cow. Instead, it spends billions of dollars enforcing laws pegged at shutting down the industry and inhibiting marijuana's adherents."

In April 2010, the Field Poll of California reported that 56 percent of likely 2010 voters would approve the Tax Cannabis initiative. The *Seattle Times* conducted a national poll that showed that two-thirds of Americans believe the "war on drugs" is a failure, while 53 percent agreed that marijuana should be legalized.

6. Data from Asset Forfeiture Annual Report 2008, California Department of Justice.

7. Martin Ball, ed., *Voyaging to DMT Space in Entheologues* (n.p.: Kyandara Publishing, 2009), 49. Rick Strassman, the foremost DMT researcher and longtime lay Buddhist, says, "At least three-quarters, maybe 80–90 percent, of the monks had had an LSD experience, and the vast majority of them, probably every one of them, felt that their LSD experience was their first real glimpse that there was another way of looking at reality."

8. Jack Kornfield, "Psychedelic Experience and Spiritual Practice," in *Entheogens and the Future of Religion,* ed. Robert Forte (San Francisco: Council on Spiritual Practices, 1997), 119–36. The comment about the vows, from page 120, is as follows: "The precept in Theravaden Buddhism . . . is to refrain from using intoxicants to the point of heedlessness, loss of mindfulness, or loss of awareness. It does not say not to use them and it is very explicit." See also the discussion of levels of Buddhist practice and which ones should use no drugs and which ones can use drugs, as well, at www.entheoguide.net/wiki/ReligionBuddhism.

9. Roland Griffiths, William Richards, Una McCann, and Robert Jesse, "Psilocybin Can Occasion Mystical-Type Experiences Having Substantial and Sustained Personal Meaning and Spiritual Significance,"

Psychopharmacology 187, 3 (2006): 268–83. Also in *Psychedelic Medicine: New Evidence for Hallucinogenic Substances as Treatments,* vol. 2, eds. Michael J. Winkelman and Thomas B. Roberts (Westport, Conn.: Praeger Publishers, 2007): 227–254.

10. Robert Forte, "A Conversation with Gordon Wasson," in *Entheogens and the Future of Religion,* ed. Robert Forte (San Francisco: Council on Spiritual Practices, 1997), 73.

11. Andrew Sewell and John Halpern, "Response of Cluster Headaches to Psilocybin and LSD," in *Psychedelic Medicine: New Evidence for Hallucinogenic Substances as Treatments,* eds. Michael J. Winkelman and Thomas B. Roberts (Westport, Conn.: Praeger, 2007), 97–124.

12. See www.Clusterbusters.com. "The Clusterbusters are a small, but growing, international group of Clusterheadache sufferers actively investigating the use of indole-ring entheogens and other natural substances to treat their disease. Our mission is to investigate indole-ring entheogens as possibly the most effective treatment yet found for Clusterheadaches, and to educate physicians, medical researchers, sufferers, and the public on the efficacy, advantages and disadvantages of this and other treatments."

13. Charles Grob, et al., "A Pilot Study of Psilocybin Treatment for Anxiety in Advanced-Stage Cancer Patients," *Archives of General Psychiatry* (January 2011), http://archpsyc.ama-assn.org (search on the article title).

14. For a commentary on the value of the therapy, see Charles Savage, "LSD, Alcoholism and Transcendence," The Psychedelic Library, www.psychedelic-library.org/savage.htm.

15. Alicia Danforth, James Fadiman, and Sophia Korb, "Students and Psychedelics: Motives, Methods, Meltdowns and Mind-Manifesting Miracles" (presented at the Science of Consciousness Conference, Santa Rosa, California, October 21–23, 2009).

16. See John Markoff, *What the Dormouse Said: How the 60s Counterculture Shaped the Personal Computer Industry* (New York: Viking Penguin, 2005). The central premise is that the personal computer owes its genesis and development to the interweaving of psychedelic experiences and computer innovation in the San Francisco Bay area in the 1960s and 1970s.

17. Quoted by Thomas Redlinger, "Sacred Mushrooms Pentecost," in *Entheogens and the Future of Religion,* ed. Robert Forte (San Francisco: Council on Spiritual Practices, 1997), 106. The concerns raised by the use of psychedelic mushrooms were well stated by two Christian missionaries, Eunice Pike and Florence Cowan. They said, "How can one effectively present the message of divine revelation to a people who already have, according

to their beliefs, a means whereby anyone who so desires may get messages directly from the supernatural world via a more spectacular and immediately satisfying way than Christianity has to offer?"

18. Susie Mandrak, "UN Advisor: Drug Money Propped Up Banks During Crisis," *Observer,* London (December 13, 2009). Mandrak wrote, "Antonio Maria Costa, head of the UN Office on Drugs and Crime, said he has seen evidence that the proceeds of organized crime were 'the only liquid investment capital' available to some banks on the brink of collapse last year. He said that a majority of the $232 billion of drug profits were absorbed into the economic system as a result." Find it at http://crooksandliars.com/susie-mandrak/un-advisor-drug-money-propped-banks-d.

19. Rick Strassman, "Biomedical Research with Psychedelics: Current Models and Future Prospects," in *Entheogens and the Future of Religion,* ed. Robert Forte (San Francisco: Council on Spiritual Practices, 1997), 159.

20. Mary Oliver, "The Summer Day," *New and Selected Poems,* vol. 1 (Boston: Beacon Press, 1992).

Chapter 20. Beyond LSD—Way Beyond

1. Don José Campos, *The Shaman and Ayahuasca.* Studio City, Calif.: Divine Arts, 2011.

Chapter 21. Behaviorial Changes After Psychedelic Therapy

1. Charles Savage, Ethel Savage, James Fadiman, and Willis Harman, "LSD: Therapeutic Effects of the Psychedelic Experience," *Psychological Reports,* vol. 14 (1964): 111–20.

2. J. J. Downing and W. W. Wygant Jr., "Psychedelic Experience and Religious Belief," in *Utopiates: The Use and Users of LSD-25.* Richard Blum, ed. (New York: Atherton Press, 1964).

3. James Fadiman, "Behavior Change Following Psychedelic (LSD) Therapy," Dissertation, Stanford University, 1965. This dissertation can be read or downloaded at www.proquest.com or at www.jamesfadiman.com.

Chapter 22. A Questionnaire Study of Psychedelic Experiences

1. J. N. Sherwood, M. J. Stolaroff, and W. W. Harman, "The Psychedelic Experience—A New Concept In Psychotherapy," *Journal of Neuropsychiatry* 4 (1962): 69–80.

2. K. S. Ditman, M. C. Hayman, and J. R. B. Whittlesey, "Nature and Frequency of Claims Following LSD," *Journal of Nervous and Mental Diseases* 134 (1962): 346–52.

INDEX

Page numbers in *italics* represent tables and illustrations.

Books of Related Interest

DMT: The Spirit Molecule
A Doctor's Revolutionary Research into the Biology of
Near-Death and Mystical Experiences
by Rick Strassman, M.D.

Inner Paths to Outer Space
Journeys to Alien Worlds through Psychedelics and
Other Spiritual Technologies
*by Rick Strassman, M.D., Slawek Wojtowicz, M.D.,
Luis Eduardo Luna, Ph.D., and Ede Frecska, M.D.*

LSD: Doorway to the Numinous
The Groundbreaking Psychedelic Research into
Realms of the Human Unconscious
by Stanislav Grof, M.D.

Tryptamine Palace
5-MeO-DMT and the Sonoran Desert Toad
by James Oroc

Psychedelic Healing
The Promise of Entheogens for Psychotherapy and Spiritual Development
by Neal M. Goldsmith, Ph.D.

Salvia Divinorum
Doorway to Thought-Free Awareness
by J. D. Arthur

The Shamanic Wisdom of the Huichol
Medicine Teachings for Modern Times
by Tom Soloway Pinkson, Ph.D.

The Acid Diaries
A Psychonaut's Guide to the History and Use of LSD
by Christopher Gray

INNER TRADITIONS • BEAR & COMPANY
P.O. Box 388 • Rochester, VT 05767
1-800-246-8648
www.InnerTraditions.com

Or contact your local bookseller